Fashion Patternmaking Techniques
[Vol. 3]

How to Make Jackets, Coats and Cloaks for Women and Men

Antonio Donnanno

Illustrations by
Elisabetta Kuky Drudi

PROMOPRESS

*We reserve a special thanks to Gianni Pucci
for allowing us to publish the photographs
of his fashion runway shows.*

Hoaki Books, S.L.
C/ Ausiàs March, 128
08013 Barcelona, Spain
T. 0034 935 952 283
F. 0034 932 654 883
info@hoaki.com
www.hoaki.com

Fashion Patternmaking Techniques [Vol. 3]
How to Make Jackets, Coats and Cloaks
for Women and Men

ISBN: 978-84-16504-18-3
D.L.: B 13313-2018
Printed in Turkey

Reprinted: 2017, 2018, 2020

Translation: Katherine Kirby
Drawings by Elisabetta Kuky Drudi
Cover design: spread: David Lorente
Cover photo design: Burberry Prorsum s/s 2019
Cover image: Gianni Pucci

PREFACE

This third text is the last in a series of studies on clothing patterns for men and women. In this book, we address patternmaking for women's outerwear and complete the selection previously offered for men with the inclusion of overcoats and jackets.

Divided into seven chapters, this volume continues the technical and educational training presented in the first two books. Once again, we have included the in-depth explanations necessary to clarify the patternmaking process and the graphic preparations that are of great importance when studying these procedures to make them comprehensible and easy to follow.

The range of garment types covered in these books is vast. This manual presents a study of all the essential principles for jackets, coats, overcoats and capes. We have also included the most up-to-date creative lines and newest cuts presented by designers, in addition to the classics that never go out of style. Sizing, an indispensable topic for industrial patternmakers, is fully covered.

I would like to express my sincerest thanks to all my collaborators who, with their talents and spirit of research, have made this series possible.

In particular, I would like to thank Professor Marisa Cassera, the best patternmaking teacher and practicing pattern and garment maker that I know; my daughter Emanuela, fashion designer and expert in computer graphics and digital page layouts; and Nadia Gregis, who collaborated on the drafting and correction of the text.

I would like to conclude by saying that I hope my book, the fruit of years of study and research, will help and encourage young people to enter the fascinating world of fashion with the right skill set, artistic sense and good taste - precisely what creators of Italian fashion are known for.

TABLE OF CONTENTS

Chapter one
PAGE 5 JACKETS AND WAISTCOATS

Chapter two
PAGE 61 HEAVY JACKETS AND WINTER JACKETS

Chapter three
PAGE 77 OVERCOATS AND TOPCOATS

Chapter four
PAGE 105
CAPES AND CLOAKS

Chapter five
PAGE 127 MEN'S JACKETS AND OVERCOATS

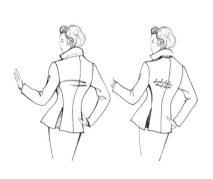

Chapter six
PAGE 153 CORRECTIONS

Chapter seven
PAGE 165 PATTERN SPREADING AND LAYOUT

JACKETS AND WAISTCOATS

Jackets 6
Jacket lines and lengths. 7
Suits and casual jackets. 8
Waistcoats 9
Variations on the basic bodice. 10
Women's double-breasted waistcoat 11
Double-breasted waistcoat with lapels 11
Edge-to-edge waistcoat 12
Sports waistcoat. 12
Maxi waistcoat. .13
Jacket measurements 14
Chart for industrial women's sizing 15
Single-breasted jacket composition. 16
Terminology 17
Basic jacket block 18
Inset sleeve block 19
Positions and sizes for jacket darts. 20
Overlaps and lapels. 22
Jacket collar 23
Variations on the sports collar. 24
Jacket with step collar. 25
Jacket with shawl collar. 26
Shaped shawl collar 27
Double-breasted shawl collar 27
Wide shawl collar. 28
Collarless lapel .29
Double collarless lapel. 30
Seam allowances. 31
Loose-fitting jacket 32
Loose-fitting jacket sleeve 33
Princess cut jacket. 34
Jacket with side panels 35
Bolero 36
Collarless bolero 36
Crop bolero with collar 37
Bolero with collar and closure 37
Jacket with yoke 38
Jacket with yoke and side panels. 39
Jacket with raglan sleeves 40
Attaching the raglan sleeves 41
Crop jacket with creative raglan sleeves. . . .42
Jacket with raglan yoke sleeves 43
Kimono jacket - back. 44
Kimono jacket - front 45
Swing jacket - back. 46
Swing jacket - front. 47
Safari jacket 48
Jacket pattern layout. 49
Jacket overlap. 50
Linings and inners. 51
Inner reinforcements 52
Sleeve and collar reinforcements 53
Jacket construction 54
Raglan sleeve jacket construction. 55
Jacket collar assembly 56
Padding on the shoulders and sleeves 57
Jacket lining 58
Jacket layout for checked fabric 59
Creative jacket exercises 60

JACKETS

INTRODUCTION

JACKETS

A women's jacket is the upper part of a suit or a matching outfit set. Its precursor was a type of form-fitting, decorated doublet worn by men of the Roman Empire, called a synthesis. Jackets as we know them, however, were first made in the Middle Ages by sewing various types of fabric together with needle and thread.

In France in the 1300s, the jacque was a common type of jacket made of humble materials worn by the poor.

In the 1600s, young men wore the frock-coat, a jacket similar to a tailcoat.

Towards the end of the 1800s, women's jackets take on the form of a redingote, with a straight cut down to the hips. These coats were worn by women over long, wide skirts.

Long coats over open skirts began to appear at the start of the 1900s, with a pinafore in a different fabric on the upper, as did cropped boleros and jackets that recede in the front worn over very high corsets.

As time went on, jacket shapes and outlines slowly changed and took on a wide variety of forms and silhouettes according to the dictates of fashion. Various cuts, volumes, lengths, fabrics and embellishments were used, based on the garment's intended use and the wearer's personal style.

Today, women's jackets may be classic, single-breasted or double-breasted, just like those for men. They can be fitted or loose, and cropped above the waist (bolero) or long, extending down to just above the knee (a 7/8 jacket). There may be three buttons, with the lapels meeting just below the bust line, or two buttons, with the lapels meeting at the waist or hip line. A jacket may be collarless or have a collar that's rounded, in the shape of a V or a number of other forms. It may feature different types of lapels and there might be welt or applied pockets, or have none at all.

There are also casual, sporty styles such as jerkins, safari jackets, parkas, windbreakers and snow jackets for women, which in recent years have expanded into an array of products matching those found in menswear.

WAISTCOATS

Waistcoats are a common item of clothing for men: a sleeveless, tight or fitted garment to be worn under a jacket. However, women's versions also exist which are frequently worn without a jacket, over a skirt or pants. A waistcoat can be single- or double-breasted, overlapping, with or without a collar, have a rounded or V shaped neckline and come in various lengths.

The fabric may match the skirt, pants or suit it is to be worn with, or contrast in terms of colour and material. The back may include a buckled cinch in the back, as often seen in men's versions, and the front may feature small pockets. The front may be fastened with buttons or be left open.

The Fontana sisters. Ph: Federico Garolla.

Jacket lines and lengths

The shape and length of a jacket may vary according to the dictates of fashion and according to the occasion on which it will be worn. The back of a jacket may include a split vent in the centre, two side vents, a box pleat or no vent at all.
The fabric used for jackets varies according to the season and the trends. Summer looks may include the use of linen, cotton, cool wool or silk, while winter may bring woollen gabardine, ottoman, tweed, vicuna, etc.

Main jacket types

Men's style jacket (also called a blazer)
Jackets or blazers, inspired by menswear, may be single- or double-breasted. Single-breasted blazers may have three buttons with the lapels overlapping at the waist or below. Double-breasted blazers may have six buttons, with the lapels meeting below the bust, four buttons, with the lapels meeting at the waist, or two buttons, with the lapels meeting below the waist, near the hips.
The shape of the lapels and the neckline for both single- and double-breasted blazers is incredibly varied, and may include: notched, peaked, shawl, etc.
The classic length for a jacket is just below the hipline (3-5 cm / 1.18-1.97"), varying according to the styles of the time.
These jackets often have smooth or overlapping vents sewn into the back (single vent) or on the sides (double vents).

The Chanel
Created by the French seamstress and designer Coco Chanel, this jacket is single-breasted and approximately 50-60 cm (19.68-23.62") long. It features a slightly widened collar, dual-seam sleeves with a cuff vent and the bottom hem of the front is either straight or rounded. These jackets are almost exclusively made of thick wool tweed or other raised fabrics in pastel tones and usually feature solid colour trimmings that coordinate with the base fabric.

The bolero
This is a short type of jacket that extends no further than the waist line. It can be without a fastening or have one or two buttons at the top. Boleros may be made with or without a collar and with or without sleeves.

The spencer
A typical form-fitting jacket for both men and women, the Spencer features youthful lines and long sleeves. It falls just below the waist, but it may be worn with a skirt and it is ideal when paired with trousers. The Spencer may have a single or double breast, various collar styles, narrow or broad lapels and, for particularly elegant occasions, it may be enriched by the application of contrasting colour satin fabric.

The 3/4 length jacket
This jacket comes in various cuts and lines. Its length falls to the upper thigh, 12-15 cm (4.7-5.9") below the hip line.

The 7/8 length jacket
This jacket extends down to the lower part of the thigh, about 5-10 (2-3.9") cm above the knee. It should always be 3-5 cm (1.18-1.97") above the hem of a skirt.

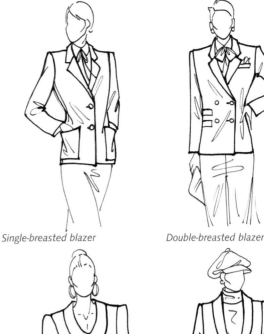

Single-breasted blazer *Double-breasted blazer*

Above-the-waist bolero *Shawl collar jacket*

Below-the-waist spencer *Cardigan style jacket*

3/4 length jacket *7/8 length jacket*

Suits and casual jackets

The suit jacket

The classic suit is the pairing of a menswear-style jacket or blazer (single- or double-breasted) with a skirt that is either straight or has a vent in the front or back. Today, the suit jacket is reinterpreted by designers to reflect their personal versions with diverse lines.

This jacket may be substituted by a smaller jacket that hits 15 cm (5.9") from the waistline at most. It may be single- or double-breasted, have a shawl collar, envelope lapels or another creative style. The sleeves may have one or two seams, gathering at the armscye, pleats, raglan or kimono in style and have fitted or loose wrists. In addition to the classic pencil shape, the skirt may have the usual pleats, soft or straight box pleats, have a flared outline or be a modified circle skirt, etc. The suit may also be made up of a jacket and trousers (suit trousers) and by a jacket and dress.

The swing jacket

A type of jacket that is loose-fitting, especially in the back, with kimono sleeves and a 3/4 length, generally speaking. These jackets were common in the late 1940s and the early 1950s, but even today they are sometimes brought back by designers with varied lapels and lengths.

The safari jacket

The safari jacket is usually in cotton or linen fabric with large patch pockets on the hips and bust, folds and epaulettes. It was once commonly used in colonised African countries. Today, it's worn as a summer jacket by both men and women.

The parka

Parkas are loose-fitting, hooded jackets made of sealed fabric that cover the buttocks, extending 35-40 cm (13.8-15.7") down from the waist. There are drawstrings at the waistline and at the bottom hem and there are large pockets on the front of the hips and bust.

The casual jacket

This is an item of clothing for both men and women, characterised by its length: no longer than approximately 65-70 cm (25.6-27.6"). These loose-fit jackets are generally casual or sporty with wide shoulders. They feature large pockets and original patterns. The sleeves may be tailored, raglan or kimono in style and often come in creative designs, while the closure may be single- or double-breasted and fastened with a zip or buttons.

Materials used to make casual winter jackets range from gabardine, different weight cloths, raised fabric, houndstooth, natural tartans, and, for the more youthful versions, lined denim, etc. Casual spring/summer jackets may be in combed or printed fabric, denim, etc.

Puffer jackets

The puffer jacket features the essential characteristics and is in breathable chintz fabric, padded with goose down or synthetic materials, layered with mouflon and an inner lining. Generally it features lively inserts and motifs and is decorated with overlapping stitching that forms patterns and designs while having the main function of keeping the padding in place. The closure is usually a thick plastic zip, hidden by a flap kept flat by press studs. Collars are almost always mandarin style or square, higher than usual, and closed with press studs or with the same zip that runs down the length of the jacket. The tailored or raglan sleeves feature an elastic band or cuff and are frequently removable.

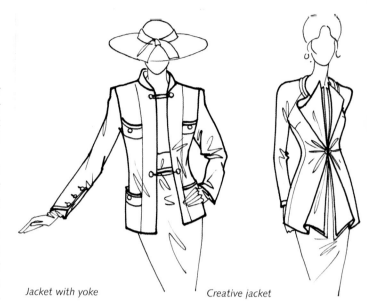

Jacket with yoke   Creative jacket

Modern swing jacket   Safari jacket

Parka   Puffer jacket

Waistcoat

A women's waistcoat (sometimes called a gilet) is a type of form-fitting bodice without sleeves. It may come with or without a front button fastening and may be worn under a jacket or simply with a skirt or pair of trousers.

A dress shirt, t-shirt or just undergarments may be worn under a waistcoat.

Created as menswear, in vogue in the 1600s and onward, the waistcoat is the evolution of a rather long, brocade, satin or damask doublet. It came with or without sleeves, with pockets and a v-shaped neckline from which the jabot of a lace shirt was visible.

A waistcoat may be single- or double-breasted, a v-shape or rounded neckline, with or without a collar (which may be lapels or a shawl collar). There may be two pockets on the front, while the back may feature a clasp.

Waistcoats are often in the same fabric as the skirt/trousers they're worn with, but they may be in a contrasting material.

Sports gilets feature a zip in the front and generally have a mandarin collar. They're usually made of a sealed, waterproof cotton canvas, wool or fleece.

Designers often include waistcoats in their collections in different shapes and lengths, including maxi gilets that fall to the ankle, frequently using prized materials.

Single-breasted waistcoat

Double-breasted with lapels

Double-breasted waistcoat

Maxi waistcoat

Open waistcoat

Sports waistcoat

VARIATIONS ON THE BASIC BODICE

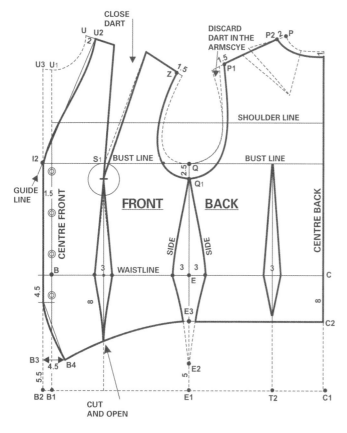

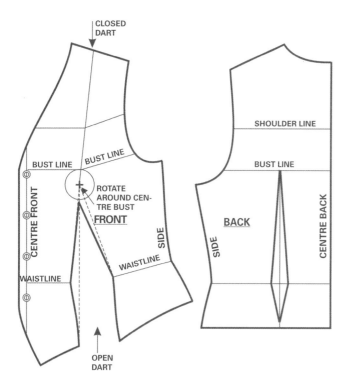

Measurements: Size 42, as in the chart.

Ease: As found under "waistcoat" in the ease chart 8-10 cm /3.1-3.9".

- Trace the base of the bodice with darts, with an 8-10 cm/3.1-3.9" ease and eliminate the shoulder dart, elongating the dart along the waistline as in the figure.
- Q-Q1 lower the armscye by 2-3 cm/0.79-1.2".
- Discard the dart of the back shoulder into the armscye.
- Taper shoulder points P1 and Z by 1-2 cm/0.39-0.79".
- U1-U3 1.5-2 cm/0.59-0.79" extension for fastening.
- U-U2 2 cm/0.79".
- P-P2 equal to U-U2, 2 cm/0.79".
- C-C2 6-8 cm/2.36-3.15".
- E-E3 equal to C-C2.
- B2-B3 5-7 cm/1.97-2.76".
- B3-B4 4-5 cm/1.57-1.97".
- Draw U2-I2-B4 and B4-E3-C2, carefully connecting with a curve.

DOUBLE-BREASTED WAISTCOAT

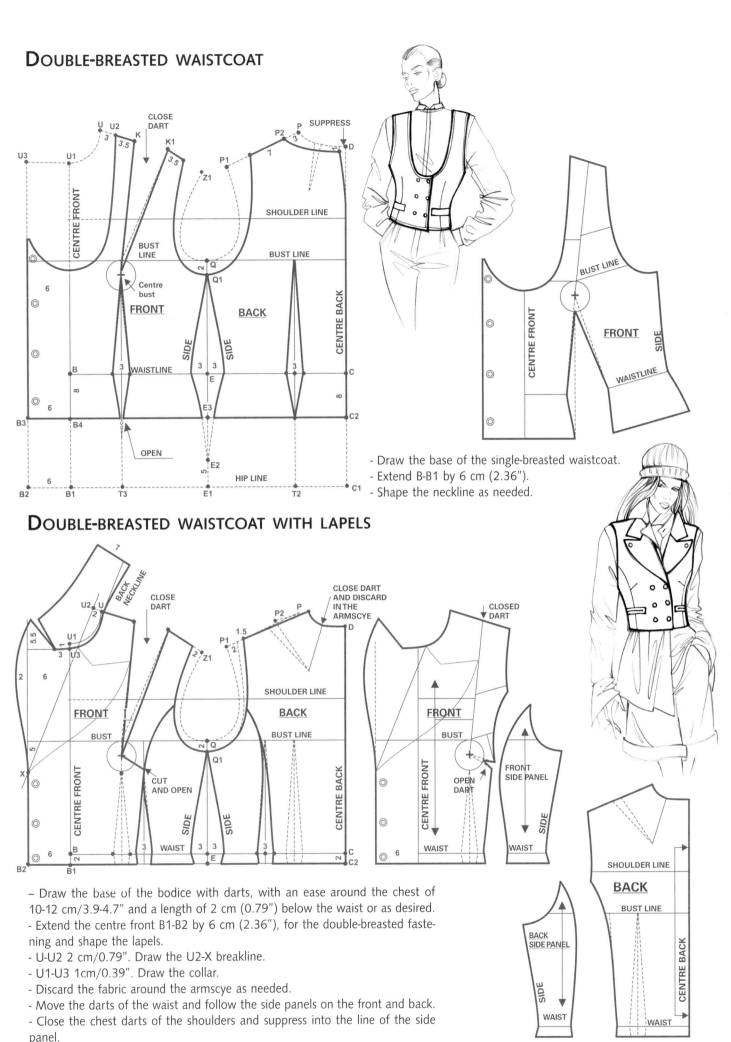

- Draw the base of the single-breasted waistcoat.
- Extend B-B1 by 6 cm (2.36").
- Shape the neckline as needed.

DOUBLE-BREASTED WAISTCOAT WITH LAPELS

– Draw the base of the bodice with darts, with an ease around the chest of 10-12 cm/3.9-4.7" and a length of 2 cm (0.79") below the waist or as desired.
- Extend the centre front B1-B2 by 6 cm (2.36"), for the double-breasted fastening and shape the lapels.
- U-U2 2 cm/0.79". Draw the U2-X breakline.
- U1-U3 1cm/0.39". Draw the collar.
- Discard the fabric around the armscye as needed.
- Move the darts of the waist and follow the side panels on the front and back.
- Close the chest darts of the shoulders and suppress into the line of the side panel.
- Suppress the shoulder dart behind, in the armscye.

11

Edge to edge waistcoat

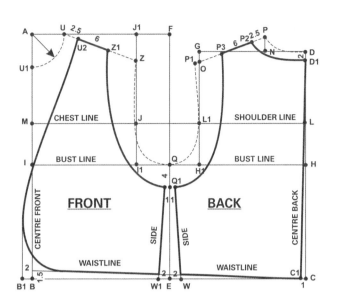

- Draw the base of the bodice without darts, with a chest ease of 8-10 cm/3.1-3.9".
- U-U2 2.5 cm/0.98". - P-P2 equal to U-U2.
- U2-Z1 6 cm/2.36". - P2-P3 equal to U2-Z1.
- Q-Q1 4 cm/1.57". - E-W and E-W1 2 cm/0.79".
- B-B1 2 cm/0.79". - C-C1 1 cm/0.39".
- Join the pieces as illustrated.

Sports waistcoat

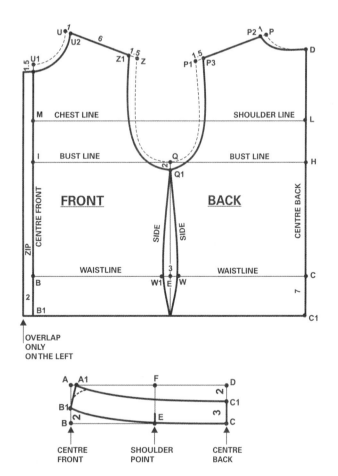

- Trace the base of the bodice without darts, with a bust ease of 10 cm/3.9" (more if padded).
- U-U2 1 cm. - P-P2 equal to U-U2.
- Z-Z1 1.5 cm/0.59". - P1-P3 equal to Z-Z1.
- Q-Q1 2 cm/0.79". - E-W and E-W1 1-1.5 cm/0.4-0.59".
- B-B1 5-7 cm/2-2.8". - C-C1 5-7 cm/2-2.8".
- Extend the centre front by 2 cm/0.79", only on the left side, for the zip cover flap.
- Trace the mandarin collar as explained in the first volume, with the collar measurements and height as desired.

MAXI WAISTCOAT

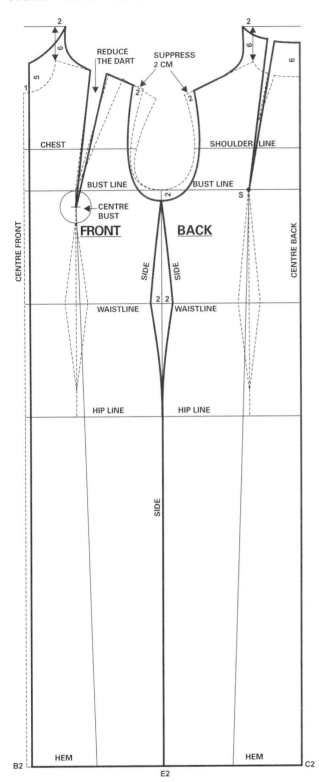

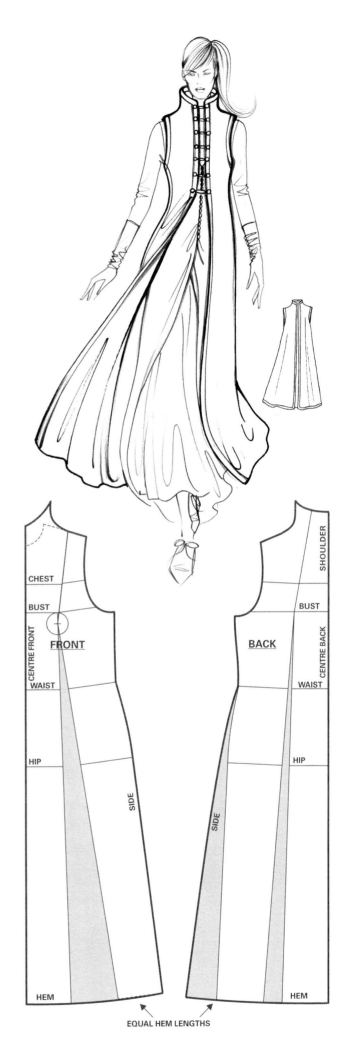

- Draw the base of the darted dress, with the ease of the waistcoat [10 cm (3.9") bust and hips] in the desired length.
- Reduce the bust dart by half.
- Raise the front and back collar by the desired measurements.
- Elongate the bust dart and that of the back collar to the bust line and elongate one side to the centre of the back.
- Cut along this line and open the bottom, closing the dart.
- Bring the width of the bottom of the back to be equal to the front, broadening along the side.

JACKET MEASUREMENTS

The measurements used to create a jacket are the same as for shirts, that is:

Neck circumference; Bust circumference; Hip circumference; Back shoulders width; Front torso width; Bust divergence; Back waist width; Front waist width; Bust depth; Sides depth; Total jacket depth.

Tailoring standards dictate that, before taking any measurements, it is important to check that the woman being measured is wearing her regular bra and that she is not wearing any bulky clothing that could throw off the measurements. In addition, it's helpful to tie a ribbon or a cord around the waist and the hips to have a precise point of reference.

Measurements should be immediately written down on the appropriate chart, along with any other characteristics or abnormalities, in order to appropriately modify the base pattern and avoid errors or inaccuracies.

All measurements must be carefully checked against the chosen pattern before proceeding to the pattern layout and cutting of the fabric.

.

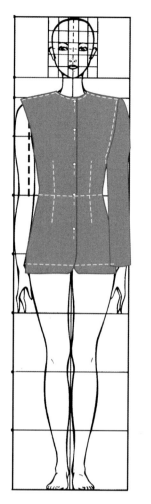

Jacket measurements, size 42 (ours)

- Neck circumference . . . . 37 cm (14.6")
- Bust circumference . . . . 92 cm + 1.2 cm ease (36.2 + 0.47" ease)
- Waist circumference . . . . . 68 cm + 6 cm ease (26.8 + 2.36" ease)
- Hip circumference . . . 92 cm + 1.2 cm ease (36.22 + 0.47" ease)
- Back shoulder width. . . . 36.5 cm + 3.5 cm ease (14.4 + 1.4" ease)
- Back waist width. . . . . 40 cm + 0.5-1 cm ease (15.7 + 0.20-0.39" ease)
- Front waist depth. . . . 41.5 cm + 0.5-1 cm ease (16.3 + 0.20-0.39" ease)
- Armscye. . . . . 9.2 cm + 1-1.5 cm ease (3.62 + 0.39-0.59" ease)

Jacket fit

Because jackets are generally worn over a shirt or a blouse and are usually lined, the fit should be looser than the wearer's torso and a fitted shirt. The ease values may vary based on the consistency of the fabric and the type of pattern. The diagram at right shows the ease allowances for the base of the bodice with respect to the base of the jacket.

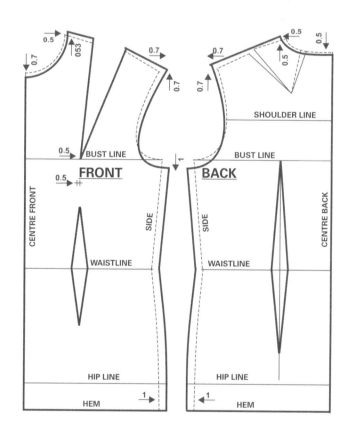

CHART FOR INDUSTRIAL WOMEN'S SIZING

WOMEN'S SIZE CHART, WITHOUT EASE ALLOWANCES

Circumference measurements	CM/IN	CM/IN	CM/IN	CM/IN	CM/IN	CM/IN
SIZE	**40**	**42**	**44**	**46**	**48**	**50**
Torso circumference	84/33.07"	86/33.86"	89/35.04"	92/36.22"	96/37.80"	100/39.37"
Bust circumference	89/35.04"	92/36.22"	96/37.80"	100/39.97"	105/41.34"	110/43.31"
Waist circumference	66/25.98"	68/26.77"	72/28.35"	76/29.92"	81/31.89"	86/33.86"
Hip circumference	89/35.04"	92/36.22"	96/37.80"	100/39.37"	105/41.34"	110/43.31"
Length of front torso *(including darts)	36.1/14.21"	37.1/14.61"	38.9/15.31"	40.5/15.94"	42.5/16.73"	44.5/17.52"
Length of back shoulders	35.3/13.90"	36.5/14.37"	37.9/14.92"	39.5/15.55"	41.5/16.34"	43.5/17.13"
Neck circumference	36/14.17"	37/14.57"	38/14.96"	39/15.55"	40/15.75"	41/16.14"
Back neckline	7.5/2.95"	8/3.15"	8.5/3.35"	9/3.54"	10/3.94"	11/4.33"
Length and width measurements						
HEIGHT	**164/64.57"**	**166/65.35"**	**168/66.14"**	**170/66.93"**	**172/67.72"**	**174/68.50"**
Bust divergence	17/6.69"	18/7.09"	19/7.48"	20/7.87"	21/8.27"	21/8.27"
Shoulder width	12/4.72"	13.5/5.31"	13.5/5.31"	14/5.51"	14.5/5.71"	15/5.91"
Back waist width	39.1/15.39"	40/15.75"	40.9/16.10"	41.8/16.46"	42.7/16.81"	43.6/17.17"
Front waist width	40.4/15.91"	41.5/16.34"	42.6/16.77"	43.7/17.20"	44.8/17.64"	45.9/18.07"
Bust depth	21.8/8.58"	22.5/8.86"	23.2/9.13"	23.9/9.41"	24.6/9.69"	25.1/9.88"
Side depth	19.6/7.72"	20/7.87"	20.4/8.03"	20.8/8.19"	21.2/8.35"	21.6/8.50"
Crotch depth	23.5/9.25"	24/9.45"	24.6/9.69"	25.2/9.89"	25.8/10/16"	26.5/10.43"
Knee depth	57.5/22.64"	58.5/23.03"	59.5/23.43"	60.5/23.82"	61.5/24.21"	62.5/24.61"
Outer leg length	102/40.16"	104/40.94"	105/41.34"	106/41.73"	107/42.13"	108/42.52"
Upper arm circumference	28/11.02"	29/11.42"	30/11.81"	31.5/12.40"	33/12.99"	35/13.78"
Wrist circumference	18/7.09"	19/7.48"	20/7.87"	20/7.87"	21/8.27"	21/8.27"
Sleeve length	57/22.44"	58/22.83"	59/23.23"	60/23.62"	61/24.02"	61/24.02"

*Control measurement

EASES BASED ON THE TYPE OF GARMENT

TYPE OF GARMENT	Costumes and bodysuits	Tops and bodices	Shirts, dresses and waistcoats	Boleros, shaped jackets	Loose-fitting jackets, shaped coats	Outerwear	Dusters, Macs, Capes	Padded heavy jackets
Torso circumference	-4 /-2 (-1.57/-0.79")	0 / 2 (0 / 0.79")	4 / 8 (1.57 / 3.15")	10 / 12 (3.94 / 4.72")	14 / 16 (5.51 / 6.30")	18 /20 (7.09 / 7.87")	22 /24 (8.66 / 9.45")	28 / 32 (11.02 / 12.60"
Bust circumference	-4 /-2 (-1.57/-0.79")	0 / 2 (0/0.79")	4 / 8 (1.57 /3.15")	10 / 12 (3.94 / 4.72")	14 / 16 (5.51 / 6.30")	18 /20 (7.09 / 7.87")	22 /24 (8.66 / 9.45")	28 / 32 (11.02 / 12.60"
Waist circumference	-2.5 / 1 (0.98/ 0.39")	0 / -1.5 (0/ -0.59")	2.5 / 4 (0.98 /1.57)	5 / 6 (1.97 / 2.36")	8 / 10 (3.15 / 3.94")	-	-	-
Hip circumference	-4 /-2 (-1.57/-0.79")	0 / 2 (0/0.79")	4 / 8 (1.57/ 3.15)	10 / 12 (3.94 / 4.72")	14 / 16 (5.51 / 6.30")	18 /20 (7.09 / 7.87")	22 /24 (8.66 / 9.45")	28 / 32 (11.02 / 12.60"
Upper arm circumference	-1.5 / -0.5 (-0.59 / 0.20")	0 / 1 (0 / 0.39")	1 / 1.5 (0.39 / 0.59")	1.5 / 2 (0.59- 0.79")	2.5 / 5 (0.98 / 1.97")	3.5 / 7 (1.38 / 2.76")	4.5 / 8.5 (1.77 / 3.35")	6 / 10 (2.36 / 3.94")
Back shoulders width	-1.5 / -0.5 (-0.59 / 0.20")	0 / -0.5 (0 / -0.20")	1 - 2 (0.39- 0.79")	2.5 - 3.5 (0.98 - 1.38")	3.5 - 4 (1.38 - 1.57")	4.5 - 5 (1.77 - 1.99")	5 - 5.5 (1.99 - 2.17")	7 - 8 (2.76 - 3.15")
Front torso width	-1.5 / -0.5 (-0.59 / 0.20")	0 / -0.5 (0 / -0.20")	1 - 2 (0.39-0.79"	2.5 - 3.5 (0.98 - 1.38")	3.5 - 4 (1.38 - 1.57")	4.5 - 5 (1.77 - 1.99")	5 - 5.5 (1.99 - 2.17")	7 - 8 (2.76 - 3.15")
Waist width (front and back)	-	-	-	1 (0.39")	2 (0.79")	2 (0.79")	2 (0.79")	3 / 4 (1.18 / 1.57")

SINGLE-BREASTED JACKET COMPOSITION

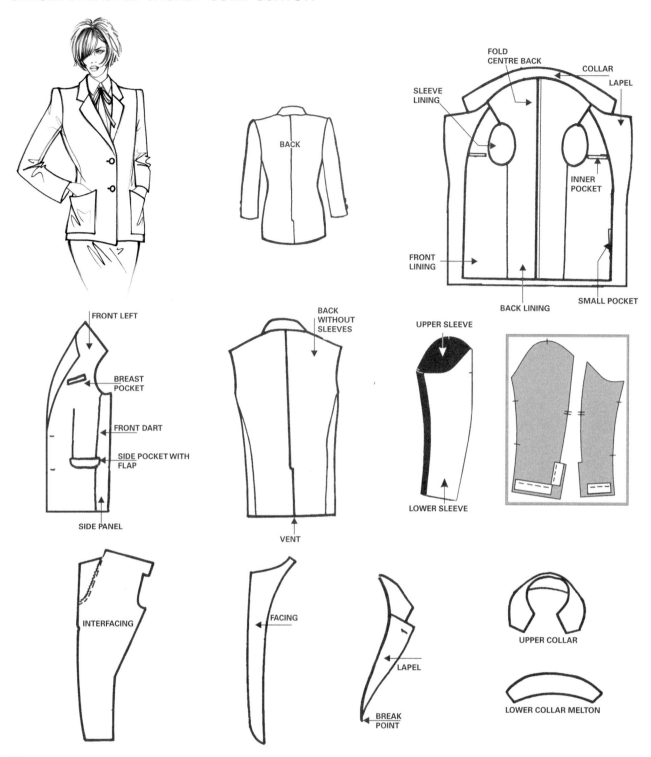

BACK

FOLD CENTRE BACK

COLLAR

LAPEL

SLEEVE LINING

INNER POCKET

FRONT LINING

BACK LINING

SMALL POCKET

FRONT LEFT

BREAST POCKET

FRONT DART

SIDE POCKET WITH FLAP

SIDE PANEL

BACK WITHOUT SLEEVES

VENT

UPPER SLEEVE

LOWER SLEEVE

INTERFACING

FACING

LAPEL

BREAK POINT

UPPER COLLAR

LOWER COLLAR MELTON

TYPES OF LAPELS FOR SINGLE-BREASTED JACKETS

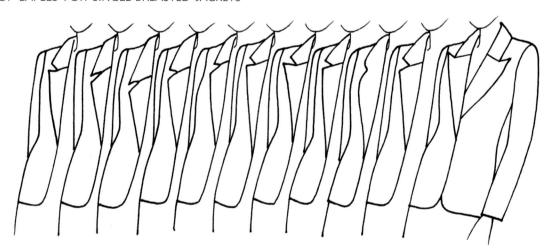

Terminology

Fabric details

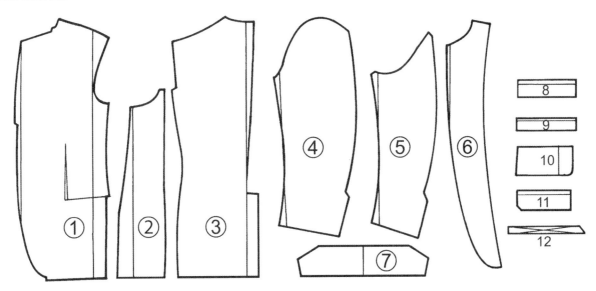

Lining and inner details

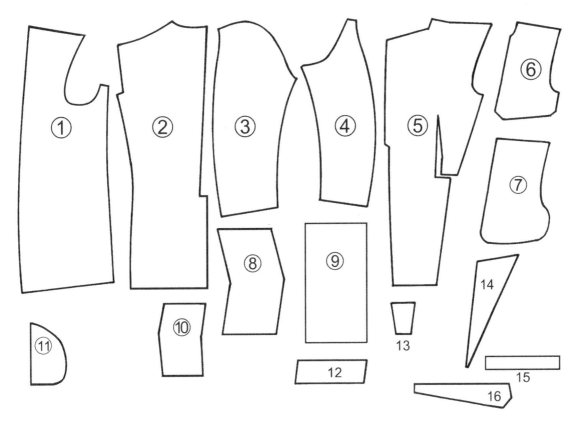

Fabric details
1) Front
2) Side
3) Back
4) Above sleeve
5) Under sleeve
6) Facing
7) Collar cover
8) Lower pocket welt
9) Upper pocket welt
10) Flap
11) Inner pocket
12) Front dart portion
Lining and placket details
1) Front

2) Back
3) Upper sleeve
4) Under sleeve
5) Camelhair body
6) Horsehair
7) Plush-covered cotton
8) Cotton lining, inner pocket
9) Cotton lining, side pocket
10) Cotton lining, breast pocket
11) Pear-shaped pocket
12) Camelhair back reinforcement
13) Camelhair shoulder gusset
14) Pad-stitched lapel reinforcement
15) Camelhair waist reinforcement
16) Front camelhair reinforcement

BASE JACKET BLOCK

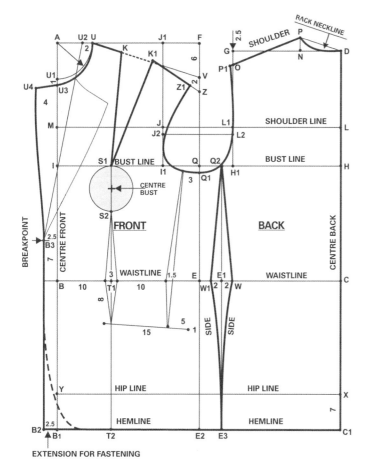

Measurements: Size 42, as in the table.

Ease: As in the chart, under "Shaped jacket".

- Draw a right angle triangle, ABC, where:
- A-B Front waist length + jacket pattern ease. (e.g.: 41.5 + 1 = 42.5 cm).
- B-C Bust semi-circumference + ease (e.g.: 92 + 12 = 104 : 2 = 52 cm).
- C-D Back waist length + ease. (i.e.: 40 + 1 = 41 cm).
- D-C1 Back jacket length (e.g.: 68 cm/26.77").
- Join D-C1 and write CENTRE BACK.
- B-B1 equal to C-C1.
- Join A-B1 and write CENTRE FRONT.
- B1-C1 equal to B-C.
- Join B1-C1 and write HEM LINE.
- B-E half of B-C. - B1-E2 half of B1-C1.
- A-F equal to B-E.
- Join F-E2 and write CENTRAL SIDE LINE.
- D-H half of C-D (e.g.: 41 : 2 = 20.5 cm).
- H-I Parallel to B-C. Write BUST LINE.
(This line is found approx. 3-5 cm/1.18-1.97" from the centre bust).
- E2-E3 4 cm/1.57", if you would like the back to be more fitted.
- Q-Q2 4 cm/1.57".
- Join Q2-E3. MOVED SIDE LINE.
- C-X Hip height (e.g. 20 cm).
- Trace X-Y. HIP LINE.
- D-G half of shoulder length + ease.
(e.g.: 36.5 + 3.5 = 40 : 2 = 20 cm).
- H-L 1/3 D-H. (e.g.: 21 : 3 = 7 cm).

- Trace L-M. SHOULDER LINE and CHEST LINE.
- H-H1 equal to D-G. (20 cm/7.87").
- H1-I1 underarm section length + ease* (e.g.: 12.4 cm/4.88").
- Draw G-H1 parallel to D-H.
- Draw I1-J1 parallel to G-H1.
- Draw the centre bust.

Back

- G-O 2.5 cm/0.98".
- D-N 1/3 D-G + 1 cm/0.39" (e.g.: 20 : 3 = 6.6 + 1 = 7.6 cm). (Without dart).
- N-P 2.5 cm/0.98". - Trace D-P.
- Join P-D with a contoured curved line.
- P-P1 passing by O, shoulder length + 1 cm/0.39". (e.g.: 13 + 1 = 14 cm).
- Mark point Q as half of H-I.
- Q-Q1 1 cm/0.39" (or more for lower armscye).
- Draw the armscye P1-L1-Q1, carefully creating the curve.
- L1-L2 equal to Q-Q1.
- Draw L2-J2. Sleeve reference.

Front

- A-U 1/3 D-G of the back (e.g.: 20 : 3 = 6.6 cm).
- Draw the curve U-U1 with measurement A-U, centred on A.
- I-I1 equal to H-H1 - 0.5 cm/0.20" (e.g.: 20 - 0.5 = 19.5 cm).
- I-S1 1/2 Bust divergence + 0.5 cm/0.20". (e.g.: 19 : 2 = 9.5+0.5= 10 cm).
- F-V 6 cm/2.36".
- Join U-V.
- U-K 1/3 P-P1 of the back +1 cm/0.39" (e.g.: 14 : 3 = 4.7 + 1 = 5.7 cm).
- K-K1 Difference between bust circumference and torso circumference. (e.g.: 92 - 86 = 6 cm).
- K1-S1 equal to K-S1. Join.
- V-Z 1/3 of F-V (e.g.: 6 : 3 = 2 cm).
- K1-Z1 equal to P-P1 of the back minus U-K (e.g.: 14 - 5.7 = 8.3 cm)
- Draw the front sleeve hole Z1-J-Q1, carefully creating the curve.

Lapel

- Trace the 2.5 cm/0.98" extension of the centre front B2-B3 for the fastening.
- Draw B2-B3, up to the height of the desired break point for the lapel (e.g.: 7 cm/2.76" from the waist).
- Draw point U2, 2 cm/0.79" from U.
– Join U2-B3. BREAKLINE.
- Lower the front collar by 1-1.5cm/0.39-0.59", point U3.
- U3-U4 4 cm/1.57" or as desired.
- Join U4-B3 and join with the bottom line with a curve as desired.

Waist darts

The waist darts and side tapering are determined by the difference between hip and waist, which is distributed proportionally along the line of the waist dart and on the side line, in addition to the creation of a small 1.5 cm/0.59" dart, with peaks on the armscye and pocket line.

The underarm area is calculated as follows: 1/5 Semi-circumference of the bust including the ease + 2 cm/0.79". (e.g.: 52 : 5 = 10.4 + 2= 12.4 cm).

INSET SLEEVE BLOCK

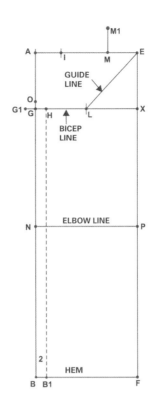

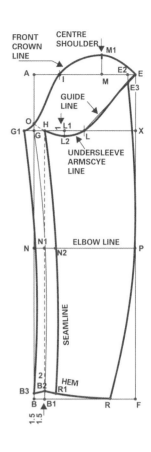

Measurements: - Arm circumference 29 cm/11.42"
- Arm length 58 cm/22.83"

On the left hand side of a piece of pattern paper, draw a rectangle with points A-B-E-F, where:
- A-E is equal to BASE BODICE SECTION +1/2 SECTION. (e.g.: 12.4 + 6.2 = 18.6 cm).
- A-B Sleeve length measurement (e.g.: 58 cm/22.83").
- A-G equal to the measurement of L2-P1 minus 1 cm/0.39" from the base of the back bodice. (e.g.: 12.5-1 = 11.5 cm).
- Trace G-X parallel to A-E.
- A-N half of A-B+2 (e.g. 58 : 2 = 29 + 2 = 31 cm). ELBOW LINE.
- A-M 2/3 of A. CENTRE SHOULDER. (e.g.: 18.4 x 2 = 36.8 : 3 = 12.3 + 1 = 13.3 cm).
- M-M1 1/3 A-G. (e.g.: 10.5 : 3 = 3.5 cm).
- A-I 1/4 A-E. (e.g.: 18.6 : 4 = 4.6 cm).
- G-H 2 cm/0.79".
- Trace H-B1 parallel to A-B.
- X-L half of G-X. (e.g.:18.6 : 2 = 9.3 cm).
- Trace the guide line E-L.
- L-L1 half of H-L.- L1-L2 1 cm/0.39".
- G-O 1.5 cm/0.59".
- G-G1 equal to G-H, 2 cm/0.79".
- Draw the front sleeve cap E-M1-I-O-G1, shaping it carefully.
- Draw the back sleeve cap E-L-L2-H-O, shaping it carefully.
- B-B1 2 cm/0.79". - B1-B2 1.5 cm/0.59" - B2-B3 2 cm/0.79".
- B3-R 1/2 length of bottom of sleeve (e.g.: 13.5 cm).

Undersleeve
- E-E2 1.5 cm/0.59" (or a different measurement, as needed).
- B2-R1 equal to B2-B3.
- Connect R-E3 and R1-H with a curved line.

Open sleeve
- Copy the undersleeve E3-P-R-R1-H-L2-L-E3 and position it on the E-F fold line on the front part. Draw the sleeve cap line, shaping it carefully. Check the measurement of the entire sleeve cap, which should be greater than the measure of the armscye, by a variable amount, based on the type of fabric used.

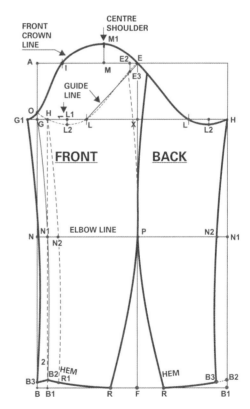

NB: To have the correct balance of the sleeve, the centre back should be adjusted, moving it towards the front or back by a few millimetres based on the subject's anatomy or posture.

POSITIONS AND SIZES FOR JACKET DARTS

The jacket's bust dart may be moved or modified in various ways, depending on the pattern.
Changes may be necessary to conceal the darts, as well as give the pattern the correct proportions and fit, with the garment's best possible appearance as the ultimate goal.
The bust dart, according to the pattern and the wearer's anatomy, may be: 1) Eliminated; 2) Reduced; 3) Absorbed into the seams; 4) Moved to another, better hidden position.

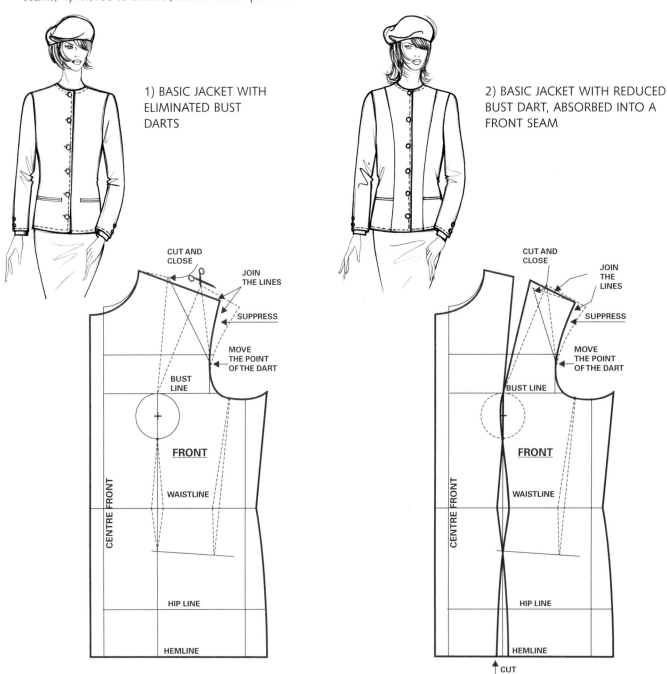

1) BASIC JACKET WITH ELIMINATED BUST DARTS

2) BASIC JACKET WITH REDUCED BUST DART, ABSORBED INTO A FRONT SEAM

1) Eliminating the darts
The bust darts can be eliminated from jackets with a roomy, loose fit.
- Draw the base of the jacket pattern, with ample measurements and ease.
- Shift the dart point to the line of the armscye.
- Cut along the second traced bust dart line and close the section until the sides meet.
- Connect both the shoulder line and the armscye line.

2) Reduction of the dart
Reducing the front bust dart is generally done for jackets with a front seam in order to give shape to the figure.
- Trace the base of the jacket pattern with ample measurements and ease.
- Trace a line from the dart point, dividing it evenly in half.
- Shift the dart point to the armscye line.
- Cut along the second line of the drawn bust dart and close the section until the sides meet.
- Join both the shoulder line and the armscye line.

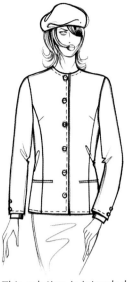

3) BASIC JACKET WITH A REDUCED BUST DART, ABSORBED INTO THE SIDE SEAM

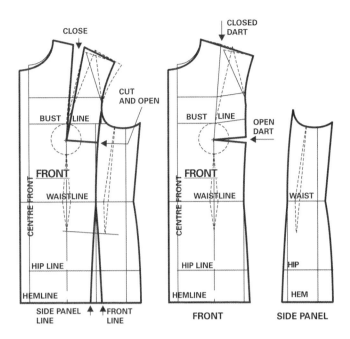

This solution is intended for subjects with a significant difference between the bust circumference and the hip circumference.
- Reduce the size of the bust dart by half or by the necessary measurement.
- Draw the side line as required by the pattern.
- Draw a line from the centre of the bust to the side line.
- Close the bust dart along the shoulder and open it on this new line. Then, make sure it is absorbed into the seam.

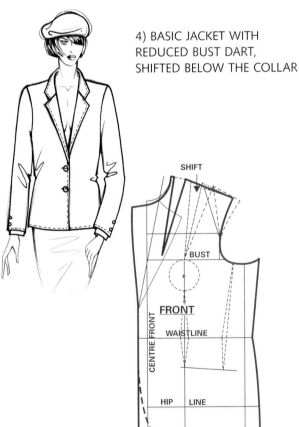

4) BASIC JACKET WITH REDUCED BUST DART, SHIFTED BELOW THE COLLAR

5) BASIC JACKET WITH DARTS ALONG THE BREAKLINE

Moving the bust dart in this way is intended primarily for jackets with a more masculine cut worn by subjects with larger busts, who require a dart in any case.
- Draw the jacket base block with the reduced dart.
- Shift the extracted dart to under the collar and lapels, in the least visible place possible.

This dart is used to give a rounded shape to the lapel when it's folded.
- Trace the jacket base block with eliminated, reduced or other alternative bust darts.
- On the lapel's breakline, draw a slightly curved, 1-1.2 cm/0.39-0.47" dart.

Overlaps and lapels

A garment's overlap is the placement of one of the front plackets over the other, which characterizes the shape and form of the fastening and the style of the pattern.

The overlap may come in two forms: 1) with a simple fastening, called single-breasted; 2) with a double fastening, called double-breasted.

The measurement of the placket and its overlap may vary according to the pattern, the garment type and style.

Single-breasted

For double-breasted jackets, the overlap of the two front panels ranges from 2.5 cm to 3 cm (1-1.2").

For coats and outerwear, the overlap ranges from 4 cm to 5 cm (1.6-2").

Execution:

- Extend the centre front B1-B2 by 2.5 cm/0.98" and give the bottom the desired shape.
- Mark the position of the first button on the overlap B3, at the desired height, as seen in the illustration.
- From point U on the neck, extend the shoulder line by 2-2.5 cm/0.79-0.98", based on the height of the collar stand.
- Trace the breakline U2-B3.

Double-breasted

For double-breasted jacket and coat patterns, the two front panels overlap by 7-8 cm/2.76-3.15".

Execution:

- Extend the centre front B1-B2 by 7-8 cm/2.76-3.15".
- Mark the position of the first button on the overlap line B3, at the desired height, as seen in the illustration.
- From point U on the collar, extend the shoulder line by 2.5 cm/0.98", based on the height of the collar.
- Draw the breakline U2-B3.

Lapels (or revers)

The lapel is the upper part of the front of the bodice that folds over at the neckline. It is a continuous elongation of the placket; the visible part of the lapel is essentially the inner facing of the jacket that is turned to face outwards.

Lapels may come in different shapes and widths according to the pattern and the style of the garment; for this reason, the measurements are not indicated in the base block.

Execution:

- Lower point U1 by the desired measurement, based on the position and size of the collar and the shape of the lapel.
- Trace the collar extension U4 with the desired shape and width.
- Join U4 with B3, adjusting the shape smoothly.
- To check that the lapel is in keeping with the pattern and that it has the right size and positioning, after having constructed the exterior part, fold the lapel along the breakline and, if necessary, apply any necessary corrections.

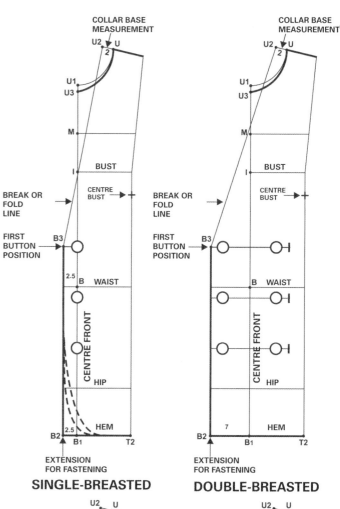

SINGLE-BREASTED   **DOUBLE-BREASTED**

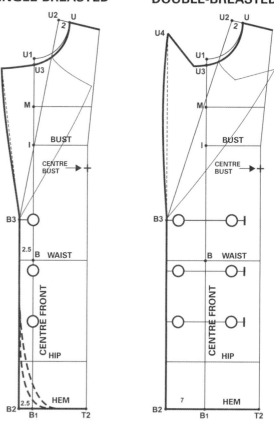

SINGLE-BREASTED   **DOUBLE-BREASTED**

JACKET COLLAR

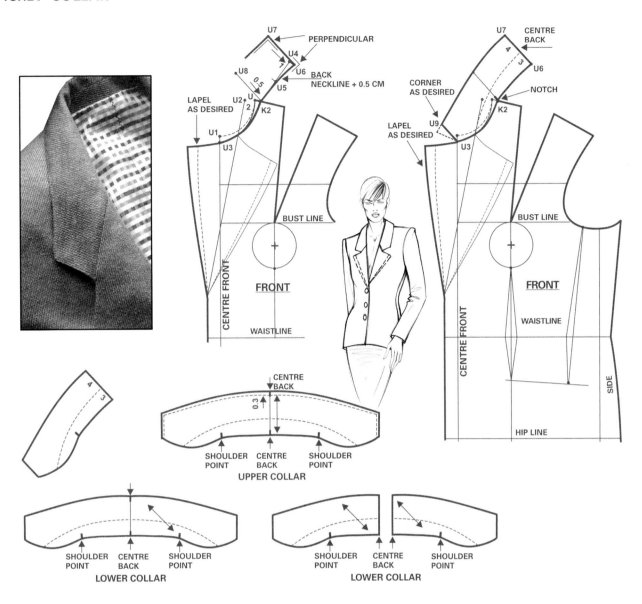

- Trace K2-U4 with K2 shifted away from U by 0.5 cm/0.20" and with a measurement equal to that of the back neckline increased by 0.5 cm (0.20").
- U4-U5 equal to half of K2-U4.
- U4-U6 1 cm/0.39".
- Join with a curved line U6-K2.
- Draw U6-U7 at a right angle from the line U6-K2, with the desired collar measurement (e.g.: 7 cm/2.76").
- K2-U8 equal to U6-U7.
- Draw U3-U9 with the desired angle and measurement (e.g.: 4 cm/1.57").
- At about 3 cm/1.18" from U6, towards U7, trace a dotted

line until you reach the breakline. This is the collar fold line, which must always be hidden under the collar.
- Smoothly connect all the lines and take the collar up again on another piece of paper.
- The upper collar must be 0.3-0.5 cm/0.12-0.20" bigger than the under collar, to hide the seam.
- The under collar may be made up of two detached pieces.

Flatter collars with different shapes

To achieve a flatter collar or one with a different shape and size, you can begin with the collar base shown above.
- Divide the part of the neckline behind the collar into 4 equal parts, drawing 4 lines from the external edge to the internal edge.
- Cut along these lines and lengthen the top part by 0.5-1 cm/0.20-0.39", according to how flat you would like it to be.
- Connect the upper part at the desired distance and with the desired shape.

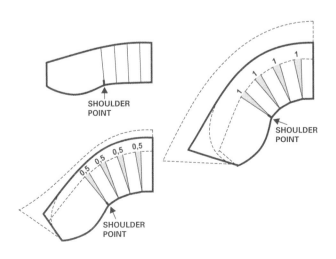

VARIATIONS ON THE SPORTS COLLAR

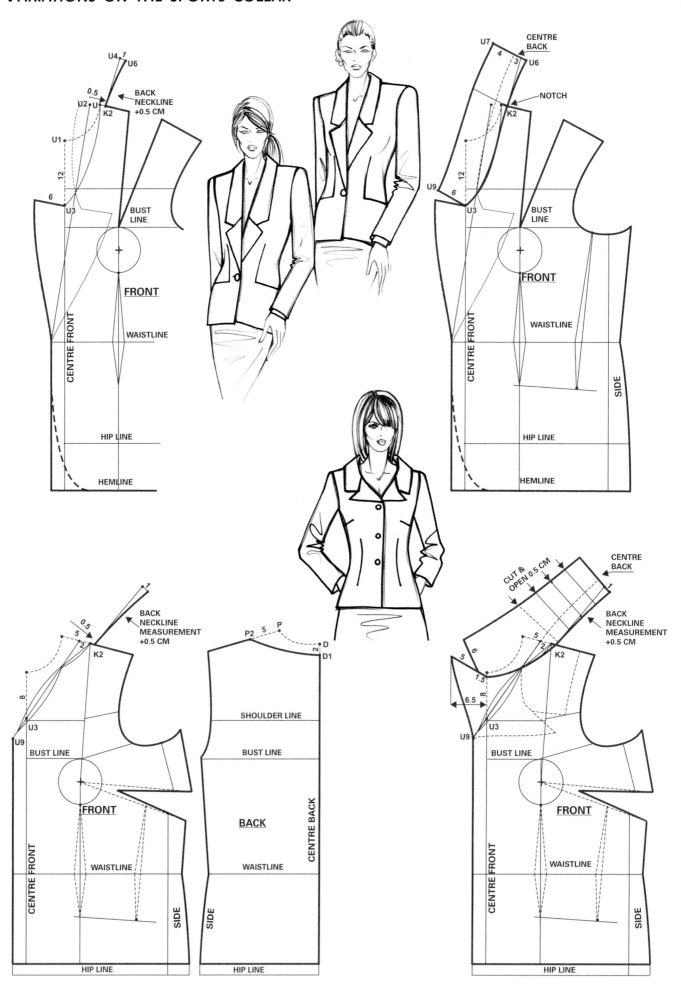

JACKET WITH STEP COLLAR

- Trace the basic jacket block with darts in ample measurements and ease. Shift the bust dart to 2 cm/0.79" from the first shoulder point.
- K2-U4 with K2 shifted away from U by 0.5 cm/0.20", with a measurement equal to that of the back neckline plus 0.5 cm/0.20".
- U4-U5 equal to half of K2-U4. - U4-U6 2 cm/0.79".
- Join U6-K2 with a curved line.
- Draw U6-U7 at a right angle to U6-K2, with the desired measurement for the collar (e.g.: 7 cm/2.76").
- K2-U8 equal to U6-U7.
- Draw U3-J with the desired angle and measurement (e.g.: 6 cm/2.36").
- J-J1 half of J-U3 or as desired.
- Draw J1-U9 with the desired measurement and angle.
- At around 2.5-3 cm/0.98-1.81" from U6, towards U7, trace a dotted line until the breakline. This line is where the collar is to be folded (remember that the collar should always be larger on the upper layer than the lower layer).
- Smoothly connect all the lines as in the illustration and take up the collar on a new piece of paper.
- The upper collar should be 0.3-0.5 cm/0.12-0.20" larger than the under collar in order to hide the seams.

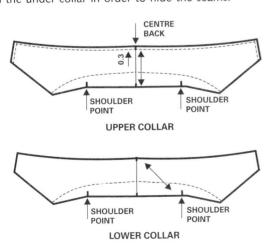

UPPER COLLAR

LOWER COLLAR

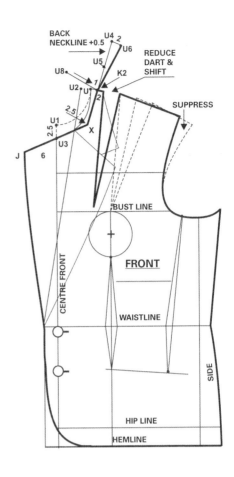

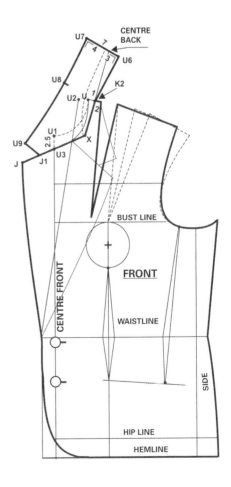

JACKET WITH SHAWL COLAR

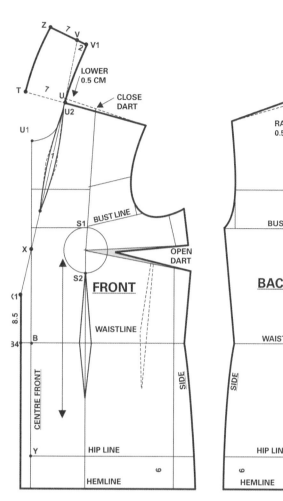

- Draw the base jacket block with the appropriate
measurements, ease and desired length.
- Lower the first front shoulder point U by 0.5 cm/0.20".
- Raise the first back shoulder point P by 0.5 cm/0.20".
- Draw the extension of the centre front for the fastening.
- Draw the breakline U2-X-X1 according to the desired lapel
angle (e.g.: 8.5 cm/3.35" from the waist).
- U-V back neckline length + 0.5 cm/0.20".
- V-V1 1.5-2 cm/0.59-0.79".
- V1-Z 7 cm/2.76" or another measurement, as desired.
- U2-T equal to V1-Z.
- Draw U2-V1 with a curved line.
- Connect Z-T-X1 with a curved line, according to the contour
desired for the collar.
Dart hidden under the shawl collar
- Trace a 15-16 cm/5.91-6.30" dart along the breakline,
starting from U2, with a width of 0.6-1 cm/0.24-0.39".
- Create a slight curve along the sides of the dart.
This dart is used to give the correct shape to the jacket's shawl
collar (which is not sewn on shirts and dresses).

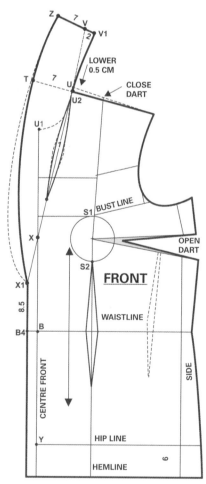

SHAPED SHAWL COLLAR

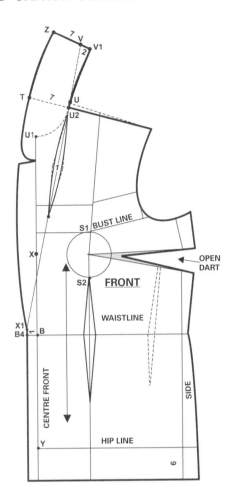

DOUBLE-BREASTED SHAWL COLLAR

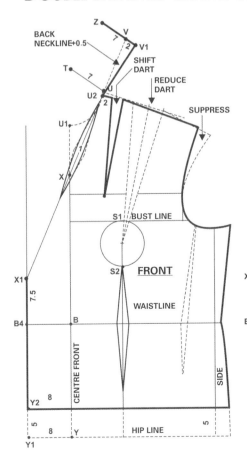

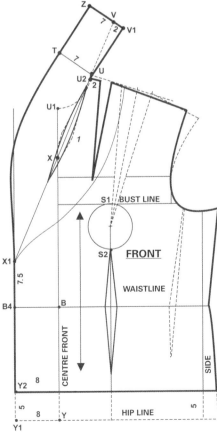

- Draw the base of the jacket pattern as shown, with the desired length.
- Extend the centre front by 6.5-8 cm/2.56-3.15" for the double-breasted overlap.
- Draw the breakline with an angle as shown in the illustration, X1-U2-V.
- Reduce the bust dart and shift it 2 cm/0.78" from the neckline, hidden under the collar.
- Draw the upper part of the collar as shown in the single-breasted illustration.
- Draw the desired shape of the shawl collar: Z-TX1-Y2.

WIDE SHAWL COLLAR

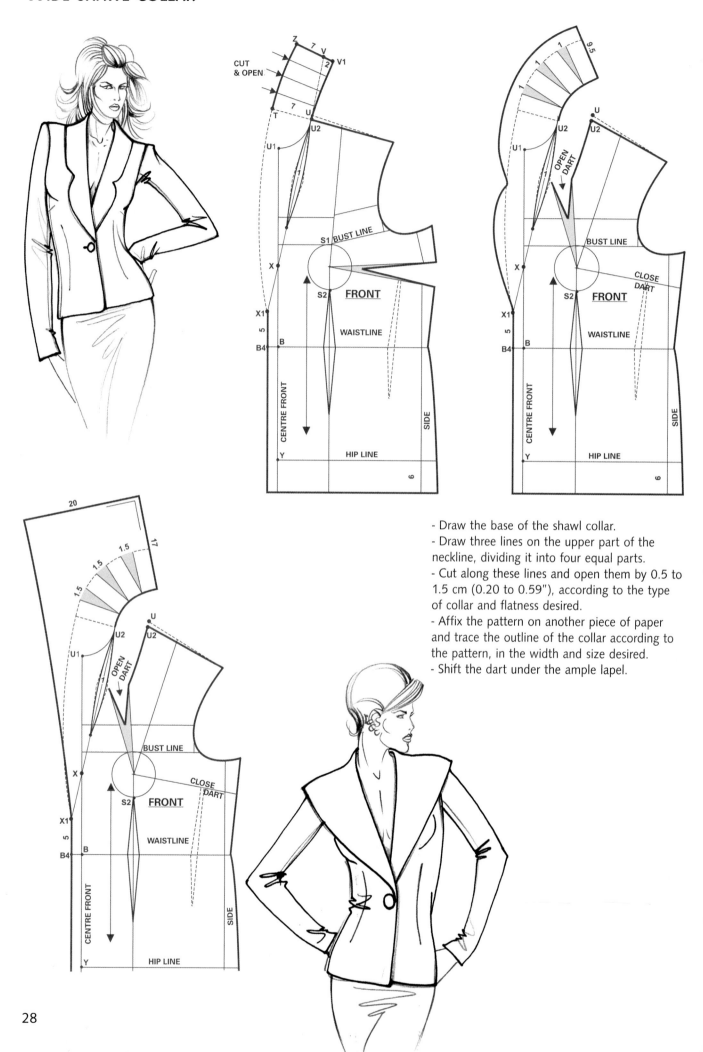

- Draw the base of the shawl collar.
- Draw three lines on the upper part of the neckline, dividing it into four equal parts.
- Cut along these lines and open them by 0.5 to 1.5 cm (0.20 to 0.59"), according to the type of collar and flatness desired.
- Affix the pattern on another piece of paper and trace the outline of the collar according to the pattern, in the width and size desired.
- Shift the dart under the ample lapel.

Collarless lapel (envelope collar)

Double-breasted jacket

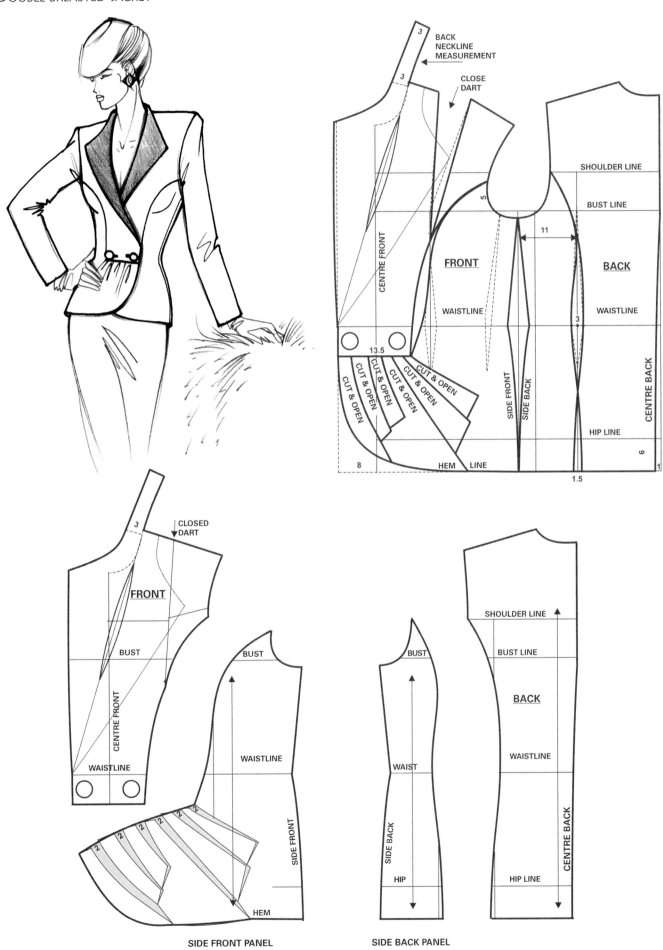

BACK NECKLINE MEASUREMENT

CLOSE DART

3

3

CENTRE FRONT

FRONT

5

SHOULDER LINE

BUST LINE

11

BACK

WAISTLINE

WAISTLINE

3

SIDE FRONT

SIDE BACK

CENTRE BACK

13.5

CUT & OPEN

CUT & OPEN

CUT & OPEN

CUT & OPEN

CUT & OPEN

HIP LINE

8

HEM LINE

6

1.5

1

CLOSED DART

3

FRONT

BUST

BUST

CENTRE FRONT

WAISTLINE

WAISTLINE

SIDE FRONT

2 2 2 2 2

HEM

SIDE FRONT PANEL

SHOULDER LINE

BUST LINE

BUST

BACK

WAIST

WAISTLINE

SIDE BACK

CENTRE BACK

HIP

HIP LINE

SIDE BACK PANEL

Double collarless lapel (envelope collar)

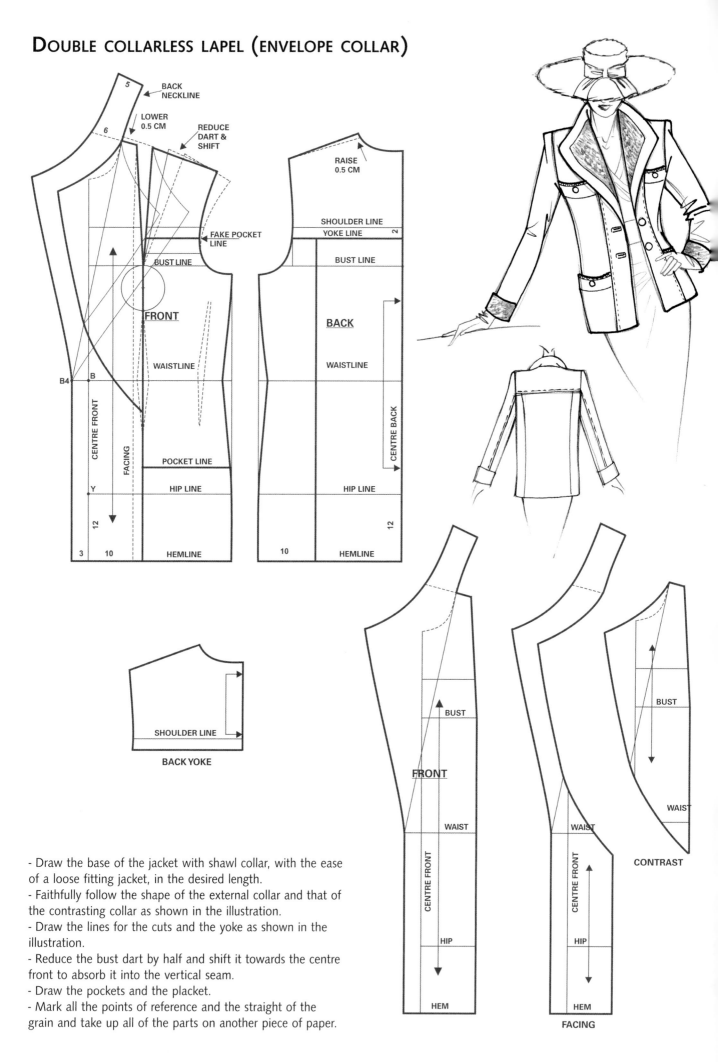

BACK NECKLINE

LOWER 0.5 CM

REDUCE DART & SHIFT

5

6

FAKE POCKET LINE

BUST LINE

FRONT

WAISTLINE

B4   B

CENTRE FRONT

FACING

POCKET LINE

Y

HIP LINE

12

3   10   HEMLINE

RAISE 0.5 CM

SHOULDER LINE
YOKE LINE   2

BUST LINE

BACK

WAISTLINE

CENTRE BACK

HIP LINE

12

10   HEMLINE

SHOULDER LINE

BACK YOKE

BUST

FRONT

WAIST

CENTRE FRONT

HIP

HEM

BUST

WAIST

CENTRE FRONT

HIP

HEM

FACING

BUST

WAIST

CONTRAST

- Draw the base of the jacket with shawl collar, with the ease of a loose fitting jacket, in the desired length.
- Faithfully follow the shape of the external collar and that of the contrasting collar as shown in the illustration.
- Draw the lines for the cuts and the yoke as shown in the illustration.
- Reduce the bust dart by half and shift it towards the centre front to absorb it into the vertical seam.
- Draw the pockets and the placket.
- Mark all the points of reference and the straight of the grain and take up all of the parts on another piece of paper.

Seam allowances

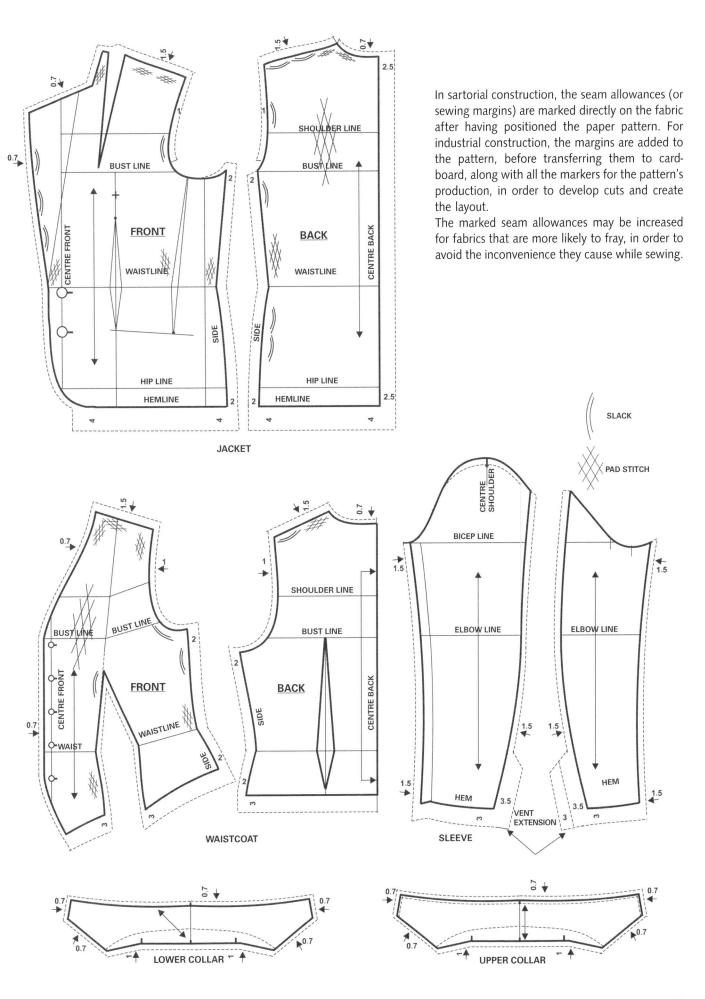

In sartorial construction, the seam allowances (or sewing margins) are marked directly on the fabric after having positioned the paper pattern. For industrial construction, the margins are added to the pattern, before transferring them to cardboard, along with all the markers for the pattern's production, in order to develop cuts and create the layout.

The marked seam allowances may be increased for fabrics that are more likely to fray, in order to avoid the inconvenience they cause while sewing.

JACKET

WAISTCOAT

SLEEVE

SLACK

PAD STITCH

LOWER COLLAR

UPPER COLLAR

LOOSE-FITTING JACKET

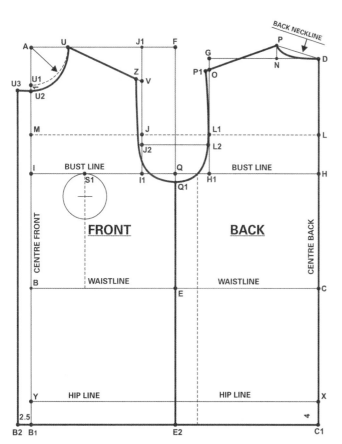

Measurements: Size 42, as in the women's sizing table.

Ease: As in the chart, under "Loose-fitting jacket".

- Draw a right angle, ABC, with:
- A-B equal to the front waist length + loose-fitting jacket ease of 2 cm/0.79". (e.g.: 41.5 + 2 cm = 43.5 cm).
- B-C bust semi-circumference + ease. (e.g.: 92 + 14 cm = 106 : 2 = 53 cm).
- C-D back waist length + ease. (e.g.: 40 + 2 cm = 42 cm).
- D-C1 back jacket length (65 cm/25.59").
- Join D-C1 (CENTRE BACK).
- B-B1 equal to C-C1.
- Join A-B1 (CENTRE FRONT).
- B1-C1 equal to B-C.
- Join B1-C1. HEM LINE.
- B-E half of B-C. B1-E2 half of B1-C1.
- A-F equal to B-E.
- Join F-E-E2 (CENTRAL SIDE LINE).
- D-H half of C-D (e.g.: 42 : 2 cm = 21 cm).
- H-I parallel to B-C, write BUST LINE.
- C-X side height (e.g.: 20 cm/7.87").
- D-G half of shoulder length + ease. (e.g.: 36.5 + 4.5 = 41 : 2 = 20.5 cm).
- H-L 1/3 D-H. (e.g.: 21 : 3 = 7 cm).
- Trace L-L1. SHOULDER LINE.
- H-H1 equal to D-G. (20 cm/7.78").
- H1-I1 armscye length + ease* (e.g.: 12.4 cm/4.88").
- Draw G-H1 parallel to D-H.
- Draw I1-J1 parallel to G-H1.
- I-M equal to H-L. Draw L-M parallel to H-I.

Back
- G-O 2 cm/0.79".
- D-N 1/3 of DG + 1 cm/0.39" (e.g.: 20.5 : 3 = 6.8 + 1 = 7.8 cm).
- N-P 2.5 cm/0.98". Trace D-P.
- P-P1 passing through O. Make it the shoulder length + 1 cm/0.39" (e.g.: 13 + 1 = 14 cm).
- Join P-D with a curved, shaped line.
- Mark the point Q at half of H-I.
- Q-Q1 1-2.5 cm/0.39-0.98" (based on the proportions).
- Draw armscye P1-L1-Q1, carefully creating the curve.
- L1-L2 equal to Q-Q1.
- Draw L2-J2. SLEEVE REFERENCE.

Front
- A-U 1/3 D-G (e.g.: 20.5 : 3 = 6.8 cm).
- Trace the U-U1 curve with the A-U measurement, centred on A.
- I-I1 equal to H-H1 - 0.5 cm/0.20". (e.g.: 20.5 - 0.5 = 20 cm).
- I-S1 1/2 Bust divergence + 0.5 cm/0.20" (e.g.: 19 : 2 = 9.5 + 0.5= 10 cm).
- F-V 6 cm/2.36".
- Join U-V.
- U-Z equal to P-P1 of the back, minus 0.5 cm/0.20" (13.5 cm/5.31").
- Draw the curved armscye section Z-J2-Q1.
- U1-U2 1-1.5 cm/0.39-0.59".
- U2-U3 2.5 cm/0.98".
- B1-B2 equal to U2-U3 2.5 cm/0.98".
- Join U3-B2.

LOOSE-FITTING JACKET SLEEVE

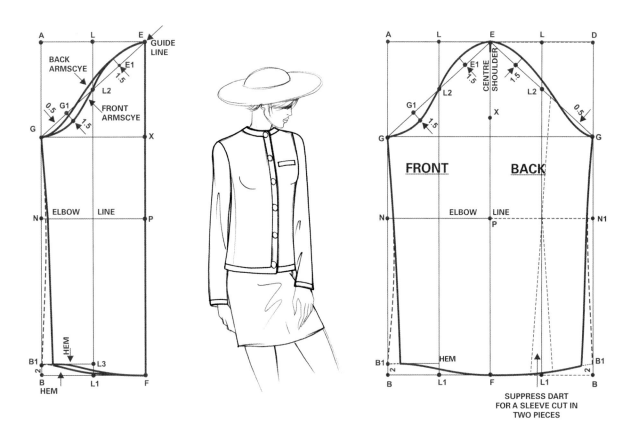

Measurements: Size 42, as in the women's sizing table.

Ease: As in the chart, under "Loose-fitting jackets".

- Trace a angle, A-B-E-F, where:
- A-B is the sleeve length from the centre back (e.g.: 60 cm/23.62").
- A-E is equal to the bodice underarm measurement + 1/2 of the underarm (e.g.: underarm 12.5 + 6.25 = 18.75 cm).
- A-G is equal to L2-P1 of the bodice + 1/3 of the bodice. (e.g.: 12.5 + 4.25 = 16.75 cm).
- Trace G-X.
- Join G-E with a diagonal line.
- A-N half of A-B + 2 cm/0.79". Join N-P.
- A-L half of A-E. Trace L-L1.
- L3 2 cm/0.79" from L1.
- E1 half of E-L2.
- G1 half of G-L2.
- B-B1 2 cm/0.79".
- Draw E-L2-G with a curved line as in the illustration.
- Draw E-G1-G with a curved line as in the illustration.
- Draw B1-F with a curved line.
- Draw B1-L1-F with a curved line.
- Take up the sleeve for the front and back and trace the entire sleeve, as in the illustration.

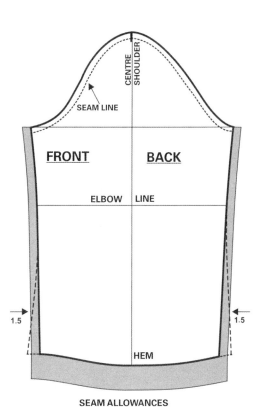

NB: To have the correct sleeve balance, the centre back should be adjusted, moving it towards the front or back by a few millimetres based on the subject's anatomy or posture.

PRINCESS CUT JACKET

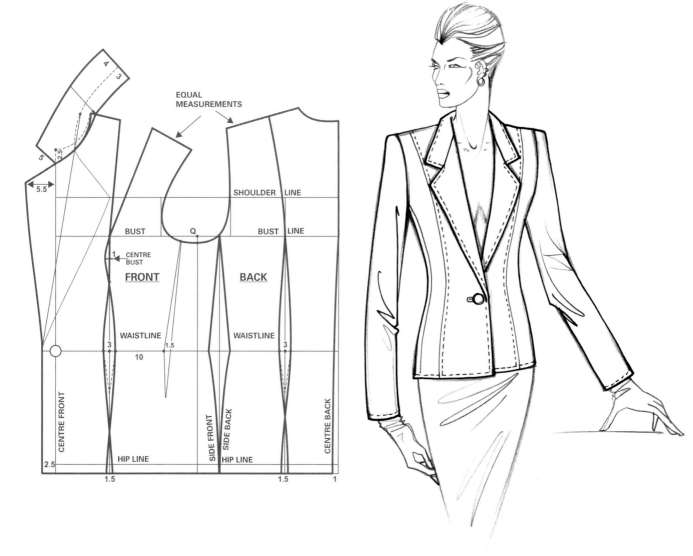

Measurements: Size 42, as in the table.

Ease: As in the chart, under "Fitted Jacket".

- Draw the jacket base block with darts and the appropriate ease.
- Draw the SIDE FRONT line, following the lines of the waist dart and giving the bottom edge a slight curve, if desired.
- Shape the SIDE FRONT line at the bust point, extending it by 1 cm/0.39" to give it a better fit.
- Draw the SIDE BACK line, starting from the same measurement of the front shoulder, following the waist dart lines and shaping the bottom hem to match the front.
- If you would like a more slender effect for the jacket, you can shift the bust dart towards the side, before tracing the side panel.

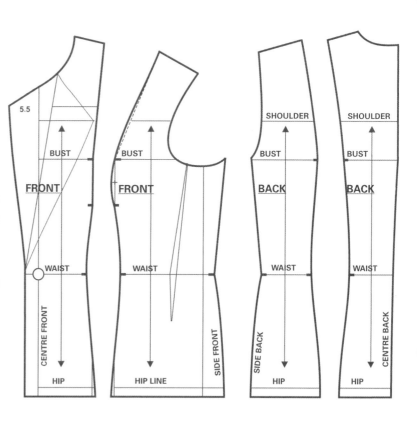

JACKET WITH SIDE PANELS

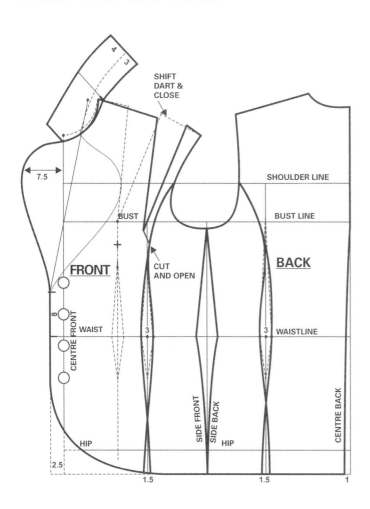

FRONT

SHIFT DART & CLOSE

7.5

BUST

CUT AND OPEN

CENTRE FRONT

WAIST

8

HIP

2.5

1.5

SHOULDER LINE

BUST LINE

BACK

WAISTLINE

SIDE FRONT

SIDE BACK

HIP

CENTRE BACK

1.5   1

Measurements: Size 42, as in the table.
Ease: As in the chart, under "Fitted jacket".

- Draw the basic jacket with darts block, with the appropriate ease and desired length and shape.
- Shift the bust and waist darts towards the armscye (reducing it 1.5-3 cm/0.6-1.2") in order to move them closer to the side panel.
- Draw the lines of the front and SIDE BACKs according to the illustration or as desired, passing through the waist dart smoothly.
- Close the bust dart and open it along the SIDE FRONT line.
- Set the reference points and take the parts of the pattern up again on another piece of paper.

NB: The side panel can be separate or whole. In the latter case, the discarded pieces from the waist will be divided equally among the waist darts.

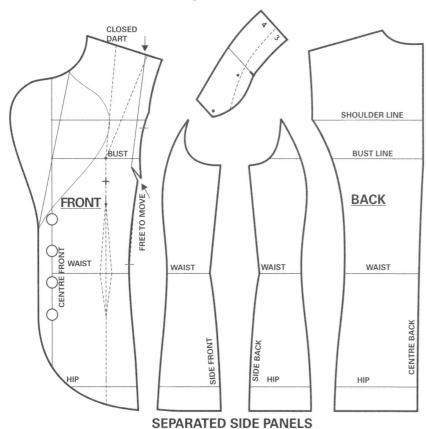

CLOSED DART

FRONT

BUST

FREE TO MOVE

CENTRE FRONT

WAIST

HIP

WAIST

SIDE FRONT

WAIST

SIDE BACK

HIP

SHOULDER LINE

BUST LINE

BACK

WAIST

HIP

CENTRE BACK

SEPARATED SIDE PANELS

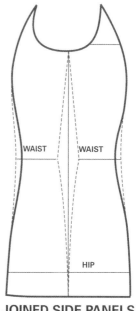

WAIST   WAIST

HIP

JOINED SIDE PANELS

Bolero

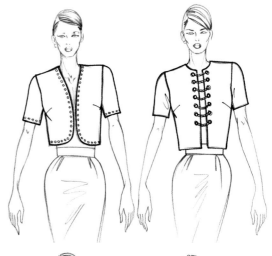

The bolero

The bolero is a short button-less jacket which follows the bust line without extending down to the waist. It can have short or long sleeves and come with or without a collar.

It originated from the popular dress of Spain and in the late 1800s then came back into in fashion in a reduced size. Rich with ornamentation and embroidery, it was often made of transparent muslin in the same colour as the dress it was worn with in summer, or in fur in the winter.

In the 1950s, it evolved once again to be worn over sleeveless dresses with deep necklines, to cover the arms and the décolleté.

Collarless bolero

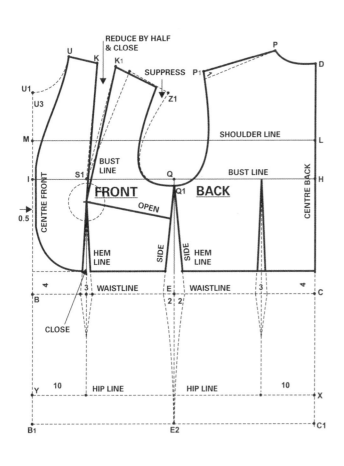

- Draw the basic jacket block with the proper ease for a bolero.
- Reduce the bust dart by approximately half and discard the difference in the armscye.
- Draw the shape of the collar as desired.
- Draw the bottom of the bolero in the desired length.
- Draw the waist darts and taper the sides as desired.
- Draw the dart lines on the side.
- Close the bust dart and the waist dart, making both of them merge into the dart on the side.
- Reduce the side dart on the bust circle.

36

CROP BOLERO WITH COLLAR

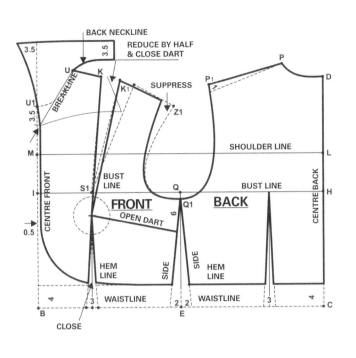

BACK NECKLINE

REDUCE BY HALF & CLOSE DART

3.5

3.5

U

K

U1

3.5

BREAKLINE

K1

SUPPRESS

P1

P

D

Z1

SHOULDER LINE

M

L

BUST LINE

S1

I

CENTRE FRONT

BUST LINE

Q

FRONT

6

Q1

BACK

H

CENTRE BACK

OPEN DART

0.5

HEM LINE

SIDE

SIDE

HEM LINE

4

3

WAISTLINE

2

2

WAISTLINE

3

4

B

E

C

CLOSE

BOLERO WITH COLLAR AND CLOSURE

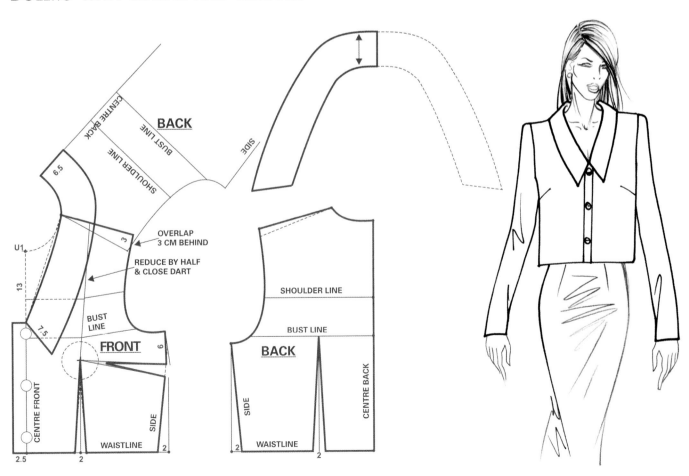

CENTRE BACK

BACK

BUST LINE

SHOULDER LINE

SIDE

6.5

3

OVERLAP 3 CM BEHIND

REDUCE BY HALF & CLOSE DART

U1

13

7.5

BUST LINE

FRONT

6

CENTRE FRONT

SIDE

2.5

2

WAISTLINE

SHOULDER LINE

BUST LINE

BACK

SIDE

CENTRE BACK

2

WAISTLINE

2

JACKET WITH YOKE

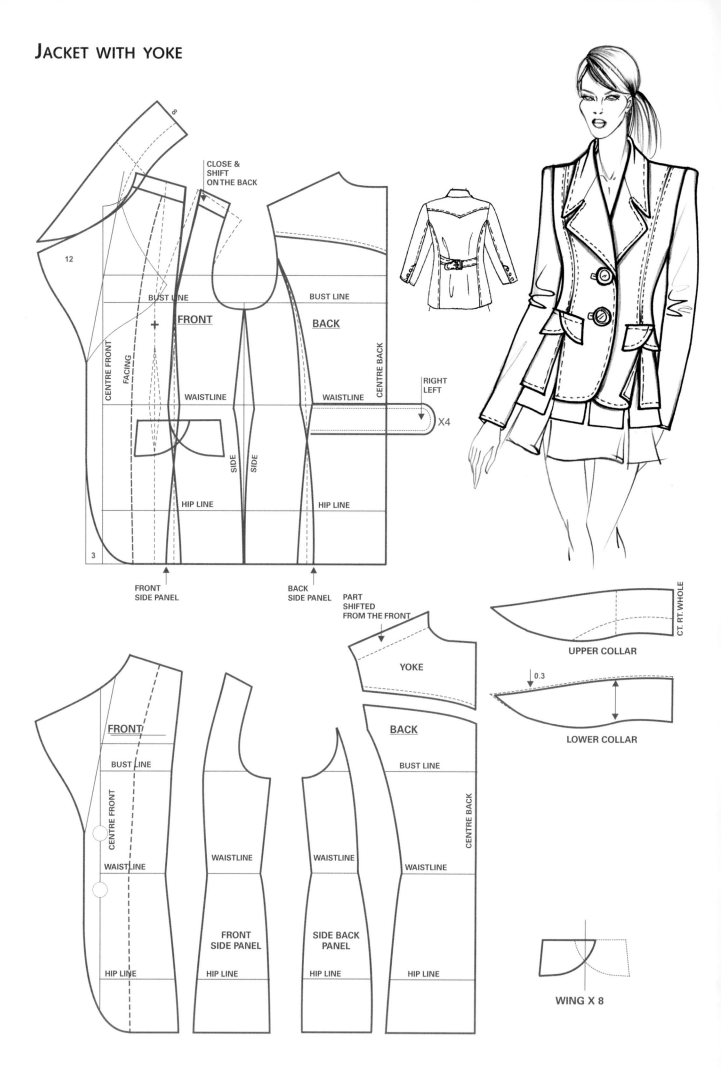

8

12

CLOSE &
SHIFT
ON THE BACK

BUST LINE

BUST LINE

FRONT

BACK

CENTRE FRONT

FACING

CENTRE BACK

WAISTLINE

WAISTLINE

RIGHT
LEFT

X4

SIDE

SIDE

HIP LINE

HIP LINE

3

FRONT
SIDE PANEL

BACK
SIDE PANEL

PART
SHIFTED
FROM THE FRONT

YOKE

CT. RT. WHOLE

UPPER COLLAR

0.3

LOWER COLLAR

FRONT

BUST LINE

CENTRE FRONT

WAISTLINE

WAISTLINE

FRONT
SIDE PANEL

HIP LINE

HIP LINE

WAISTLINE

SIDE BACK
PANEL

HIP LINE

BACK

BUST LINE

CENTRE BACK

WAISTLINE

HIP LINE

WING X 8

38

Jacket with yoke and side panel

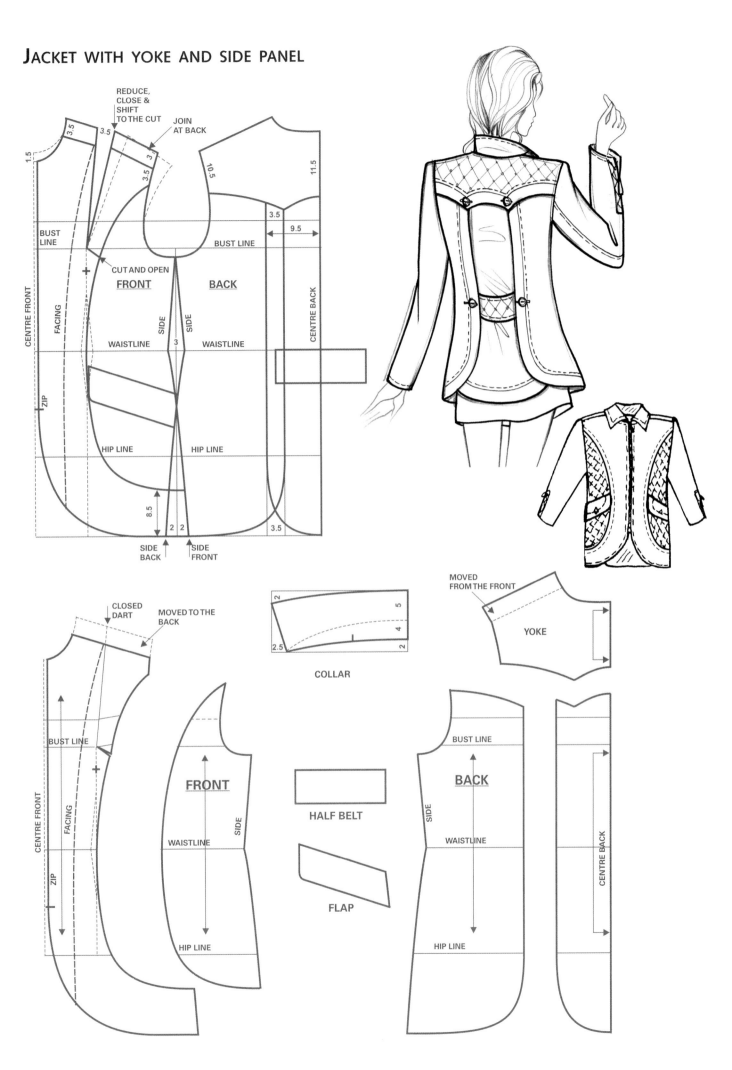

Top-left pattern diagram labels:

REDUCE, CLOSE & SHIFT TO THE CUT

JOIN AT BACK

3.5 3.5 3 3.5

1.5

10.5 11.5

3.5

BUST LINE

9.5

BUST LINE

CUT AND OPEN

FRONT BACK

CENTRE FRONT

FACING

SIDE SIDE

CENTRE BACK

WAISTLINE 3 WAISTLINE

ZIP

HIP LINE HIP LINE

8.5

2 2

SIDE BACK SIDE FRONT

3.5

Lower-left pattern diagram labels:

CLOSED DART

MOVED TO THE BACK

BUST LINE

CENTRE FRONT

FACING

FRONT

SIDE

WAISTLINE

ZIP

HIP LINE

Collar:

2

5

2.5

4

2

COLLAR

Centre pieces:

HALF BELT

FLAP

Yoke:

MOVED FROM THE FRONT

YOKE

Back pattern:

BUST LINE

BACK

SIDE

WAISTLINE

CENTRE BACK

HIP LINE

39

JACKET WITH RAGLAN SLEEVES

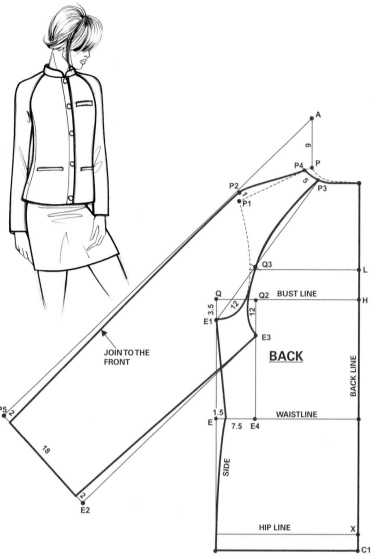

- Carefully measure the sleeve and the bodice on another piece of paper.
- Draw the base of the jacket with or without darts and make the appropriate changes, then separate the back half from the front half.

Back
- Draw a perpendicular line P-A in the desired measurements, based on the angle you would like the sleeve to have.
- Draw A-P2-P5, deviating from point P1 by 1 cm/0.39", with P2-P5 equal to the sleeve length taken from the centre back.
- Q-E1 3-8 cm/1.18-3.15", based on the armscye depth desired.
- E-E4 7.5 cm/2.95".
- Draw E4-Q2.
- P4-P3 5 cm/1.97" or as desired.
- Draw the guide line P3-E1.
- 12 cm/4.72" from E1 towards P3, passing through the meeting point of the curves. Point Q3.
- Draw the curved line E1-Q3-P3.
- Q3-E3 equal to Q3-E1.
- Draw E3-Q3-P3.
- Draw E2-E3 parallel to P5-P2.
- Adjust the bottom of the sleeve according to the design.
- Smoothly draw the external and internal lines of the sleeve and the bodice.
- Carefully take up the sleeve and the bodice again.

Front
- On the front half, draw a perpendicular line (U-A) in the desired measurements, equal on the front and back, based on the angle you would like the sleeve to have.
- Draw A-Z1-Z2 deviating from point Z by 1 cm/0.39", with Z-Z1 equal to the sleeve length (60 cm/23.62") measured from the centre back, equal on the back.
- Q-E1 3-8 cm/1.18-3.15" according to the desired drop, as on the back.
- E-E4 6.5 cm/2.56". Trace the line E4-Q2.
- From E1 towards U3, 9 cm/3.54", passing along the meeting point Q3.
- U2-U3 4-5 cm/1.57-1.97".
- Draw a curved line, E1-Q3-U3.
- Draw E2-E3-E5 parallel to Z1-Z2, with equal measurements to E2-E5 on the back minus 0.5-1 cm/0.20-0.39".
- Q3-E5 equal to Q3-E1.
- Draw E5-Q3-U2.
- Adjust the bottom of the sleeve according to the design.
- Smoothly draw the external and internal lines of the sleeve and the bodice.

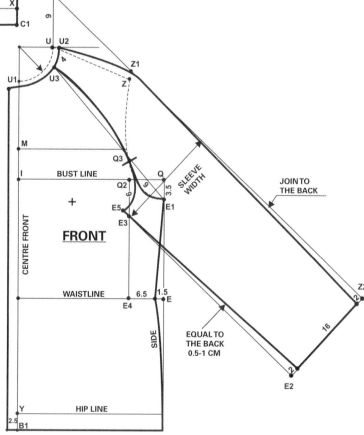

ATTACHING THE RAGLAN SLEEVES

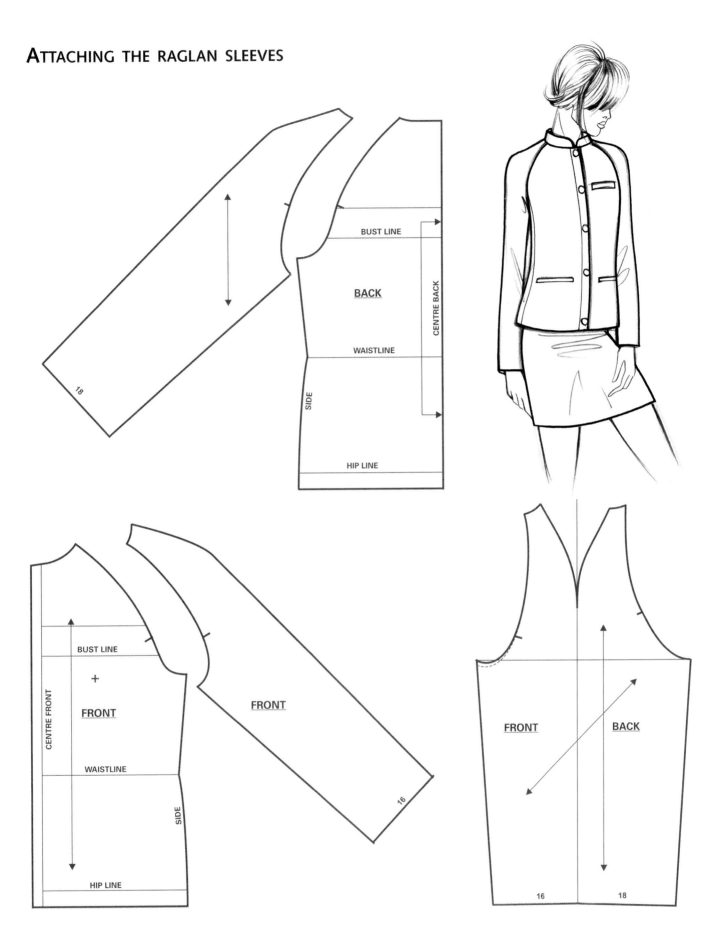

After having drawn the front and back sleeves, take up single parts of the bodice and the sleeves on another sheet of paper, including the reference points for the seams.

Raglan sleeves can have a central seam or they can be made of a single piece of fabric.

For sleeves made of one piece of fabric, eliminating the seam, join the back to the front along the outer edge, as shown in the illustration.

Uniting the sleeves will create a dart in the shoulder area, which should be rounded to avoid angles or defects.

This sleeve may be positioned on the bias or crosswise to the grain, based on the type of fabric and the pattern.

CROP JACKET WITH CREATIVE RAGLAN SLEEVES

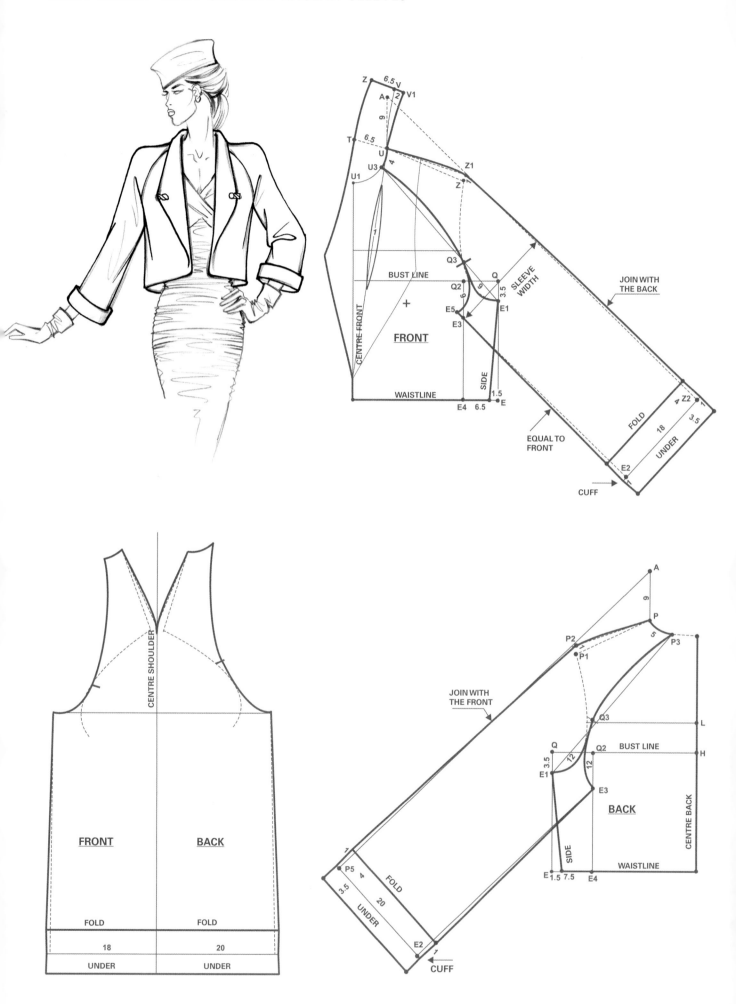

JACKET WITH RAGLAN YOKE SLEEVES

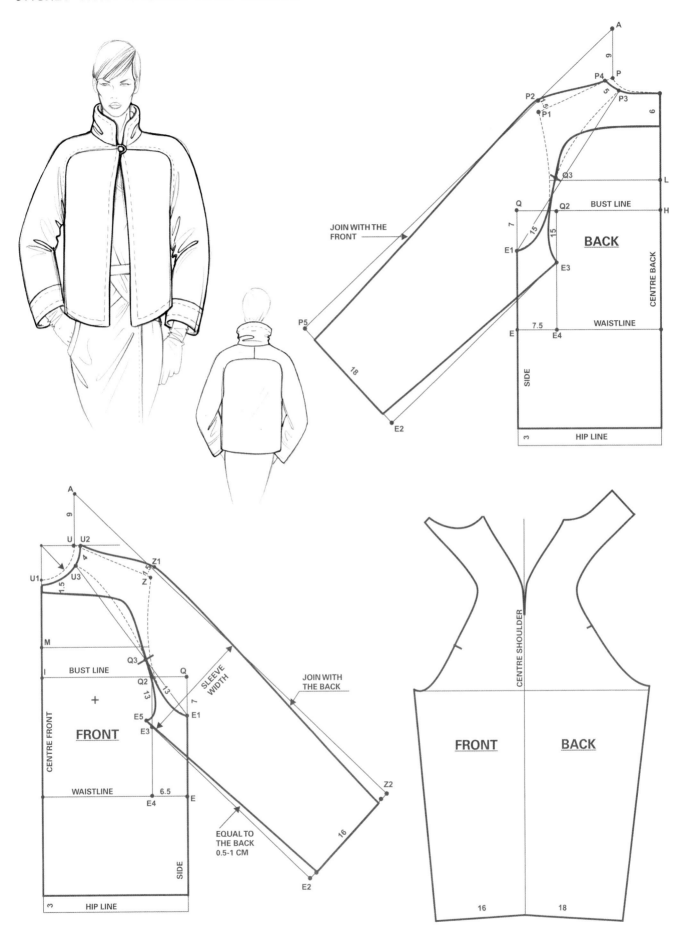

Raglan yoke sleeves are based on raglan sleeve construction, varying the way the sleeve is attached to the bodice, which should reflect the curvature shown in the illustration on the front and the back.

KIMONO JACKET - BACK

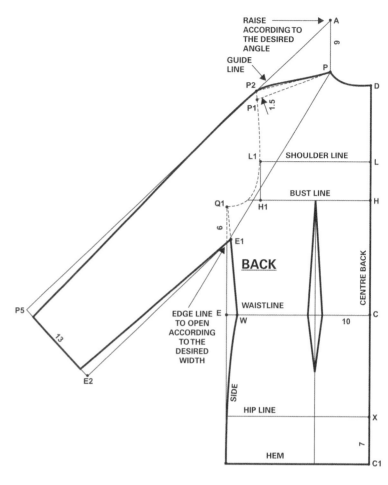

- Trace the base block of the jacket with darts, including the appropriate ease.
- Create the waist darts and taper the sides as necessary, then adjust the length to the desired measurements and separate the back from the front.
- From point P, draw a perpendicular line 6 cm to 12 cm (2.36-4.72") long, according to the desired angle for the sleeve (in this case, 9 cm / 3.54").
- From A, connect to P2, 1-1.5 cm/0.39-0.59" from P1, drawing a straight line from A-P5.
- P2-P5 = sleeve length measurement from the shoulder point.
- From point Q1, drop 6 - 12 cm (2.36-4.72") down, marking point E1 (in this case, 6 cm/2.36").
- Draw the diagonal line P-E1.
- Draw E1-E2 parallel to P2-P5.
- Draw the hem line P5-E2 and adjust the length of the bottom of the sleeves with the front 2 cm/0.79" larger than the back.
- Cut along diagonal line E1-P, opening up as needed (according to the pattern, e.g.: 8 cm/3.15") and connect the separate parts with a curved line.

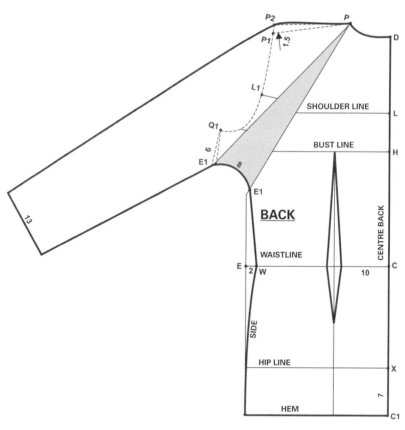

Kimono jacket - front

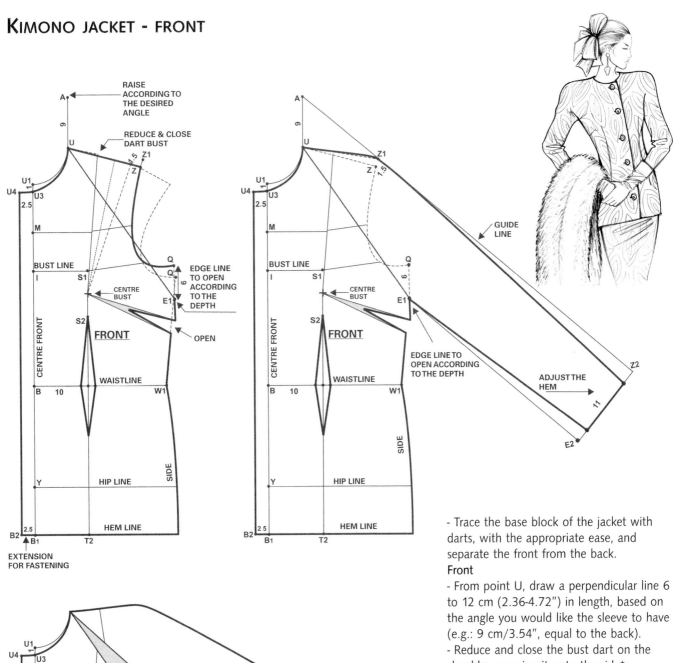

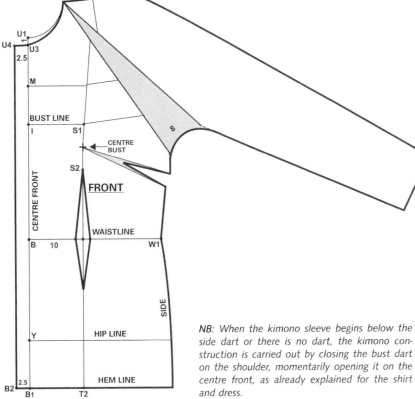

NB: *When the kimono sleeve begins below the side dart or there is no dart, the kimono construction is carried out by closing the bust dart on the shoulder, momentarily opening it on the centre front, as already explained for the shirt and dress.*

- Trace the base block of the jacket with darts, with the appropriate ease, and separate the front from the back.

Front

- From point U, draw a perpendicular line 6 to 12 cm (2.36-4.72") in length, based on the angle you would like the sleeve to have (e.g.: 9 cm/3.54", equal to the back).
- Reduce and close the bust dart on the shoulder, opening it onto the side*.
- From A, passing through Z1 at 1-1.5 cm/0.39-0.59" from Z, draw a straight line (A-Z2).
- Z1-Z2 = sleeve length from the shoulder point, equal to the back.
- From point Q drop from 4 cm to 16 cm (1.57 to 6.30"), based on the desired sleeve length (in this case, 6 cm/2.36" equal to the back) and mark point E1.
- Draw the diagonal line U-E1.
- Draw E1-E2 parallel to Z1-Z2.
- Draw the bottom Z2-E2 at a right angle to Z1-Z2, adjusting the length of the bottom of the sleeve, making it 2 cm/0.79" smaller than the back.
- Cut along the diagonal line E1-U, then open as on the back, according to the requirements of the pattern (e.g.: 8 cm/3.15", equal to the back) and connect the separate parts with a curved line.
- Check the pattern by overlapping the front over the back.

Swing jacket - back

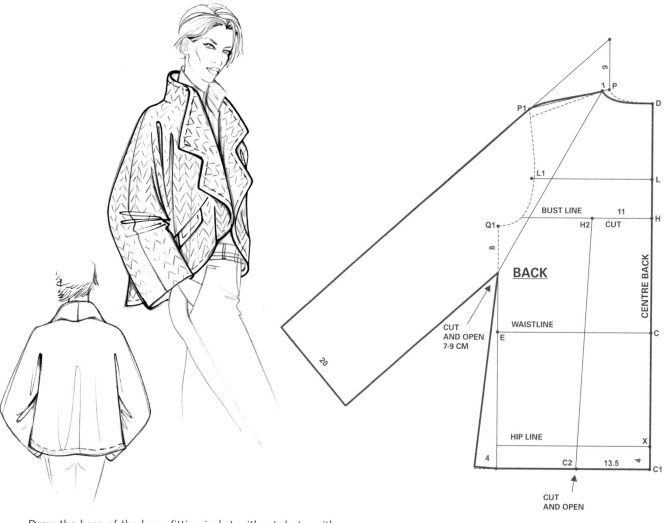

- Draw the base of the loose-fitting jacket without darts, with the appropriate ease.
- Draw the 9 cm/3.54" perpendicular line from point P and follow the sleeve's angle.
- Draw the collar, shifted away by 1 cm/0.39".
- Elongate the bottom by 4 cm/1.57" along the side.
- Draw H2-C2, cut along these lines, elongate by 4 cm/1.57" and connect to the bottom.
- Elongate the undersleeve by the desired measurements.

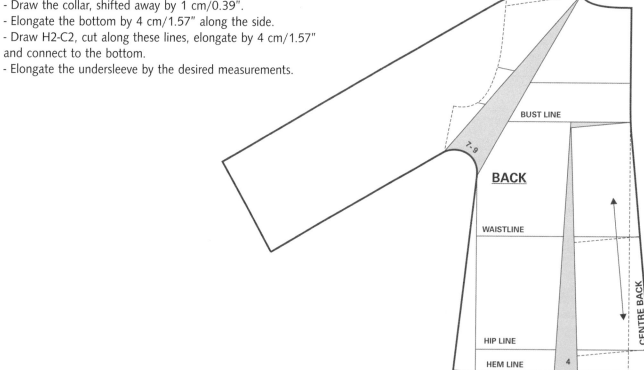

SWING JACKET - FRONT

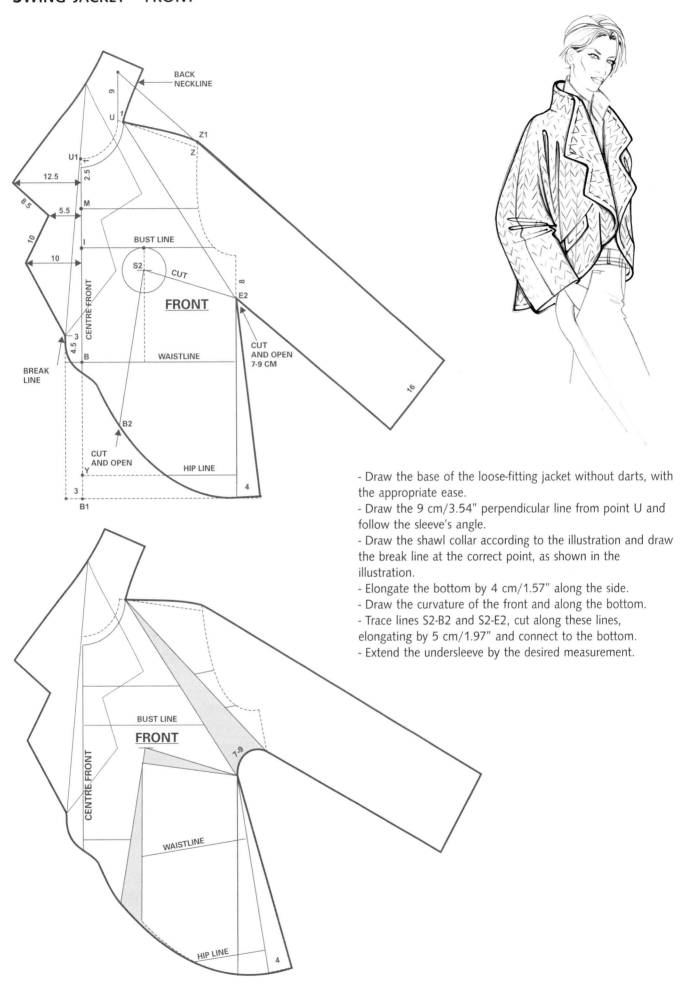

BACK NECKLINE

9

U 1

Z1

Z

U1 1

2.5

12.5

8.5

5.5 M

10

I

BUST LINE

10

S2 CUT

CENTRE FRONT

FRONT

8

E2

CUT AND OPEN 7-9 CM

3

4.5

B

WAISTLINE

BREAK LINE

B2

CUT AND OPEN

Y

HIP LINE

3

4

16

B1

BUST LINE

FRONT

CENTRE FRONT

7-9

WAISTLINE

HIP LINE

4

- Draw the base of the loose-fitting jacket without darts, with the appropriate ease.
- Draw the 9 cm/3.54" perpendicular line from point U and follow the sleeve's angle.
- Draw the shawl collar according to the illustration and draw the break line at the correct point, as shown in the illustration.
- Elongate the bottom by 4 cm/1.57" along the side.
- Draw the curvature of the front and along the bottom.
- Trace lines S2-B2 and S2-E2, cut along these lines, elongating by 5 cm/1.97" and connect to the bottom.
- Extend the undersleeve by the desired measurement.

SAFARI JACKET

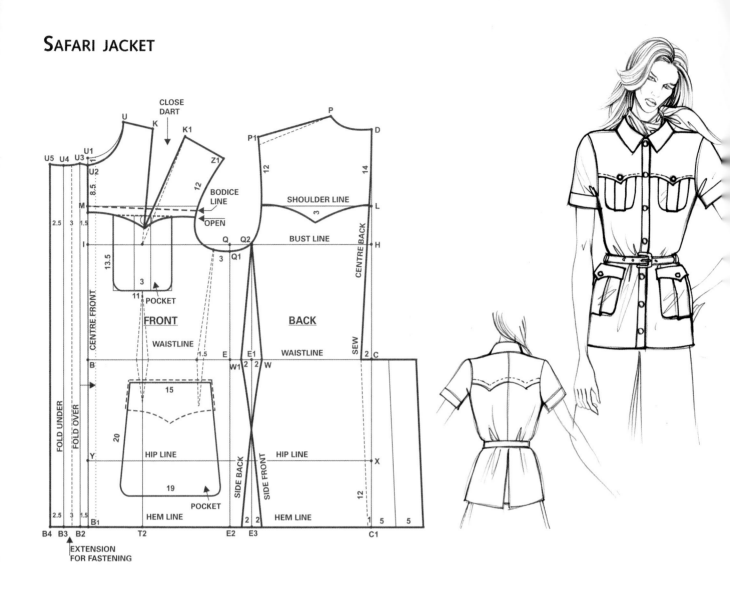

Measurements: Size 42, as in the women's sizing table.

Ease: As in the chart, under "Loose-fitting jacket".

- Draw the basic block of the jacket with darts, with the ease of a loose-fitting jacket (see chart).
- Draw the 2-3 cm/0.79-1.2" inward curve of the waist on the back and the 2-2.5 cm/0.79-0.98" side tapering on the waist.
- Trace the extension of the centre back for the bottom fold/ vent.
- Extend the length of the bottom along the side by 2-3 cm/0.79-1.18" for extra spaciousness.
- Extend the double overlap on the front for the fastening, as shown in the illustration.
- Draw the lines of the yoke on the front and back at the desired height and with the desired outline.
- Take up the front and back yoke, the lower bodice block and the pockets once again.
- Close the bust dart of the front yoke.
- Construct the expandable pocket and the folded recess.

NB: The part of the dart remaining on the bodice may be absorbed into the seams when uniting it with the yoke.

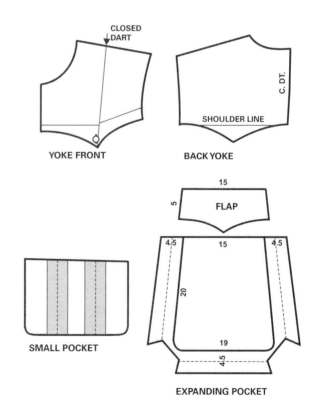

Jacket pattern layout

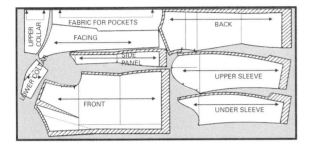

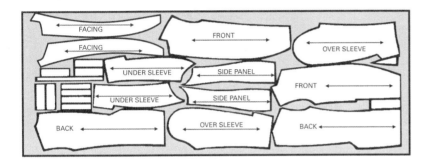

SARTORIAL LAYOUT

INDUSTRIAL LAYOUT

Whether or not the jacket's parts are perpendicular depends entirely on the arrangement of the paper pattern on the fabric. Thus, if you would like a garment that "falls" perfectly, it is necessary to proceed with extra caution during this activity.

After having prepared the fabric, that is, after having wet (if necessary), ironed and marked it, keep in mind that when the fabric is doubled during the layout, the folded edge will be facing the person working and that the two straight sides should line up perfectly. The pattern is then applied as follows: starting from the left edge, the pattern is arranged along the fabric's folded edge (that is, the edge that is intact).

Carefully following the indications, arrange the model so that the straight of the grain or the bias, indicated on the various pieces of the pattern, line up perfectly with the straight of the grain and the bias of the fabric. If you ignore this basic rule, a garment's missing "line" cannot ever be restored.

Start applying the most important pieces, in order: front, back, sleeve, etc. All should be in the same direction, making sure that there isn't too much space between one piece and another, which would be a waste of fabric. Only leave the space necessary for the seams, hems, etc. This isn't a fixed rule: it may be that by moving the front or the back, you are unable to carve out sufficient space for the sleeve, the pocket, etc. In this case, move the various pieces of the pattern until they all fit, while using the least amount of fabric possible.

Sometimes all you need is a bit of patience, as sometimes footage which at first glance didn't seem to be enough, ends up being quite abundant.

On the other hand, it is important that the tailor does everything possible to be frugal with the fabric, keeping in mind that wasting just 10 cm/3.93" of material is essentially throwing money away.

For patterned fabrics, especially those whose value derives from an original design, it's always best to avoid cuts and seams that are not absolutely essential to the shape of the jacket. Otherwise, the seams interrupt the design and ruin the value of the garment.

With striped cloth, a jacket is considered perfectly made when the lines match up precisely along the shoulder, pockets, etc. In this case it is best to cut the fabric in two steps: first the main body of the garment and then, after a fitting, the sleeves, collar and all the other smaller pieces (belts, trimming, etc.).

After the entire model (the front, back, sleeves, collar, cuffs, belts, pockets or flaps, etc.) is properly laid out and you are sure the entire pattern fits on the fabric available, begin pinning, starting with the first piece on your left.

Always remember that you must never risk cutting any pieces before thoroughly checking everything and being entirely sure that the pattern pieces fit on the fabric. The smallest shortage of fabric, just enough for a minor part of the pattern, could put the entire garment at risk. If nothing has been cut, you'll be able to address the issue. However, once the scissors have come out, there's little to do and the tailor or seamstress may even be responsible for paying the client for the wasted fabric. If carefully prepared as described above, the fabric is now ready to be cut.

Jacket overlap

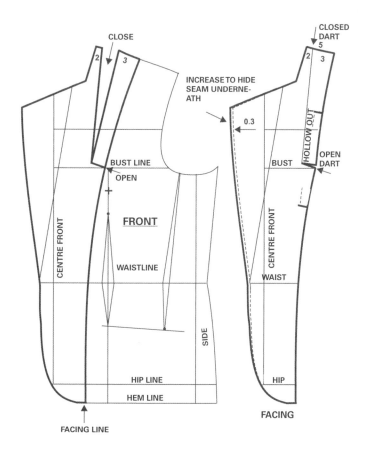

CLOSE

2   3

INCREASE TO HIDE SEAM UNDERNE-ATH

0.3

BUST LINE

OPEN

CENTRE FRONT

FRONT

WAISTLINE

SIDE

HIP LINE

HEM LINE

FACING LINE

CLOSED DART

5

2   3

HOLLOW OUT

OPEN DART

BUST

CENTRE FRONT

WAIST

HIP

FACING

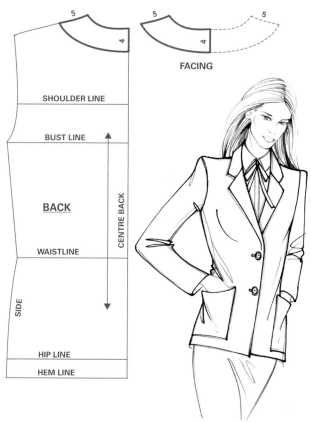

5   4

5   4   5

FACING

SHOULDER LINE

BUST LINE

BACK

CENTRE BACK

WAISTLINE

SIDE

HIP LINE

HEM LINE

NB: The line of the front placket should be enlarged by 0.3-0.5 cm/0.12 - 0.20" if you wish to hide the seam under the lapel.

INCREASE TO HIDE SEAM UNDERNEATH

0.3 - 0.5

5

5

SUPPRESS

BUST LINE

FRONT

WAISTLINE

CENTRE FRONT

SIDE

CENTRE FRONT

HIP LINE

HEM LINE

8   8

FACING LINE

FACING

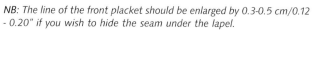

5   4

5   4

BUST LINE

BACK

WAISTLINE

SIDE

CENTRE BACK

HIP LINE

6   HEM LINE

LININGS AND INNERS

LININGS: These are specially made fabrics used to cover the inside of a garment, in order to make it presentable and improve its fit. Linings may be in cotton, wool and at times silk, but the majority are made of rayon (viscose, acetate or cuprammonium, known by the brand name Bemberg). In the past, the best linings were made of silk, but they have been substituted by a silk-rayon blend due to silk's quick deterioration and high cost.

Linings in wool or in other heavy fabrics are used for coats or sports jackets in order to increase the garment's weight and thus its insulation. The most sought-out characteristics for outerwear linings are shininess and slipperiness.

In terms of aesthetics, lining fabric may be a single colour, striped, checked, patterned or decorated in some other manner.

In industrial garment production, their use requires a careful study of their properties and behaviour during the various construction phases, especially when pressed as any variations in size may result in irreparable - or at least damaging - defects.

Traditionally, linings with specific characteristics are used to make various types of clothing:

Linings for sleeves are generally made of rayon in a light colour, in accordance with the traditional, hand-crafted tailoring methods, because they are in contact with the sleeves. In the past, when dyes weren't stable, this avoided the colour staining the shirt due to sweat on the arm. Some prefer to use a neutral coloured lining, such as pearl grey, which matches easily with any other lining tone. An exception can be made for lighter fabrics; their open structure requires an in-tone lining in order to avoid any contrasting colours from showing through.

Linings for trousers generally cover the front part of the garment down to just below the knee. They help the trousers to run smoothly over the leg and to avoid deformations at the joint and are sometimes used to improve the feel of the trousers. It is often useful to line the back as well. This is especially true for fabrics that are itchy or catch easily, such as carded or semi-carded wools. These linings are made of rayon in a tone matching that of the trousers or in a neutral colour.

Linings for pockets are usually made of a fabric called silesia: a robust material almost always in cotton, though at times in a cotton-rayon blend, pure rayon, Terylene® or other synthetic fibres. Silesia comes in various hues, but garment makers often prefer to use the usual pearl grey colour in order to avoid incurring extra costs.

Silesia textiles with different characteristics and costs can also be used, depending on their intended purpose. For example, a less expensive kind of silesia may be used on jacket pockets than is used for trouser linings, given that the wear placed on the pockets is drastically less than that of the trousers. Silesia may also be used for the waistband of classic trousers, shoulder straps, gussets, reinforcements, etc.

One of the accessories for traditional outerwear is the interfacing, which gives shape and consistency to the front of the jacket and which is made of the three types of fabric listed below:

CAMEL HAIR: This is the basic fabric used for the interfacing, which makes the garment a bit more rigid and give it a specific shape. The warp is in cotton, but the weft is in springy fibres which give it a good amount of elasticity, similar to that of wool or goat hair. Traditional camel hair is now often substituted with materials that are easier to find and less expensive.

HORSE HAIR: This fabric features a cotton warp and a weft made of the hairs from horses' tails and manes, which is notably springy. It is used in the upper part of the interfacing, which lies across the chest and shoulder, and serves to fill the garment while also giving greater flexibility and spring-back to the front, in a point where camel hair alone wouldn't be enough. This fabric's height is limited by the length of the fibres used, and generally tends to span from 35 to 45 cm/14 to 18".

Because of the fabric's high level of shrinkage, it is essential to immerse the pieces in 50-60°C (122-140°F) before cutting it, thus avoiding any subsequent problems.

Traditionally it was in a sort of brushed cotton, but today it is more commonly found in a non-woven fabric version, which covers the roughness of the horse hair and makes this part of the interfacing softer. Being devoid of warp and weft, these non-woven fabrics are less resistant to shaping, easily adapting to the form of the bodice.

STAY TAPE: These strips of cotton, almost always white in colour, are placed along the garment's edges and seams to ensure that the fabric doesn't become deformed in those points, altering the shape and size of that particular aspect. The tape is made from pieces of fabric in various sizes, which result in equally varied types of tape:

Warp stay tape is made from pieces cut longitudinally (the direction of the warp).

Weft stay tape is made from pieces cut crosswise (the direction of the weft).

Bias stay tape is made from pieces cut on the bias, that is, at a 45° angle.

The three types of tape are easily recognized and distinguished from one another: the weft version, unlike the warp, every so often (every 100-150 cm/39.37-59.06") has overlapping selvedges, while the bias stay tape has elements with a 45° angle. All three types of tape must uphold the fabric and keep it in its original size, while also allowing a certain amount of elasticity.

REINFORCEMENTS: Usually cotton fabric is used for reinforcements, but at times linen or hemp may be used. There are two types of reinforcements: those on the edges (tape and ribbon) and those on the surfaces (interfacing, sangeant, or silesia).

MELTON: In textile jargon, this word indicates a tightly woven fabric that is felted and brushed, and which therefore has a tight, closed construction, a flat finish and almost no fraying. For clothing, it generally is used for the undercollar on a classic jacket, which is made of two parts: one in Melton fabric and the other in reinforced fabric (hemp or linen). Both parts of the undercollar are cut on the bias so that they can easily adapt to the rounded form of the neck, and they are joined with a blind stitch (stitch type 103). Melton may be substituted by a non-woven fabric that doesn't require a bias cut.

RIBBON: This material resembles warp stay tape, but it is significantly different in that it has selvedge sides which make it particularly resistant - so much so that it can prevent any deformations in the points where it is applied. Both ribbon and stay tape may be thermo-adhesive (iron-on).

INTERFACING AND SANGEANT: These are cotton fabrics, usually white, pearl grey or black, which act as reinforcements. Unlike tape and ribbon, which are placed along edges or seams, interfacing and sangeant are used on surfaces.

INNER REINFORCEMENTS

JACKET BACK AND FRONT

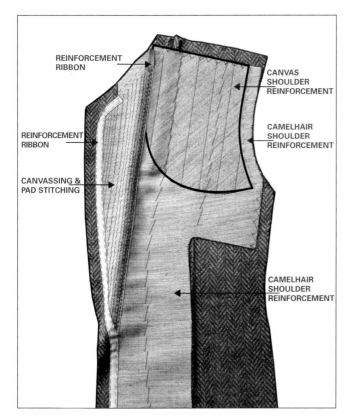

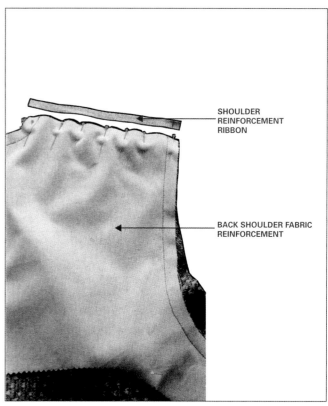

Inner reinforcements (canvassing)

In jackets and coats, inner reinforcements are found between the external fabric and the facing (or lining) in places that need extra strength. They give substance to the front, shoulders, neckline, cuffs, pockets and button fastenings, and they reinforce the edges which are stressed by tension and use, such as armscyes without sleeves and necklines without collars. The types of inner reinforcements are the same as those used for facings, but are generally narrower. Most tailors and seamstresses prefer not to make a separate pattern for inner reinforcements, but we advise you do so in order to be as precise as possible.

The materials used for canvassing, usually called camel hair, are manageable, tightly woven, crease-resistant and supple. Most are made of a blend of wool (30-40%), horse hair (7-18%) and cotton or rayon.

There are four methods used to apply them: manually, with the aid of a machine, with thermo-adhesive fabric or a mixed method. The manual method is based on hand sewing which, even if requiring much more time than the other options, is still the most common in tailoring as it will set the item apart as a well-made garment.

The other options are quicker and, even if they are often found in less valuable products, they also may be used to produce fine results. Using thermo-adhesive products eliminates seams, allowing you to complete the final product quickly.

Reinforcements on the jacket front

Whatever the method used, canvassing the front of a jacket or coat gives the garment shape and helps maintain its lines, making sure they remain unchanged over time.

The reinforcements that are applied on the front are: 1) The piece of fabric on the front which helps the garment fall along the body without defects, with straight edges and properly supported pockets; 2) The reinforcement along the shoulders, which ensures perfect draping as the garment goes from shoulder to chest; 3) The quilting and shaping of the lapel; 4) The reinforcement tape along the edges and breakline of the lapels, which helps them lay flat against the bodice.

Reinforcements on the jacket back

Reinforcements are applied to a jacket or coat's shoulders and to make sure its lines are perfect and to ensure its stability, thus avoiding the fabric being exposed to strain along the shoulder blades. Reinforcements on the back are cut out of tightly-woven fabric, brushed cotton or muslin.

The seam allowances of the reinforcement are taken into the garment seams. In this way, they need not be stabilised on the neckline with a ribbon or piece of tape. An exception is made for collarless garments, which are subjected to the most stress and thus are reinforced with a ribbon.

To develop the back shoulder, you'll need extra room to compensate for the rounded shape. To do so, you'll need to add an ease on the seam allowances. Be careful to pay close attention when sewing and pressing this portion in order to maintain its delicate shape. It may thus be advisable to reinforce the stitching with tape so as to adapt the garment's shoulders to the figure and avoid tears along the seams.

The shaped shoulder seams may seem curved after they are sewn and pressed, but this will no longer be an issue when the garment is being worn.

SLEEVE AND COLLAR REINFORCEMENTS

Sleeve reinforcements

A jacket with well-rounded sleeve caps and properly shaped cuffs at the wrist portrays the image of a properly made, hand-crafted garment.

To support the sleeve cap and to hide the edge of the seam allowance on the front, one or more strips of a wool and cotton blend or heavy wool cut on the bias (0.5 cm/0.20 in thick) are often applied.

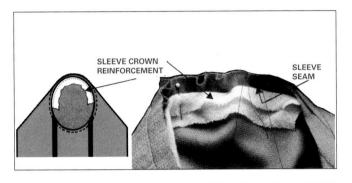

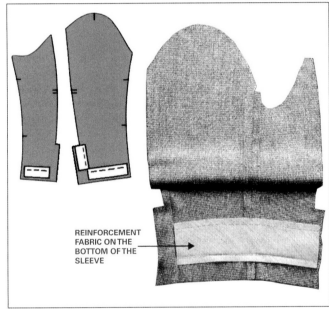

REINFORCEMENT FABRIC ON THE BOTTOM OF THE SLEEVE

RAGLAN SLEEVE INTERFACING

These strips are folded with one side a bit longer than the other and then sewn with a slip stitch (blind stitch) along the seam of the sleeve.

Collar reinforcements

A jacket's collar reinforcement is applied to the undercollar, which is canvassed to provide shape and to better support the weight of the upper collar.

The canvassing methods are the same as described for the body of the jacket and you should choose the method that is most suitable for the garment.

When the camel hair is being applied, the undercollar should be shaped with a stitch to canvas (pad stitching) by hand or by machine.

The reinforcement should further be shaped with a press with steam over a cushion.

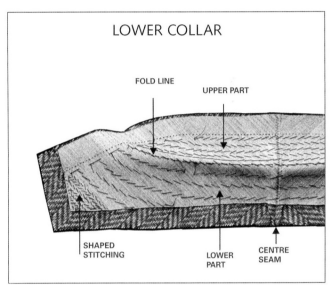

LOWER COLLAR

FOLD LINE
UPPER PART
SHAPED STITCHING
LOWER PART
CENTRE SEAM

After affixing the camel hair, fold the undercollar along the breakline and secure it with pins on an egg-shaped pressing cushion. Steam the collar in order to set the form, without ever creating a crease, let it dry completely and remove it from the cushion.

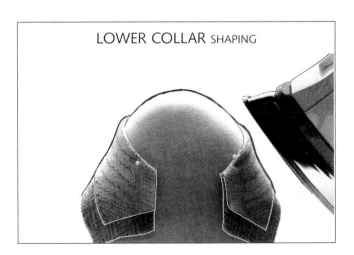

LOWER COLLAR SHAPING

JACKET CONSTRUCTION

THE INDUSTRIAL TECHNIQUE

Sleeves
1) Sew to unite the upper sleeve with the undersleeve.
2) Press the seam allowances open.
3) Apply the sangiant reinforcements at the cuff.
4) Create button holes at the cuff.
5) Sew the edges of the cuff.
6) Turn the edges of the cuff over.
7) Secure the reinforcement at the cuff.
8) Sew the elbow of the sleeve.
9) Sew the lining of the sleeve.
10) Press to open the seam on the elbow.
11) Insert the lining of the sleeve onto the fabric using a top stitch.
12) Invisible stitch the sleeve lining to the fabric.
13) Turn the sleeve over and press.

Collar
1) Trim the top and bottom parts of the collar.
2) Apply the lower collar to the upper with a T-point top stitch.
3) Sew the edges of the lower collar to the upper.
4) Turn the collar right-side-out, tacking the top collar. Press with an iron.

Flap
1) Apply and trim lining.
2) Turn the flap right-side-out and press with an iron.
3) Apply faux pocket edging to the flap.

Breast pocket
1) Apply ribbon to the pocket.
2) Fold and sew the edges.
3) Turn out and press with an iron.

Unite the lining with the external fabric
1) Construct the fore parts.
2) Construct the back parts.
3) Construct the darts on the front lining.
4) Construct the small open pocket with the applied edging on the inner pockets and related seam.
5) Construct the inner pockets with edging and seams to join the lining to the facing.
6) Sew the centre back with the application of the ribbon along the neckline.
7) Sew the front darts.
8) Apply the ribbon on the shoulder seam, press the dart allowances open, apply iron-on reinforcements on the pockets lines and the sides.
9) Mark the position of the pockets and breast pocket with cuts.
10) Sew the pockets and breast pocket to the front with a sewing machine.

11) Fold and sew the lower edging on the side pockets.
12) Close the pockets and breast pocket by applying the bag lining.
13) Baste the canvassing fabric on the straight part of the front.
14) Baste the fabric of the front inside out, by hand or with a sewing machine.
15) Tailor stitching of the lapels.
16) Sew the sides of the front right and left sides to the back.
17) Apply ribbon to the armscye.
18) Trim the lapels of the jacket front by hand.
19) Taper the canvassing from the front.
20) Line up the facing with the front and initial tacking of the front.

Lining
1) Apply the ribbon to the edges.
2) Top-stitch the ribbon on the edges.
3) Press open the seams on the front.
4) Turn the placket and points of the cuffs and baste the front and lower seams.
5) Second basting of the placket to the front.
6) Top stitch and secure the bottom hem and the placket.
7) Baste the lining to the jacket.
8) Top stitch the lining to the bottom.
9) Trim the excess lining and fabric along the armscyes and the shoulders.
10) Baste the top of the shoulders.
11) Sew the shoulders with a sewing machine and press the seams open with an iron.

Attaching the collar
1) Match the collar to the jacket and sew collar leaf.
2) Sew upper collar.
3) Baste undercollar.
4) Top-stitch the undercollar by hand.

Sleeve assembly
1) Press the turned seams with an iron to flatten them.
2) Join the sleeves to the jacket.
3) Press the upper part of the armscye with an iron to open it.

Invisible stitching of the sleeve
1) Apply the curved strip reinforcement on the inner sleeve crown.
2) Start the seam of the inner sleeve crown with chain stitch basting.
3) Baste the lining to the armscye.
4) Invisible stitch the sleeve and trim the shoulders.
5) Top stitch the lower part of the armscye.
6) Add the buttonholes (if any).
7) Top stitch the shoulders and armscye.

RAGLAN SLEEVE JACKET CONSTRUCTION

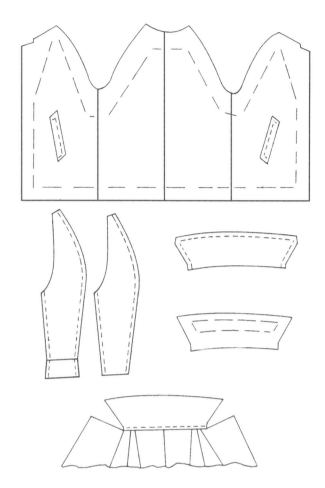

1) Sew the linings to the plackets
2) Sew the front linings to the back linings
3) Apply the ribbon to the pockets' welts
4) Re-fold the pocket welts, while topstitching
5) Mark the position of the side pockets
6) Apply the welts to the front
7) Apply the 1st part of the pocket lining
8) Apply the placket
9) Proceed with the v-shaped cuts along the sides for the pocket openings
10) Apply the 2nd part of the pocket lining
11) Turn the pocket lining inwards
12) Close the pocket welts - remove the tacking
13) Close the pocket bag
14) Stitch the sides of the pocket welts
15) Apply canvas to affix the front pocket
16) Apply canvassing, quilting it to the lapel
17) Press the lapel and the jacket front
18) Adjust the points of the lapel
19) Undo the basting along the edges
20) Apply the iron-on reinforcements to the edges of the front
21) Sew the centre back fabric seam
22) Sew the centre back lining seam
23) Sew the fabric sides
24) Open the seams on the fabric along the sides
25) Open the seams on the fabric along the centre back
26) Press the seams of the front lining
27) Press the seams of the middle front lining
28) Position the lining on the garment's fabric shell, pin in place
29) Baste the edges of the lining
30) Sew the edges
31) Sew the hem along the bottom of the garment
32) Undo the basting and turn the lining over
33) Baste the edges on the front
34) Baste the edges on the bottom
35) Baste the lapels and the breakline
36) Turn the piece over
37) Proceed to unite the lining to the outer fabric of the placket
38) Proceed to unite the lining to the outer fabric of the bottom hem
39) Turn the lining over
40) Baste the bust lining to the garment
41) Sew the lower sleeve fabric
42) Sew the upper sleeve fabric
43) Sew the lower sleeve lining
44) Sew the upper sleeve lining
45) Sew the lining and fabric of the base of the sleeve
46) Open the seams on the fabric of the sleeve
47) Invisible stitch the hems, sewing the lining to the fabric

48) Turn the sleeves out
49) Trim the upper part of the sleeve linings
50) Invisible stitch the end of the sleeves
51) Press the sleeves with an iron
52) Invisible stitch the armscye fabric + roll + lining
53) Attach the sleeves
54) Top stitch the armscye
55) Quilt the under collar
56) Trim the under collar
57) Sew the collar with a stretch stich
58) Trim the corners of the collar
59) Turn the collar over
60) Gather the seam of the collar along the fold line
61) Baste the upper collar to the under collar with the extended part of the upper collar
62) Apply the collar
63) Blind stitch along the neckline
64) Prepare the collar and collar roll - top stitching
65) Baste the collar and neckline
66) Top stitch the collar roll and neckline
67) Press the front and collar with an iron
68) Top stitch the edges of the front and the collar
69) Remove the basting and clean
70) Mark the buttonholes
71) Create the buttonholes
72) Bartack the buttonholes
73) Press the external part of the front
74) Press the external part of the back
75) Press the sleeves
76) Go back over the lining
77) Attach the buttons
78) Attach the label(s)

JACKET COLLAR ASSEMBLY

THE SARTORIAL TECHNIQUE

The lower collar

After having sewn the shoulders of the jacket and having prepared the undercollar, attach it to the neckline, sew it into position, trim the seam allowance and press with an iron. You may then add the upper collar and the facings.

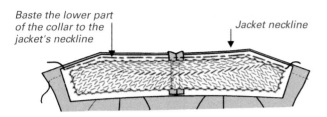

Baste the lower part of the collar to the jacket's neckline

Jacket neckline

Procedure

- Pre-stitch along the neckline of the jacket and notch to affix the corners. Place the "right" sides of the collar facing each other and, lining up the seam along the centre back, baste the lower part of the collar to the jacket until the lapel marker points, making the jacket collar conform to the neckline.

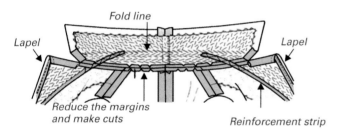

Fold line

Lapel

Lapel

Reduce the margins and make cuts

Reinforcement strip

– Sew the seams with a machine and remove the basting. Trim the seam allowances, press them open with an iron and reduce them down to 6 mm/0.24". Working on the reverse side, affix the reinforcement strips with a catch stitch, extending them beyond the internal folds of the lapels

The upper collar

The upper part of the collar should be a bit bigger than the lower collar. Thanks to this slight difference, the external seam will be hidden when the collar is turned flat, resting correctly on the back of the shoulders.

- Mark the centre of the upper part of the collar. Place right side to right side. Pin the upper part of the collar to the lower part, making sure the centre back and the markers line up, and machine sew along the seam line, starting and stopping exactly where the lower part of the collar meets the neckline.

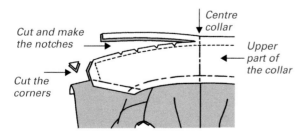

Cut and make the notches

Centre collar

Upper part of the collar

Cut the corners

Remove the basting and trim the seam allowances, cutting

those of the upper collar to 5 mm/0.20" and those of the lower collar to 3 mm/0.12". Notch the outer edges of the collar and cut the corners.

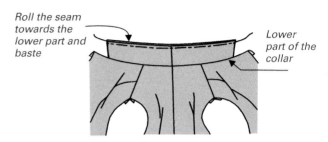

Roll the seam towards the lower part and baste

Lower part of the collar

- Bring the collar straight and roll the seam between your fingers, pushing it towards the lower side. Baste the external edges. Press the seam, working along the lower part of the collar

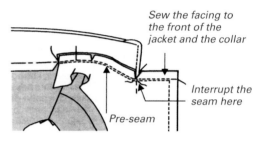

Sew the facing to the front of the jacket and the collar

Interrupt the seam here

Pre-seam

- Sew a pre-seam onto the edges of the neckline of the placket and notch the corners. With the "right" sides of fabric towards each other, baste the facing to the collar, from the corners of the lapels to the seams along the shoulders, and then along the edges of the opening.
- Sew the facing in two steps:
    1) to the edge of the shoulder to the corner of the lapel;
    2) from the corner along the upper edge of the lapel and along the opening.
- Notch the seam allowances on the collar corresponding to the seams on the shoulder of the placket and press the seam allowances open with an iron.

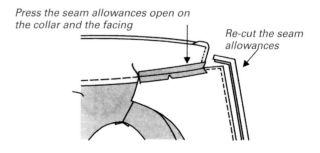

Press the seam allowances open on the collar and the facing

Re-cut the seam allowances

- Cut the jacket's seam allowance to 3 mm/0.12" and that of the facing to 6 mm/0.24", from the seam of the collar towards the bottom until the base of the lapel.
- Bring the facing towards the inside. Roll the seam towards the underside of the lapel, in the opposite direction under the lapel, so that it is not visible from the front.

Padding on the shoulders and sleeves

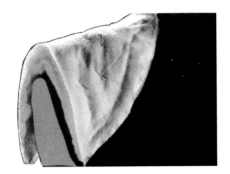

TRADITIONAL PADDING

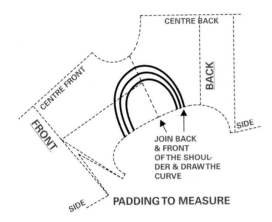

PADDING TO MEASURE

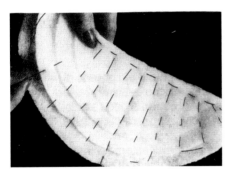

SEW THE LAYERS

POSITION & AFFIX THE PADDING

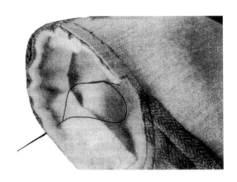

SEW THE PADDING

COMPLETED ARMSCYE

Shoulder padding

Shoulder padding can be made to the exact measurement of the armscye by using the pieces from the pattern. To adapt them to the figure as necessary, you must often adjust their measurements and thickness. If one of the wearer's shoulders is higher than the other, the padding on the lower shoulder should be thicker to compensate for the difference. If the person has sloping shoulders, the padding should be decidedly thicker than that suggested in the pattern, while square shoulders would require less padding.

In tailored garments, such as jackets and coats, the front of the shoulder padding is thicker than the back to fill in the indentation under the shoulder and to create a surface without creases. The back is thinner than the front to round out the shoulder at the height of the shoulder blades. If the chest is full, the padding should be slightly reduced on the front.

Always insert the padding each time the jacket or coat is tried on. Their shape and size may significantly change the line of the sleeves and shoulders.

To create padding in the desired thickness, cut a few graduated layers of thin material such as polyester wadding or any other material used for quilting which is substantial enough and not too soft.

For the upper part of the padding, you may use a piece of iron-on hemp fabric. Its structure is better for attaching to the fabric and thus makes it more stable and taut under the garment.

Sleeve padding

The sleeve padding is made up of strips of material that sustain the peak of the sleeve, lifting it and eliminating creases along the points where the sleeves are gathered in order to adapt to the shape of the armscye.

The padding on the sleeves is also meant to improve the way the jacket drapes. This padding may be made of the same material used to pad the shoulders, or of the padding used on neckties cut on the bias.

Jacket lining
The sartorial technique

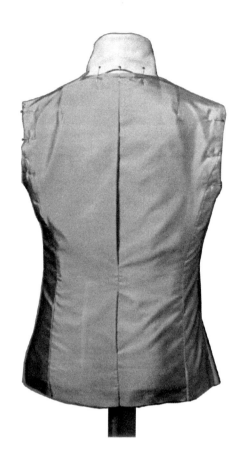

The lining should be cut and sewn along the same seam lines as the jacket. However, a few prudent details will make it more comfortable.

A fold at the centre back facilitates the range of movement of the shoulders and the upper back. Another fold is usually found between the lining and the garment's flounce hems, which allows the wearer to move comfortably without stressing the jacket and ripping the seams.

The jacket lining can be made from a separate pattern or from the same pattern as the jacket with a few necessary adjustments.

If you decide to use the same pattern paper for the sleeves and their lining, cut the lining so that it is 1.5 cm/0.59" higher in relation to the armscye. This allows the lining to rest above the seams of the armscye and prevents creases in this area. However, if the pattern for the sleeve lining is made separately, make sure that it fits appropriately by overlapping the sleeve pattern pieces over that of the lining, matching up the seamlines of the armscye.

Cut the jacket and sleeve lining 1.5 cm/0.59" longer than the garment (with the hem completed).

When applied, the finished edges of the lining will fall just below the midway point of the hems along the jacket and sleeves.

Should you need to lengthen or shorten the jacket or the sleeves, adjust the length of the corresponding linings accordingly.

Procedure

1) Sew all parts of the lining together, including the sleeves. Reinforce the seams of the armscye with two parallel rows of stitches. Fold and baste the central back fold at the top and bottom of the lining with a sewing machine. Sew a supporting seam 1 cm/0.39" from the armscye, the sleeve and the lower edges of the lining. Also place a few seams all the way to the supporting seam on the margin of the neckline.

2) Turn the jacket placket to the outside. Place the right sides together and sew the lining to the placket. On both sides of the front, leave the seam open for a length equal to twice the height of the hem (i.e., leave 10 cm/3.94" unsewn if the seam is 5 cm/1.97" high).

On the rounded edges, add the usual seams and then press them as they are.

3) Make the seam allowances on the lining and the jacket outer match up with the seams on the shoulder and the armscye and affix them with a few stitches.

Turn the lining over and run the sleeves inside the jacket. To finish, lightly press the seam allowances of the placket and facing towards the lining, using an ironing cloth.

4) Take in the raw edges of the front placket to make it neater and cleaner, if necessary. Finish the raw edges of the hem with an overlock stitch. Fold the lining underneath, along the line of support that runs along the lower edge, then pin in place so that the lining's raw edge is lined up with the upper edge of the jacket's hem.

NB: The shoulder lining must be completed before inserting the wadding to make sure it has the correct shape.

JACKET LAYOUT FOR CHECKED FABRIC

When cutting the pieces for a jacket in fabric with checks, stripes, herringbone, houndstooth or other woven patterns, lining up the designs requires careful attention when positioning the pattern on the fabric. The same is true of fabric with patterns or motifs that repeat in a series of rows, squares or blocks of colours.

Checked fabrics
For checked fabrics, each piece should be placed on the fabric, opened in one single layer.
When positioning the pattern for a plaid fabric, begin with the back so as to ensure perfect alignment.

Positioning the back
Place the waistline of the back (A) at the exact half (vertically) of the design (centre back). The bottom should fall at half or 3/4 of the check.
Pin the rest of the paper pattern, carefully double checking against the squares of the fabric.

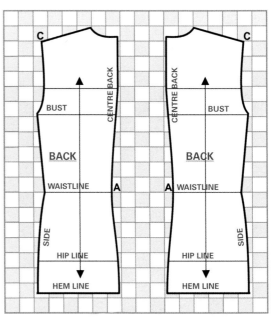

Positioning the front
The front should be positioned starting from point C, which should correspond to point C on the back. Place the rest of the pattern paper on the straight of the grain, paying careful attention that the bottom front has the same position as the back.

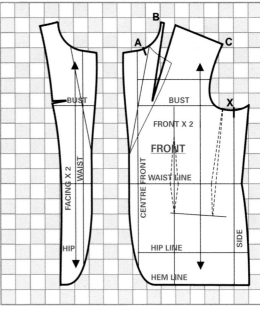

Positioning the sleeve
When positioning the sleeve, it is of utmost importance that point X corresponds to point X on the front. Place on the straight of the grain and pin.
When positioning the collar, be sure to respect points A - B - C which must be in the same position as those on the front.

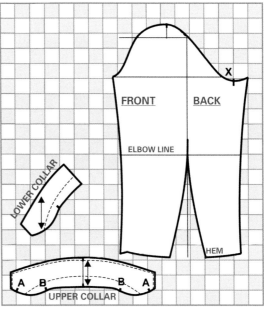

HEAVY JACKETS AND WINTER JACKETS

Heavy jackets and winter jackets 62
Base racer jacket block 63
Bomber jacket 64
Jacket with kimono cap sleeves 65
Jacket with wing cap sleeves 66
Jerkin with knit edges 68
Motorcycle jacket 69
Base puffer jacket 70
Sleeve for puffer jacket 71
Attaching the sleeve to the base 72
Wind jacket with a wing cap 73
Winter jacket 74
3/4 puffer jacket 75
Creative heavy jacket exercises 76

HEAVY JACKETS AND WINTER JACKETS

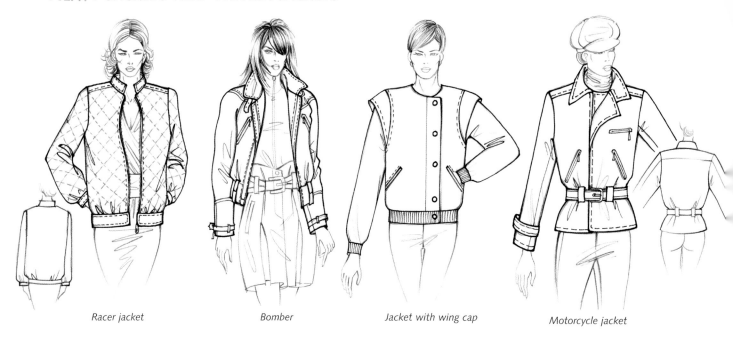

Racer jacket   *Bomber*   *Jacket with wing cap*   *Motorcycle jacket*

Heavy jackets

Heavy jackets come in men's and women's versions and are characterised by their length, which is no longer than approximately 65-70 cm (25.59-27.56").

The lines are generally sporty with roomy shoulders and an ample fit. The sleeves may be set-in, raglan or kimono and the jacket may have creative patterns or an innovative cut. But what really sets these jackets apart is the presence of visible pockets, original prints and wristbands decorated with buttons and buckles. Belts of various widths, with 1 or 2 buttons, are also common, at times including belt loops.

The fastening may be single or double breasted, with a zip or buttons. The fabrics used to make winter jackets include the entire range of gabardine, textiles of different weights, brushed fabrics, houndstooth and, for the more youthful versions, denim lined with artificial fur.

As far as spring/summer jackets are concerned, materials range from lightly combed fabric to flannel, to fresh, lively prints. They include floral patterns and plain denim, or even simply printed plastics for waterproof jackets.

Winter and puffer jackets

This type of jacket is generally worn in the winter and in the mountains.

It has a few distinctive characteristics: it is usually made of glazed or coated textiles or synthetic materials and generally has an inner lining or layer of mouflon. The sleeves are usually padded or lined as well, and may be detachable.

These jackets generally feature lively inserts, especially for winter jackets to be worn in the mountains.

They are usually fastened by a thick zip.

The necklines often feature mandarin collars which sometimes contain a hidden hood, closed in a secret compartment with a zip, to be used when it rains.

A few models come with hoods that are padded and lined with fur, some have a drawstring waist, others feature a yoke, etc.

BASE RACER JACKET BLOCK

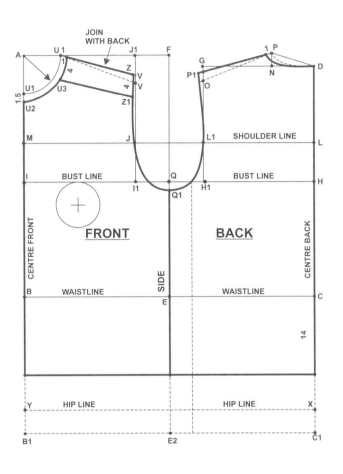

Measurements: Size 42, as in the women's sizing table.

Ease: As in the chart, under "Heavy Jackets".

- Draw the base of the "loose-fitting jacket", with bust circumference ease of 14-18 cm/5.51-7.09" (according to the padding to be used) and the desired length.
- Draw the line of the yoke Z1-U3 on the front shoulder, to join with the back, at the desired height.
- Lower the front neckline by 1-1.5 cm/0.39-0.59" for the collar.
- Move the front and back neck point by 1 cm/0.39".

BELT
- Draw a rectangle whose length is equal to half of the hip circumference taken at the height of the jacket's hem (e.g.: circ. 96 : 2 = 48 cm/18.90") and with a height equal to twice that of the desired final height (e.g.: 6 + 6 cm/2.36 + 2.36").

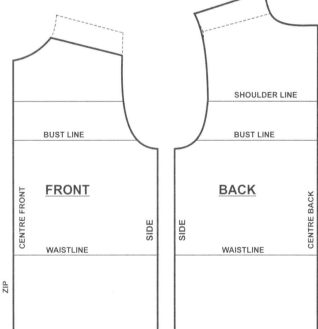

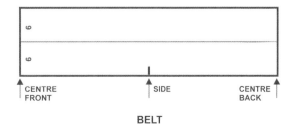

BELT

BOMBER JACKET

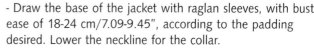

BACK

YOKE LINE

JOIN WITH FRONT

CUFF LINE

SIDE

CENTRE BACK

BUST LINE

WAISTLINE

SMALL FOLD

LOOP

10.5

16

18

26

8.5

5

3

6   6

2

P5 2

Q Q2 Q3 L H

E1 E3 E4 E

C1

P2 P1 P4 P P3

9

5

19

COLLAR

LOOP

SHOULDER

ENTIRE CENTRE BACK

2   11   10   2

FRONT

YOKE LINE

JOIN WITH BACK

CENTRE FRONT

FOLD UNDER   OVERLAP

BUST LINE

SLEEVE WIDTH

SIDE

CUFF LINE

WAISTLINE

SMALL FOLD

BAND

BELT LOOP

EQUAL TO BACK 0.5-1 CM

A

9

U U2

U1 U3 Z Z1

1.5 4

M

Q3 Q2 Q

E5 E3 E4 E

E1

E2

B1

3

7.5 5

10.5

16

16

16

16

2 Z2

NECK STRAP

½ COLLAR MEASUREMENT   CENTRE BACK

3 7   FOLD   2   IN HALF
3

WRIST STRAP

SLEEVE HEM MEASUREMENT

3 7   FOLD   2
3

NECK LOOP   WRIST LOOP   BELT LOOP

1.5   2   3
5   5   8

- Draw the base of the jacket with raglan sleeves, with bust ease of 18-24 cm/7.09-9.45", according to the padding desired. Lower the neckline for the collar.
- Lower the armscye by the desired amount (10.5 cm/4.13").
- Determine the desired length and draw the strip around the waist, according to the waist circumference.
- Draw the front and back yoke.
- Draw the cuffs on the base of the sleeve.
- Draw the flap for the fastening.
- Draw the straps for the collar and the sleeves.
- Draw the loops for the collar and the cuffs.
- Draw the collar, as shown in the illustration.

JACKET WITH KIMONO CAP SLEEVES

- Draw the base of the loose-fitting jacket, with a 14-16 cm/5.51-6.30" ease on the bust circumference, according to the fabric. Determine the desired length and draw the high collar.
- Draw the base of the sleeve for the loose-fitting jacket, suitable for the model.
- Draw a line, L-L1, on the sleeve and curve it as desired (points L-X-L1).
- Place the measurement of the piece of the sleeve crown G-L on the front armscye (points Q1-J2); position the crown of the front sleeve L-X-E on the front shoulder and join as in the figure.
- Put the measurement of G1-L1 (the portion of the sleeve crown) onto the back armscye (points Q1-L2); position the part of the sleeve crown L1-X-E on the back shoulder and join them.
- Extend the sleeve for the bottom hem.
- Draw the cuff and the waistband.

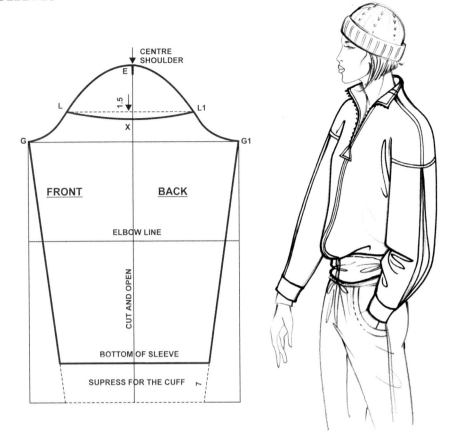

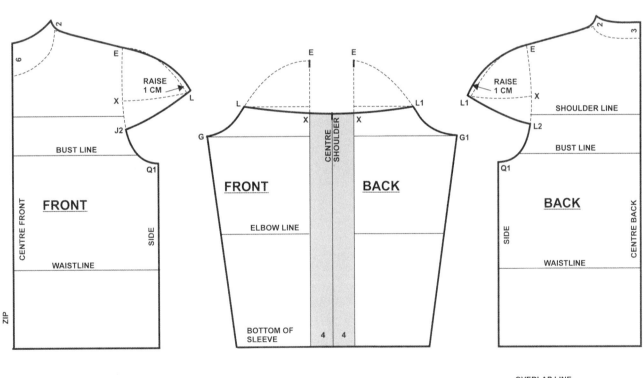

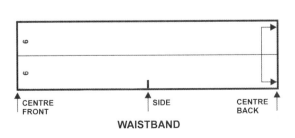

WAISTBAND

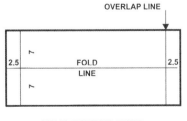

SINGLE PIECE CUFF

Jacket with wing cap sleeves

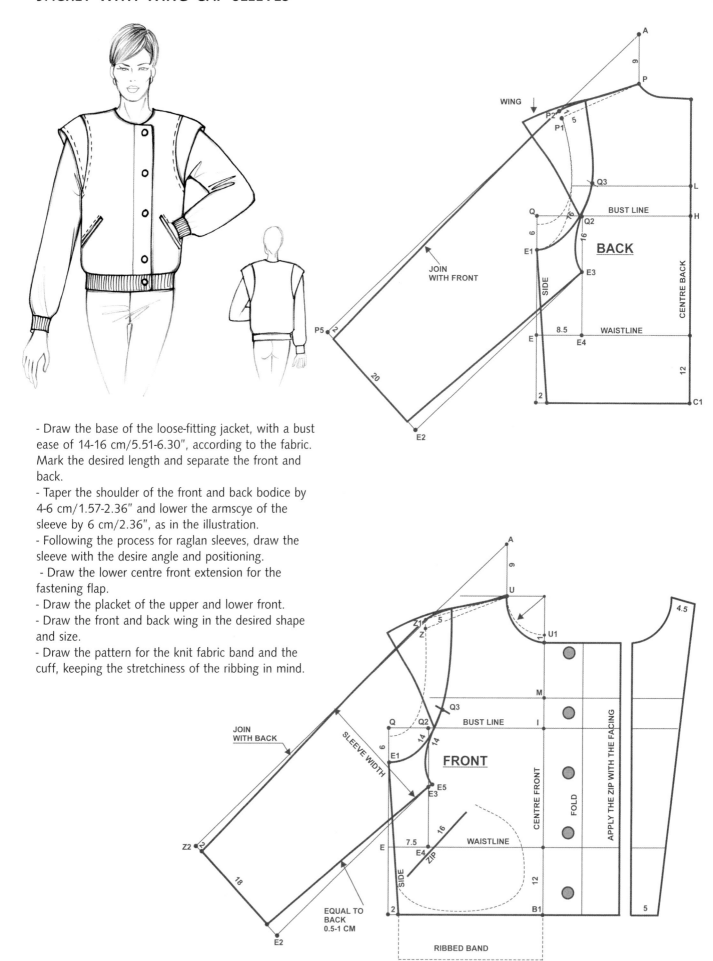

- Draw the base of the loose-fitting jacket, with a bust ease of 14-16 cm/5.51-6.30", according to the fabric. Mark the desired length and separate the front and back.
- Taper the shoulder of the front and back bodice by 4-6 cm/1.57-2.36" and lower the armscye of the sleeve by 6 cm/2.36", as in the illustration.
- Following the process for raglan sleeves, draw the sleeve with the desire angle and positioning.
- Draw the lower centre front extension for the fastening flap.
- Draw the placket of the upper and lower front.
- Draw the front and back wing in the desired shape and size.
- Draw the pattern for the knit fabric band and the cuff, keeping the stretchiness of the ribbing in mind.

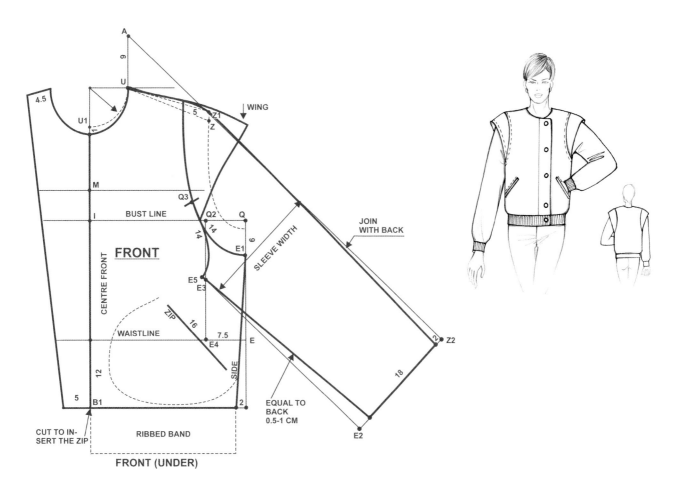

FRONT

FRONT (UNDER)

- Take up the front and back sleeves on a separate sheet of paper and join them in the centre shoulder.
- Take up the front and back sleeve wings on another piece of paper, then join them along the centre shoulder with a smooth curve.

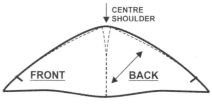

CENTRE SHOULDER

FRONT   BACK

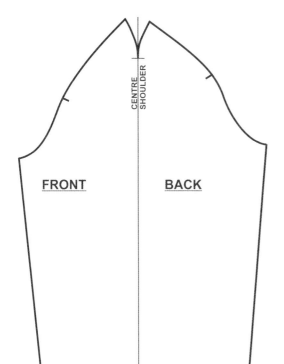

FRONT   BACK

CENTRE SHOULDER

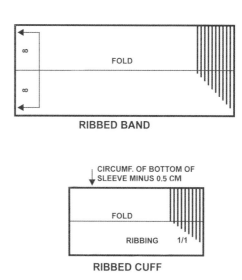

RIBBED BAND

RIBBED CUFF

CIRCUMF. OF BOTTOM OF SLEEVE MINUS 0.5 CM

FOLD

RIBBING   1/1

JERKIN WITH KNIT EDGES

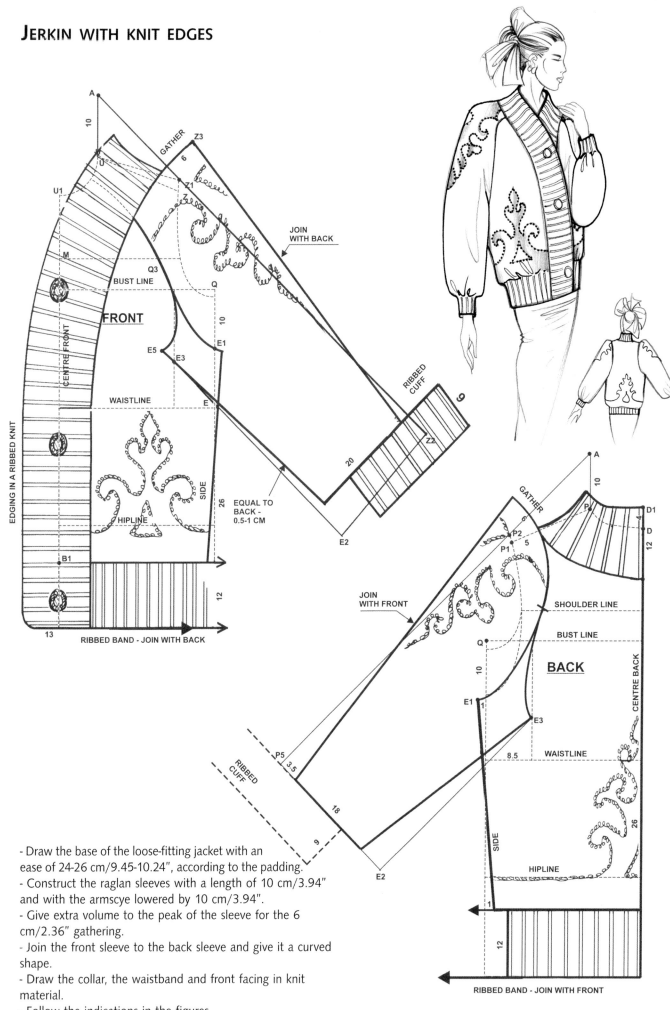

FRONT

BACK

JOIN WITH BACK

JOIN WITH FRONT

GATHER

BUST LINE

CENTRE FRONT

WAISTLINE

SIDE

HIPLINE

EDGING IN A RIBBED KNIT

RIBBED BAND - JOIN WITH BACK

RIBBED CUFF

EQUAL TO BACK - 0.5-1 CM

SHOULDER LINE

BUST LINE

CENTRE BACK

WAISTLINE

SIDE

HIPLINE

RIBBED CUFF

RIBBED BAND - JOIN WITH FRONT

- Draw the base of the loose-fitting jacket with an ease of 24-26 cm/9.45-10.24", according to the padding.
- Construct the raglan sleeves with a length of 10 cm/3.94" and with the armscye lowered by 10 cm/3.94".
- Give extra volume to the peak of the sleeve for the 6 cm/2.36" gathering.
- Join the front sleeve to the back sleeve and give it a curved shape.
- Draw the collar, the waistband and front facing in knit material.
- Follow the indications in the figures.

68

MOTORCYCLE JACKET

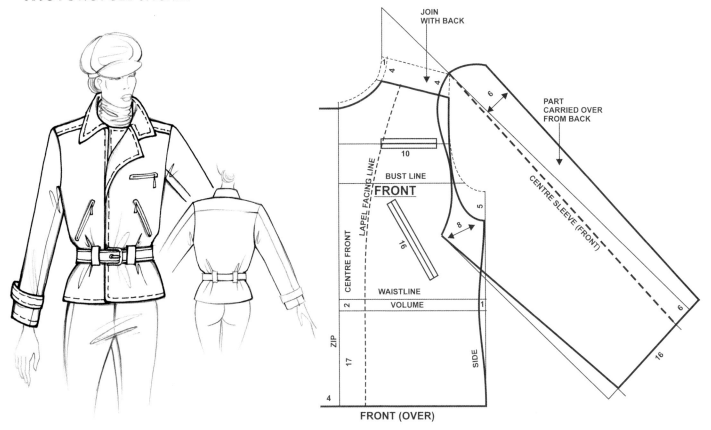

- Draw the base of the loose-fitting jacket, with a bust ease of 14-16 cm/5.51-6.30", according to the type of leather used. Create the desired length and separate the front and back.
- Lower the sleeve's armscye by 5 cm/2.0", as illustrated.
- Following the procedure used for raglan sleeves, draw the sleeve, with a 9 cm/3.54" angle.
- Draw the part of the front shoulder to bring to the back for the yoke, the part of the front sleeve to carry over to the centre front sleeve and the back yoke, as shown in the illustration.
- Draw the extension of the centre front (under) for the fastening.
- Draw the facing and the zip fastening strip for the centre front (over).
- Draw the main pocket and the small pocket with zips.

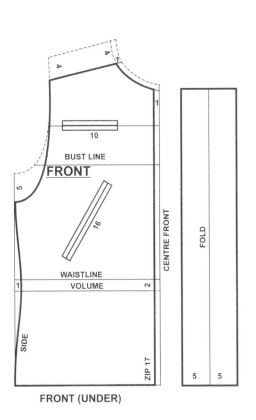

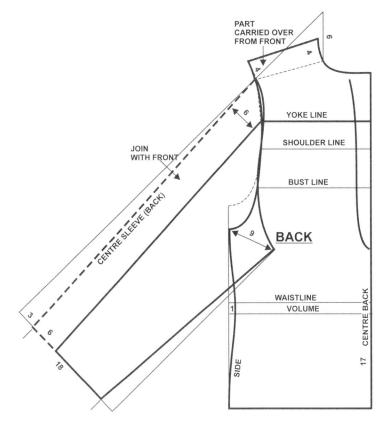

BASE PUFFER JACKET

Padded puffer jackets which are meant to be worn in the mountains should have an ease appropriate for garments made of three layers: the external fabric, the padding and the lining. In addition, it is necessary to remember that puffer jackets are often worn with heavy jumpers and dungarees.

We have used the ease found in the chart in the previous chapter for this bodice block:

For the bust circumference and hips, 30 cm/11.81"; for the length of the front and back waist, 3cm/1.18"; for the sector, 6 cm/2.36"; etc.

However, it is always prudent to check all of the measurements, including the armscye of the sleeve, with respect to the crown, and have the subject try on the sample before proceeding to the following phases.

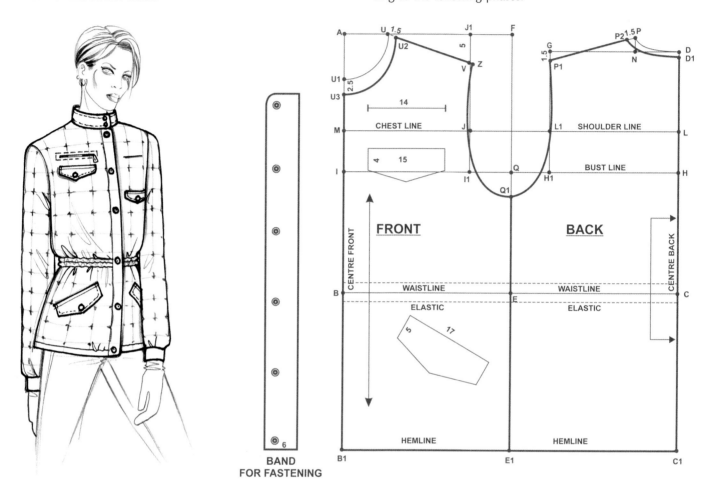

BAND
FOR FASTENING

- Draw a rectangle A-B-C-D with:
- A-B equal to the length of the front waist + 3 cm/1.18" ease (e.g.: 43 + 3 = 46 cm).
- B-C equal to the bust semicircumference + 1/2 ease of 15 cm/5.91" (e.g.: 92 + 30 = 122 : 2 = 61 cm/24.02").
- B-E half of B-C.
- Draw F-E (centre side).
- B-B1 elongation of the jacket as desired (24-28 cm/9.45-11.02"). Draw B1-C1. (hem line).
- A-U 1/6 length of the shoulders (including 10 cm/3.94" for ease). (e.g.: 38 + 10 = 48 : 6= 8 cm/3.15").
- Draw a curve from U-U1.
- C-D length of the back waist + 3 cm/1.18" ease (43 cm/16.92"). - C-H half of C-D. (21.5 cm/8.46").
- Draw H-I (bust line).
- H-L 1/3 of H-D (e.g.: 21.5 : 3 = 7.2 cm/2.83").
- Draw L-M (chest and shoulder line).
- D-G 1/2 back shoulder length + 10 cm/3.94" ease (or 2/5 of B-C -1 cm/0.39"). (e.g.: 38 + 9.5 = 47.5 : 2= 23.75 cm).

- H-H1 as D-G.
- Draw G-L1-H1.
- H1-I1 1/5 Bust semicircumference + 1/6 bust ease (5 cm/1.97") (e.g.: 46 : 5 = 9.2 + 5 = 14.2 cm/5.59").
- Draw I1-J-J1
- G-P1 1.5 cm/0.59".
- D-D1 1 cm/0.39".
- D-N 1/3 D-G (8 cm/3.15").
- N-P 2.5 cm/0.98".
- P-P1 Shoulder length + ease (according to the fabric's padding).
- P-P2 1.5 cm/0.59".
- J1-V 5 cm/1.97".
- U-U2 1.5 cm/0.59"
- U-U3 2.5 cm/0.98".
- U2-Z as P-P1.
- Q-Q1 4-5 cm/1.57-1.97".
- Connect all the points as illustrated.

Sleeve for puffer jacket

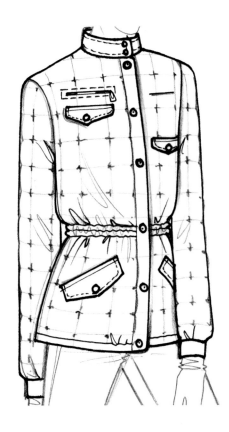

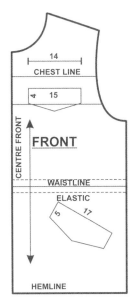

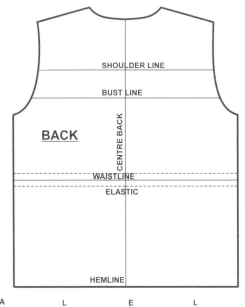

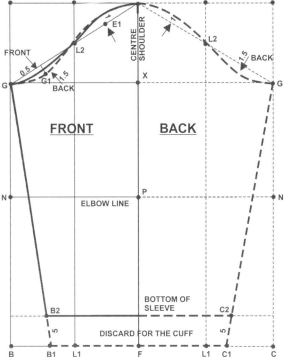

Sleeve

- Draw a rectangle A-B-E-F with:
- A-B sleeve length + 3 cm/1.81" ease
(e.g.: 58 + 3 cm = 61 cm).
- A-E = measurement of the bodice sector + 1/2 of that same sector + 2.5 cm/0.98" ease.
(e.g.: sector of 14.2 + 7.1 = 21.3 + 2.5 = 23.8 cm).
- A-G as L1-P1 of the bodice + 1 cm/0.39" (14 cm/5.51").
- Draw G-X.
- Join G-E with a diagonal line.
- A-N half of A-B + 2 cm/0.79". Join N-P.
- A-L half of A-E. Draw L-L1.
- L2 half of G-E.
- E1 half of E-L2.
- G1 half of G-L2.
- Draw E-L2-G with a curved line as in the figure.
- Draw E-G1-G with a curved line as in the figure.
- Take up the front and back sleeve and draw the entire sleeve as in the figure.
- B1-C1 sleeve width.
- B1-B2 and C1-C2 tapering for the cuff.

Collar

– Draw right triangle A-B-C with:
- A-B desired collar height (9 cm).
- B-C total length of the front and back neckline of the base.
- B-D neckline measurement from the centre front to the centre shoulder.
- E-C measurement of the fastening flap (5.5 cm/2.17").
- E-E1 3 cm/1.18". Draw B-D-C1-E1 with a curved line.
- E1-F as A-B, at a right angle to C1-E1.
- Connect A-F.

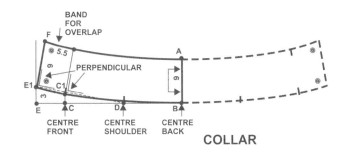

ATTACHING THE SLEEVE TO THE BASE

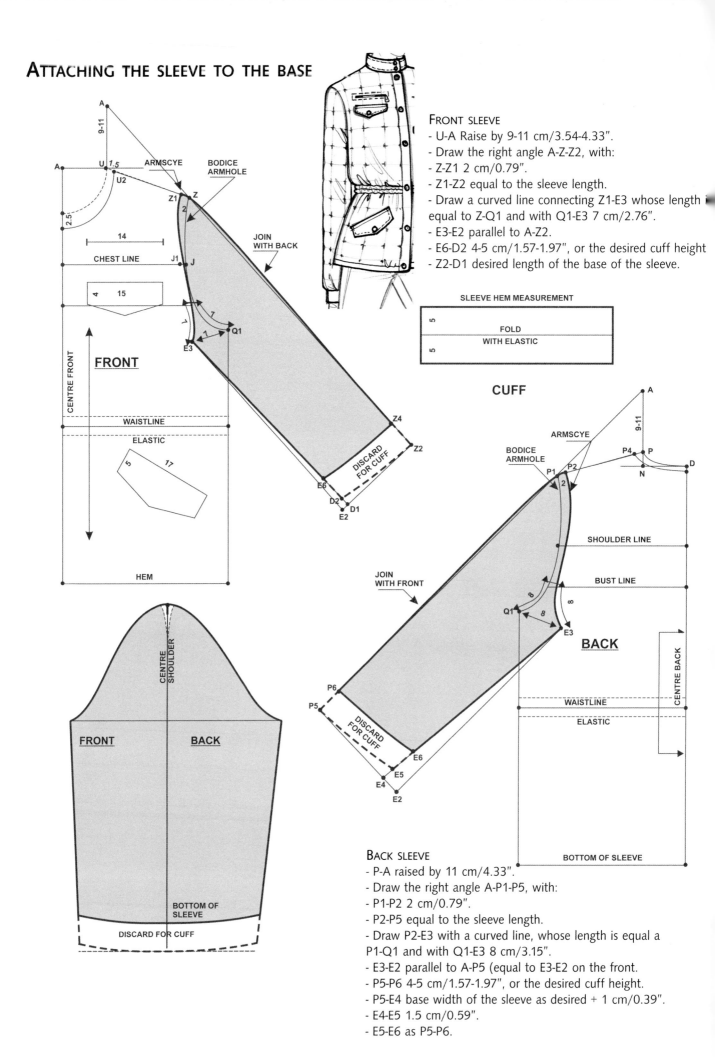

FRONT SLEEVE
- U-A Raise by 9-11 cm/3.54-4.33".
- Draw the right angle A-Z-Z2, with:
- Z-Z1 2 cm/0.79".
- Z1-Z2 equal to the sleeve length.
- Draw a curved line connecting Z1-E3 whose length equal to Z-Q1 and with Q1-E3 7 cm/2.76".
- E3-E2 parallel to A-Z2.
- E6-D2 4-5 cm/1.57-1.97", or the desired cuff height
- Z2-D1 desired length of the base of the sleeve.

SLEEVE HEM MEASUREMENT	
5	FOLD
5	WITH ELASTIC

CUFF

BACK SLEEVE
- P-A raised by 11 cm/4.33".
- Draw the right angle A-P1-P5, with:
- P1-P2 2 cm/0.79".
- P2-P5 equal to the sleeve length.
- Draw P2-E3 with a curved line, whose length is equal a P1-Q1 and with Q1-E3 8 cm/3.15".
- E3-E2 parallel to A-P5 (equal to E3-E2 on the front.
- P5-P6 4-5 cm/1.57-1.97", or the desired cuff height.
- P5-E4 base width of the sleeve as desired + 1 cm/0.39".
- E4-E5 1.5 cm/0.59".
- E5-E6 as P5-P6.

Wind jacket with a wing cap

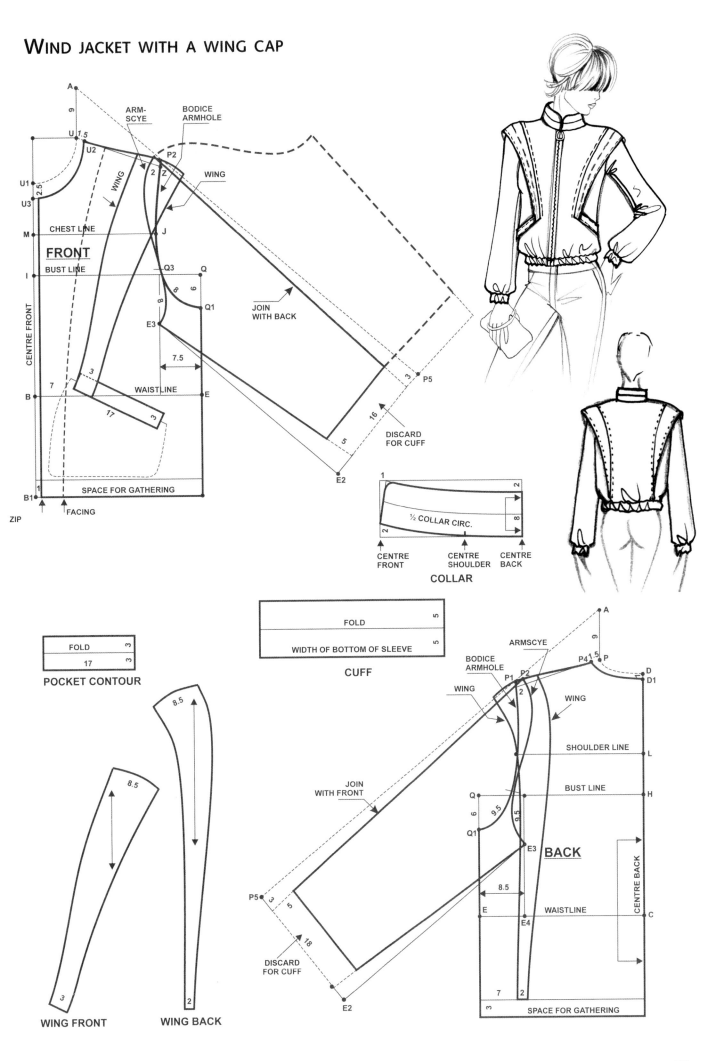

FRONT

A
9
U 1.5
U2
ARMSCYE
BODICE ARMHOLE
P2
WING
2 Z
WING
U1
2.5
U3
CHEST LINE
M
J
CENTRE FRONT
BUST LINE
I
Q3 Q
8 6
8
E3
Q1
JOIN WITH BACK
7.5
WAISTLINE
B
7
E
17
3
3
P5
16
DISCARD FOR CUFF
5
B1 1
SPACE FOR GATHERING
E2
ZIP
FACING

COLLAR

1
2
½ COLLAR CIRC.
8
2
CENTRE FRONT
CENTRE SHOULDER
CENTRE BACK

POCKET CONTOUR

FOLD 3
17 3

CUFF

FOLD 5
WIDTH OF BOTTOM OF SLEEVE 5

WING FRONT

8.5
8.5
3

WING BACK

8.5
2

BACK

A
9
P4 1.5 P
ARMSCYE
BODICE ARMHOLE
P1 P2
2
D
D1
WING
WING
JOIN WITH FRONT
SHOULDER LINE
L
BUST LINE
H
Q
6 9.5
9.5
Q1
E3
CENTRE BACK
P5 3
5
8.5
E
WAISTLINE
C
E4
18
DISCARD FOR CUFF
7 2
E2
3 SPACE FOR GATHERING

WINTER JACKET

WITH DETACHABLE SLEEVES

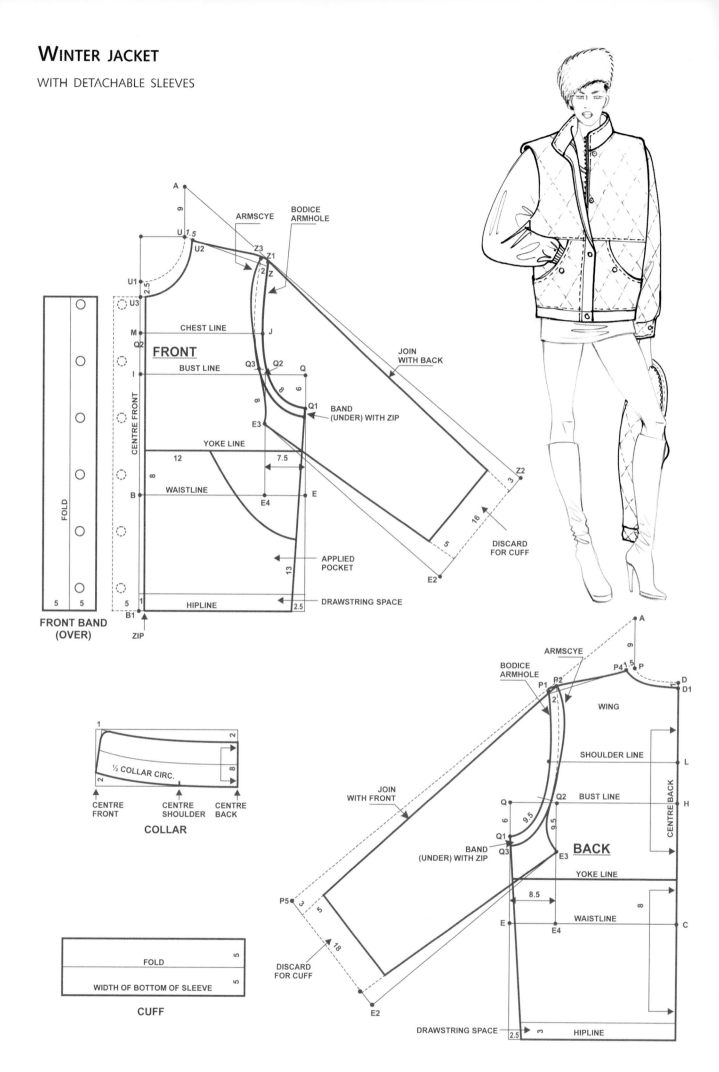

FRONT BAND (OVER)

COLLAR

½ COLLAR CIRC.

CENTRE FRONT

CENTRE SHOULDER

CENTRE BACK

CUFF

FOLD

WIDTH OF BOTTOM OF SLEEVE

ARMSCYE

BODICE ARMHOLE

CHEST LINE

FRONT

BUST LINE

CENTRE FRONT

BAND (UNDER) WITH ZIP

JOIN WITH BACK

YOKE LINE

WAISTLINE

DISCARD FOR CUFF

APPLIED POCKET

HIPLINE

DRAWSTRING SPACE

ZIP

FOLD

ARMSCYE

BODICE ARMHOLE

WING

SHOULDER LINE

JOIN WITH FRONT

BUST LINE

CENTRE BACK

BAND (UNDER) WITH ZIP

BACK

YOKE LINE

WAISTLINE

DISCARD FOR CUFF

DRAWSTRING SPACE

HIPLINE

3/4 PUFFER JACKET

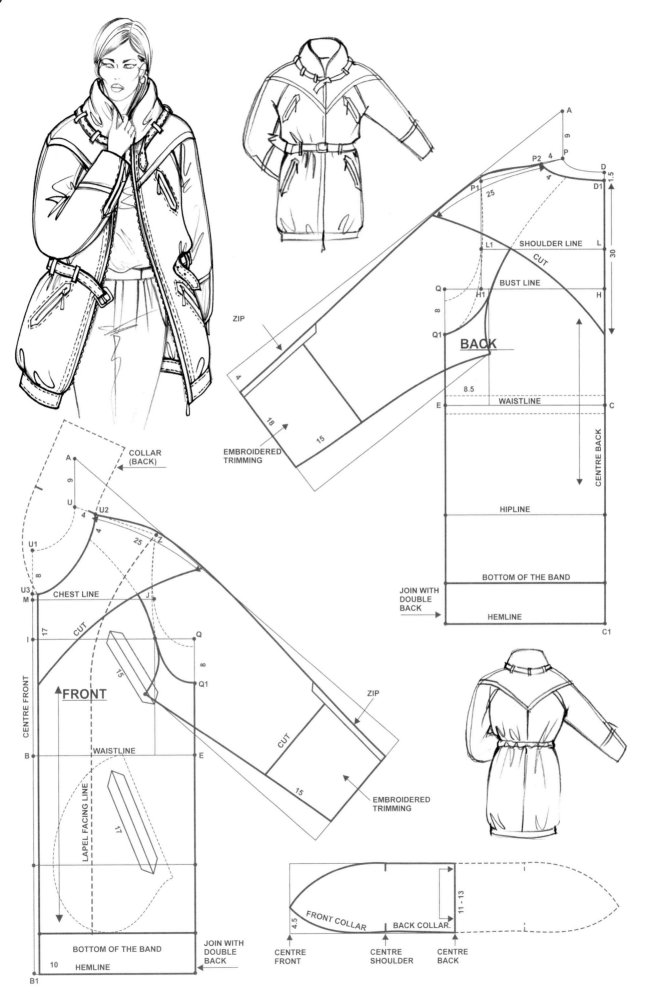

ZIP

EMBROIDERED TRIMMING

4

18

15

A

9

P2   4   P
P1
25

D
D1   1.5

SHOULDER LINE   L

CUT

30

BUST LINE

Q
H1

BACK

8

Q1

8.5

WAISTLINE

E   C

CENTRE BACK

HIPLINE

BOTTOM OF THE BAND

JOIN WITH
DOUBLE
BACK

HEMLINE

C1

COLLAR
(BACK)

A
9
U
4   U2
U1   4   25   Z
8
U3
M   CHEST LINE   J
I   17   CUT

15

FRONT

Q
8
Q1

CENTRE FRONT

CUT

B   WAISTLINE   E

15

EMBROIDERED
TRIMMING

ZIP

LAPEL FACING LINE

17

BOTTOM OF THE BAND

JOIN WITH
DOUBLE
BACK

10   HEMLINE

B1

FRONT COLLAR   BACK COLLAR.

11 - 13

4.5

CENTRE
FRONT

CENTRE
SHOULDER

CENTRE
BACK

OVERCOATS AND TOPCOATS

Overcoats and topcoats 78
Overcoat lines and shapes. 79
Base overcoat block 80
Inset sleeve for overcoats 81
Base loose-fitting coat block 82
Loose-fitting coat sleeves. 83
Double-breasted Chesterfield. 84
Double-breasted overcoat 85
Seam margins for overcoats. 86
Loden coat. 87
Base Montgomery coat block 88
Montgomery coat sleeves 89
Overcoat with horizontal seams 90

Redingote overcoat. 91
Kimono coat. 92
Kimono coat with gusset. 93
Raglan sleeve coat 94
Coat with dropped shoulders. 95
Coat with saddle raglan sleeves. 96
Overcoat with yoke 97
Creative overcoat 98
Base Mac (trench) block 100
Mac (trench) with raglan sleeves 102
Sporty mac (trench) 103
Overcoat exercises 104

Overcoats and topcoats

V. Borovikovsky, Catherine II of Russia, 1794 J. Tissot, Waiting for the Ferry, 1878

C. W. Merritt, My Daughter Die, 1902

An overcoat is an outerwear garment generally made of heavy wool fabric. It comes in versions for men and women, in various models, and is at times lined with fur or other warm materials.

The fabrics used to create overcoats are: boucle', heavy cloth, velour, brushed fabric, heavy double wool crepe, camelhair, knickerbocker material, tweed, herringbone, etc. They are also at times paired with sportier materials, such as leather inserts. The names "coat", "overcoat", "topcoat" and "cape" have all appeared in various eras to indicate garments with different qualities. However, they have always had the purpose of protecting the wearer from the cold.

Other terms were used in the past, such as *himation* and *clamide* in Greece in the 6th century B.C.; *lurna* and *tebenna* by the Etruscans in the 500s (B.C.); *toga, pallium* and *lacerna, burrus* or *cuculus, caracalla* in Ancient Rome; *paludamentum, colobium* in the 4th century A.D.; *loron* in Byzantium; *housse, gabbano* in the 12th century A.D.; *houppelande* in France; *pellanda, pelandrana, palandrana, ferraiolo, tabarro* and *barracano* in Italy in the 15th century A.D.; *giomea* in the High Renaissance; *schaube* in the 1500s in Germany; *casacca, velada* and *giamberga* in the 1600s and *zamberlucco* in the 1700s in Italy; *paltò, paletot* or *paltock* in the 19th century, which then underwent further linguistic modifications according to the model and length of the garment.

The Fontana sisters (photo: Federico Garolla)

OVERCOAT LINES AND SHAPES

The lines and lengths of overcoats vary according to the dictates of fashion and occasions on which they are worn.

In the back, they may feature a vent in the centre or a small box pleat.

The fabric used on overcoats and topcoats will vary according to the garment and the style.

Main types of overcoats and topcoats

Classic overcoat

Classic overcoats, inspired by menswear, may be double- or single-breasted.

Single-breasted coats may be straight and without seams, with the breakline of the lapel at the bust or as low down as the waist, and they may come with one, two or three buttons.

They may have transverse seams or prints, vertical seams, contouring along the waist or have the shape of a redingote or frock coat. They may be wide along the bottom or be amphora shaped and narrow at the bottom. The sleeves may be set-in, kimono style or dropped. They may come with or without a collar, with lapels similar to men's coats or with a collar that is very wide at the shoulders.

The double-breasted coat may have six buttons with the lapel's breakline under the bust, or have four buttons with the breakline near the waist. There may be vertical seams, contoured sides near the waist or be shaped like a redingote (frock coat).

The Loden overcoat

The Loden, which gets its name from the type of fabric it is made of, was created in the 1960s as menswear but then offered by designers in versions for women. Originally in bottle green and made of pure brushed wool, this type of coat stands out for its slight trapezoid shape and shoulders with flaps over the armscye to cover the seams.

The flap and the sleeve's stitching and attachment leave open space at the underarms for breathability and to allow perspiration to escape, in addition to providing better ease of movement.

On the back, there is generally an inverted pleat secured with a fly or triangle shaped piece of leather.

Heavy jacket

The heavy jacket is a type of outercoat whose length is from 3/4 (hitting at the thighs) to 7/8 and 9/10 above the knee. It comes in all the cuts and lines as a classic overcoat and even comes in the same materials.

Topcoat

The topcoat is a light item of outerwear made in various medium-weight fabrics to be worn mid-season.

This type of garment existed as early as the 18th century, though it has undergone countless changes and transformations since then.

Macintosh or trench coat

The Macintosh or trench coat is an item of outerwear for men or women, made in waterproof fabric. It comes in various lines and cuts, according to current fashions, but it is always relatively loose-fitting. It is worn as protection from the rain.

The Loden   Double-breasted coat   Single-breasted coat

Raglan-sleeve coat   The Redingote   The Montgomery

Loose-fitting coat   Mac or trench coat

BASE OVERCOAT BLOCK

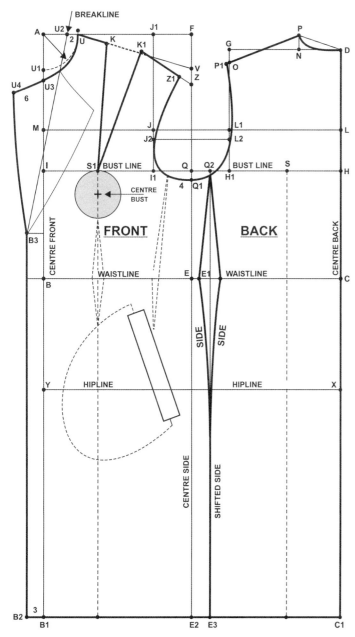

Measurements: Size 42, as in the chart.
Ease: As in the "Shaped coat" chart.
- Draw a right angle ABC, where:
- A-B Front waist length + overcoat ease.
(E.g.: 41.5 + 2 = 43.5 cm).
- B-C Bust semicircumference + ease.
(E.g.: 92 + 16 = 108 : 2 = 54 cm).
- C-D Back waist length + ease. (E.g.: 40 + 2 = 42 cm).
- D-C1 Length of the back of the overcoat.
- Join D-C1. CENTRE BACK. - B-B1 like C-C1.
- Join A-B1. CENTRE FRONT. - B1-C1 as in C-B.
- Join B1-C1. HEM LINE. - B-E half of B-C.
- B1-E2 half of B1-C1. - A-F as in B-E.
- Join F-E2. CENTRAL SIDE LINE. - D-H half of C-D. (E.g.: 42 : 2 = 21 cm). - H-I parallel to B-C. BUST LINE. (This measurement is found at approximately 3-5 cm /1.81-1.97" from the centre bust).
- E2-E3 4 cm/1.57", if you want the back to be a bit more fitted.
- Q-Q2 4 cm/1.57").
- Join Q2-E3. SHIFTED SIDE LINE. - C-X Side height (E.g.: 20 cm/7.87").

- D-G half of shoulder length + 1/2 ease. (E.g.: 36.5 + 4.5 = 41:2 = 20.5 cm/8.07").
- H-L 1/3 D-H. (E.g.: 21 : 3 = 7 cm). - Draw L-L1. SHOULDER LINE.
- H-H1 as in D-G. (20.5 cm/8.07").
- H1-I1 Sector width + ease* (E.g.: 13.3 cm/5.24"). - Draw G-H1 parallel to D-H.
- Draw I1-J1 parallel to G-H1.
- I-M like H -L. - Draw L-M parallel to H-I. - Draw the centre bust.

Back
- G-O 2.5 cm/0.98".
- D-N 1/3 DG + 1 cm/0.39" (E.g.: 20.5 : 3 = 6.8 + 1 = 7.8 cm).
- N-P 2.5 cm/0.98".
- Draw D-P.
- Join P-D with a smooth curved line.
- P-P1 passing through O, create the shoulder length + 1.5 cm/0.59". (E.g.: 13 + 1.5 = 14.5 cm).
- Mark point Q halfway between H-I.
- Q-Q1 1 cm/0.39" (or more for a lower armscye).
- Draw the armscye P1-L1-Q1, smoothly.
- L1-L2 like Q-Q1.
- Draw L2-J2. SLEEVE REFERENCE

Front
- A-U 1/3 D-G of the back (E.g.: 20.5 : 3 = 6.8 cm).
- Draw the curved line U-U1 with the measurement of A-U centred on A.
- I-I1 like H-H1-0.5 cm/0.20" (E.g.: 20.5 - 0.5 = 20 cm/7.87").
- I-S1 1/2 bust divergence + 1 cm/0.39". (E.g.: 19 : 2 = 9.5 + 1 = 10.5 cm).
- F-V 6 cm/2.36".
- Join U-V.
- V-Z 1/3 of F-V. (E.g.: 6 : 3 = 2 cm). (This measure is obtained by rotating the segment Z1-K-S1 around point S1, until reaching the opening of the dart).
- U-K 1/3 P-P1 on the back + 1 cm/0.39" (E.g.: 14.5 : 3 = 4.8 + 1 = 5.8 cm).
- K-K1 Difference between the bust circumference and the chest circumference + 0.5 cm/0.20". (E.g.: 92 – 86 = 6 + 0.5 = 6.5 cm).
- K1-S1 like K-S1. Join.
- K1-Z1 like P-P1 of the back, less U-K (E.g.: 14.5 - 5.8 = 8.7 cm).
- Draw the front armscye Z1-J-Q1 with a curved line.

Lapel
- Draw the 3-4 cm/1.18-1.57" extension of the centre front B2-B2, for the fastening.
- Draw B2-B3, until the height of the desired lapel breakline (E.g.: 8 cm/3.15" from the waist).
- Draw point U2, at 2 cm/0.79" from U.
- Join U2-B3. BREAKLINE.
- Lower the front neckline by 1.5-2.5 cm/0.59-0.98", point U3. - U3-U4 6 cm/2.36" or as desired.
- Join U4-B3 and join with lower line with a curve.

Waist dart
The darts and tapering at the waist correlate to the difference between the hips and waist, which is distributed proportionally along the bust dart and the sides, aided by the creation of a small 1.5 cm/0.59" dart, with its points on the armscye line and the pocket.

* The armscye sector is created as follows: 1/5 bust semicircumference including ease + 2.5 cm/0.98". (E.g.: 54 : 5 = 10.8 + 2.5 = 13.3 cm/5.24").

INSET SLEEVE FOR OVERCOATS

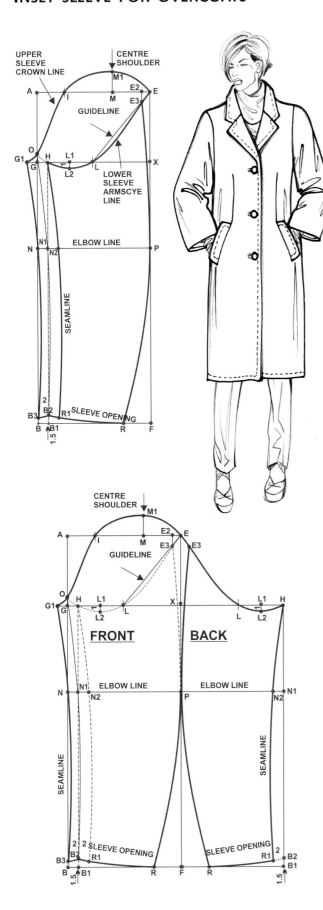

Measurements: Arm circumference 29 cm/11.42". Arm length 58 cm/22.83".

On the left side of a sheet of pattern paper, draw a rectangle, A-B-E-F, where:
- A-E, which is the bodice sector, + 1/2 sector + 1.5 cm/0.59".
(E.g.: 12.5 + 6.25 cm = 18.75 + 1.5 = 20.2 cm).
- A-B sleeve length measurement (E.g.: 58 cm/22.83").
- A-G is the measurement of L2-P1-1 cm/0.39" of the base of the back bodice. Here: 13.5 - 1= 12.5 cm/4.92").
- Draw G-X parallel to A-E.
- A-N half of A-B (E.g.: 58 : 2 = 29 + 2 = 31 cm).
 Write ELBOW LINE.
- A-M 2/3 of A-E. (E.g.: 20.2 x 2= 40.4 : 3= 13.46 cm). CENTRE SHOULDER.
- M-M1 1/3 A-G. (E.g.: 11 : 3 = 3.7 cm).
- A-I 1/4 A-E. (E.g.: 20.2 : 4 = 5 cm).   - G-H 2 cm/0.79".
- Draw H-B1 parallel to A-B. (This is the seam line, which is often shifted to the front).
- X-L half of G-X. (E.g.: 20.2 : 2 = 10.1 cm).
- Draw guide line E-L. - G-O 1.5 cm/0.59".
- L-L1 half of H-L. - L1-L2 1 cm/0.39". - G-G1 like G-H.
- Smoothly draw the arc of the front sleeve crown E-M1-I-O-G1.
- Smoothly draw the arc of the back crown E-L-L2-H-O.
- B1-B2 1.5 cm/0.59".
- B3-R 1/2 length of the cuff (E.g.:13.5 cm/5.31").

Undersleeve
- EE-E2 1.5 cm/0.59". (Or another measurement, as required).
- B2-R1 as in B2-B3.
- Connect R-E3 and R1-H with a curved line.

Open sleeve
- Copy over the undersleeve E3-P-R-R1-H-L2-L-E3 and position it on the E-F fold line of the front portion.
- Check the measurement of the sleeve's entire crown, which should be greater than the measurement of the armscye, by a variable number, according to the type of fabric used.

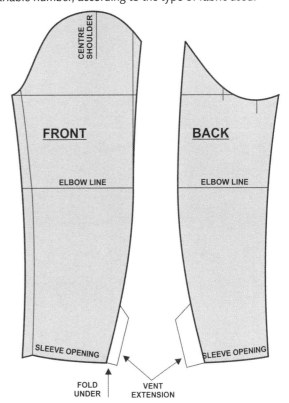

Note: *Often an opening, such as a vent, is added to the back of the sleeve along the internal seam. If so, it is necessary to add an extension on both parts of the sleeve. The extension of the upper sleeve should be folded, while that of the undersleeve continues straight under the upper part.*

BASE LOOSE-FITTING COAT BLOCK

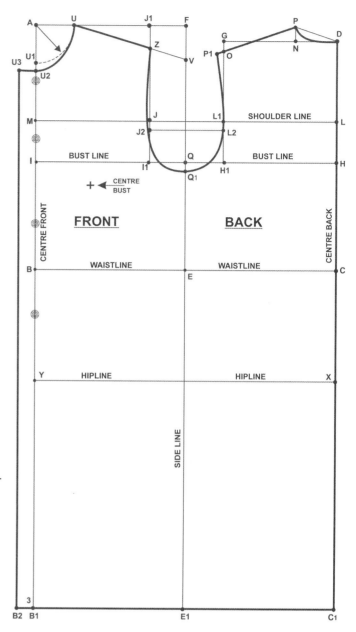

Measurements: Size 42, as in the chart on p.19.

Ease: An in the chart a p.17, "Outerwear" (18-20 cm/7.09-7.87").

- Draw a right angle ABC, where:
- A-B = front waist length + outerwear ease.
(E.g.: 41.5 + 2 = 43.5 cm).
- B-C Bust semicircumference + ease.
(E.g.: 92 +18 = 110 : 2 = 55 cm).
- C-D Back waist length + ease. (E.g.: 40 + 2 = 42 cm).
- D-C1 Length of the back of the overcoat or topcoat.
- Join D-C1. CENTRE BACK.
- B-B1 as in C-C1.
- Join A-B1. CENTRE FRONT.
- B1-C1 as in B-C.
- Join B1-C1. HEM LINE.
- B-E half of B-C. B1-E1 half of B1-C1.
- A-F as in B-E.
- Join F-E-E1. SIDE LINE.
- D-H half of C-D (E.g.: 42 : 2 = 21 cm).
- H-I parallel to B-C (55 cm/21.65") BUST LINE.
- C-X side height (e.g. 20 cm/7.87").
- D-G half of shoulder length with ease + 0.5 cm/0.20".
(E.g.: 36.5 + 4.5 = 41 : 2 = 20.5 + 0.5 = 21 cm).
- H-L 1/3 D-H (7 cm/2.76").
- Draw L-L1. SHOULDER LINE.
- H-H1 as in D-G (21 cm/8.27").
- H1-I1 sector 13.5 cm/5.31".
- I-M like H-L.
- Draw L-M parallel to H-I.

Back
- G-0 2 cm/0.79".
- D-N 1/3 of D-G + 1 cm/0.39" (7.8 cm/3.07").
- N-P 2.5 cm/0.98".
- P-P1 shoulder width + 2 cm/0.79" (15 cm/5.91").
- Point Q halfway between H-I.
- Q-Q1 2 cm/0.79".
- Draw armscye P1-L1-Q1.
- L1-L2 like Q-Q1.
- Draw L2-J2. SLEEVE REFERENCE.

Front
- A-U 1/3 D-G of the back (6.8 cm/2.68").
- Draw the curved line U-U1.
- I-I1 like H-H1 - 0.5 cm/0.20". (20.5 cm/8.07").
- F-V 6 cm/2.36".
- U-Z like P-P1 - 0.5 cm/0.20" (E.g.: 15 - 0.5 = 14.5 cm/5.71").
- Draw the armscye portion Z-J-Q1.
- U1-U2 1.5-2 cm/0.59-0.79".
- U2-U3 3 cm/1.81".
- B1-B2 like U2-U3 3 cm/1.81".

LOOSE-FITTING COAT SLEEVES

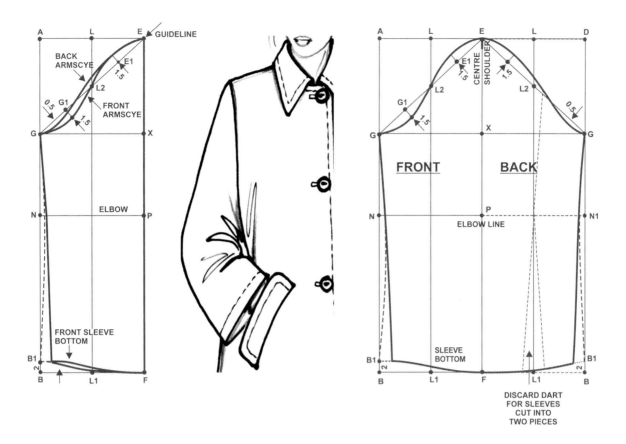

Measurements: Size 42, as in the women's size chart.

Ease: An in the chart for "Outerwear".

- Draw a rectangle, A-B-E-F, where:
- A-B Sleeve length from the centre sleeve. (E.g.: 60 cm/23.62").
- A-E like the measurement for the bodice sector + 1/2 of the same bodice sector (E.g.: sector of 13.5 cm + 6.75 = 20.25 cm).
- A-G as in L1-P1 of the bodice + 1/3 of the same bodice. (E.g.: 13 + 4.33 = 17.33 cm).
- Draw G-X.
- Join G-E with a diagonal line.
- A-N half of A-B + 2 cm/0.79".
- Join N-P.
- A-L half of A-E.
- Draw L-L1.
- L2 half of G-E.
- E1 half of E-L2.
- G1 half of G-L2.
- B-B1 2 cm/0.79".
- Draw E-L2-G with a curved line, as in the figure.
- Draw E-G1-G with a curved line, as in the figure.
- Draw B1-F with a curved line.
- Draw B1-L1-F with a curved line.
- Take up the front and back sleeve again and draw the entire sleeve as in the figure.

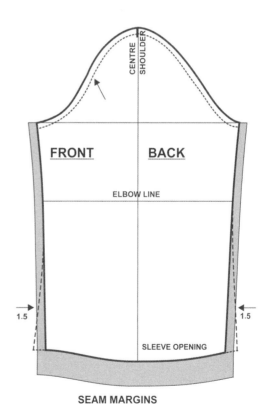

SEAM MARGINS

Note: For the correct angling of the sleeve, adjust the centre shoulder, which may be shifted towards the front or back by a few millimetres, according to the posture and conformation of the subject.

Double-breasted Chesterfield

SHOULDER POINT   CENTRE BACK

COLLAR

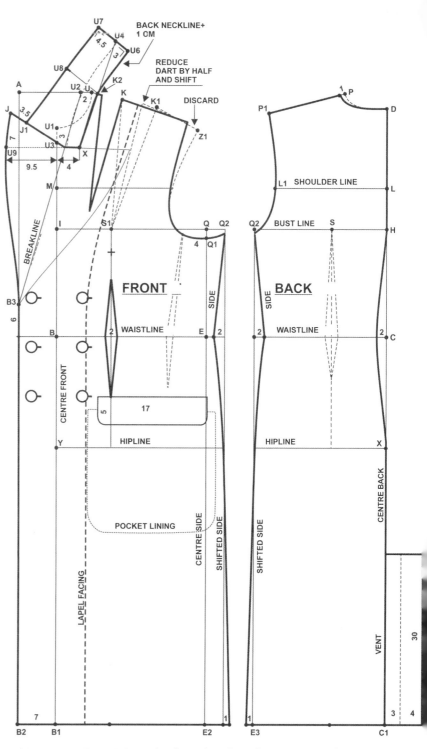

- Draw the base of the shaped overcoat with the appropriate measurements and ease. Reduce and shift the bust darts by 2 cm/0.79"from the first shoulder point.
- Extend the centre front B1-B2 by 7-8 cm/2.76-3.15" and draw B2-A.
- Draw breakline U2-B3 at the desired angle (here, 6 cm/2.36" from the waist).
- Flare the bottom by 1-1.5 cm/0.39-0.59".

COLLAR
- Draw K2-U4 with K2 shifted 0.5 cm/0.20" from U and with a measurement equal to the back neckline + 1 cm/0.39".
- U4-U6 3 cm/1.81".
- Join U6-K2 with a curved line.
- Draw U6-U7 at a right angle to U6-K2, in the desired collar measurement (E.g.: 7 cm/2.76").
- K2-U8 like U6-U7.

- Draw U3-J in the desired angle and measurement (E.g.: 9.5 cm/3.74").
- J-J1 3.5 cm/1.38" or as desired.
- J1-U9 7 cm/2.76" or as desired.
- At approx. 3 cm/1.81" from U6, towards U7, draw a dotted line until the breakline. This is the fold line for the collar, which should always have a lower part which is shorter than the upper part.
- Smoothly connect all the lines as in the figure and take up the collar on another sheet of paper.
- The upper collar must be 0.3-0.5 cm/0.12-0.20" wider than the undercollar to hide the seam.

BACK
- On the lower hemline, draw the vent in the desired measurement.
- Taper the waist along the sides like in the front and on the centre back in the desired measurement (here, 2 cm/0.79").

Double-breasted overcoat

with lapels to the waist

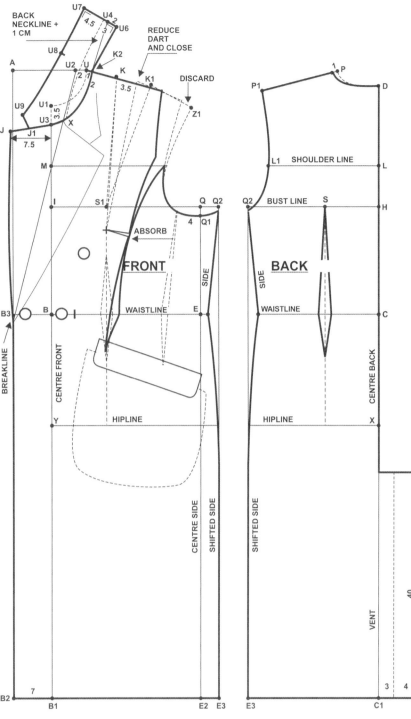

- Draw the base of the shaped overcoat with the appropriate measurements and ease.
- Reduce the bust dart and shift it 2 cm/0.79" from the first shoulder point.
- Extend the centre front B1-B2 by 7-8 cm/2.76-3.15" and draw B2-A.
- Draw breakline U2-B3 at the desired angle (here, down to the waist).
- Draw the lapel line B3-J in the desired shape.

Collar

- K2-U4 with K2 shifted from U by 0.5 cm/0.20" and with measurements equal to that of the back neckline + 1 cm/0.39".
- U4-U6 2 cm/0.79".
- Join U6-K2 with a curved line.

- Draw U6-U7 at a right angle to U6-K2, in the desired measurement for the collar (E.g.: 7-8 cm/2.76-3.15").
- K2-U8 as in U6-U7.
- Draw U3-J in the desired angle and the measurements (E.g.: 6 cm/2.36").
- J-J1 half of J-U3 or as desired.
- Draw J1-U9 in the desired angle and measurements.
- At approximately 2.5-3 cm/0.98-1.18" from U6, towards U7, draw a dotted line until the breakline.
This is the fold line for the collar. The lower part should always be smaller than the upper part.
- Smoothly connect all the lines as in the figure and take up the collar on another sheet of paper.
- The upper collar should be 0.3-0.5 cm/0.12-0.20" larger than the undercollar to hide the seam.

SEAM MARGINS FOR OVERCOATS

INDICATIONS FOR PRESSING

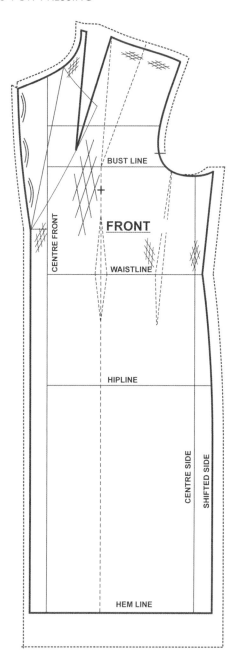

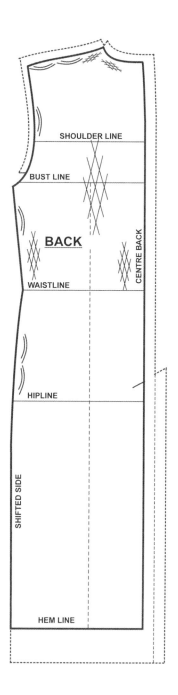

Seam margins
The seam margins should run parallel to the seam lines.
The margin on the back shoulder is optional and requires that you sew below the line of demarcation by 0.6 cm/0.24".

Pressing
As with the jacket, pressing the overcoat is essential to creating a perfect shape and fresh look.
Use the press to rectify the shoulder line from the point of meeting with the humerus; the bagginess should be taken up; you must determine the size of the neckline, flatten and adjust the darts and give the correct shape to the side panel and the armscye.

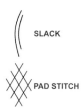

SLACK

PAD STITCH

LODEN COAT

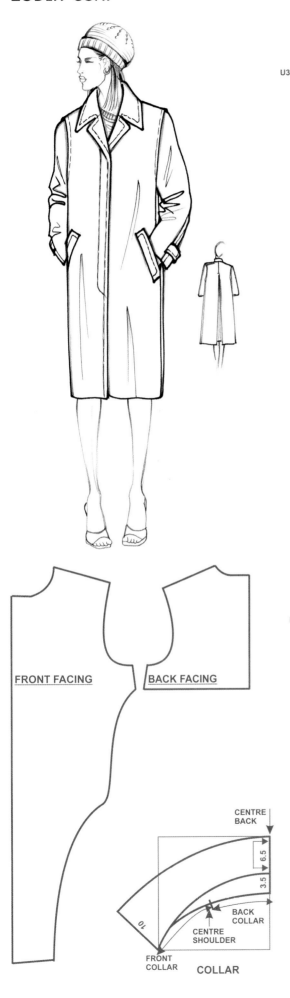

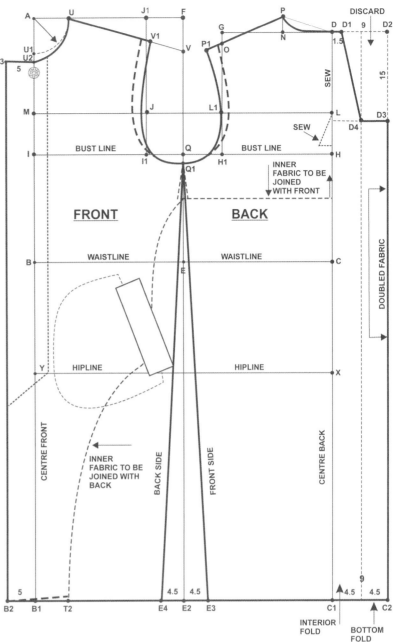

FRONT

BACK

CENTRE FRONT

BACK SIDE

FRONT SIDE

CENTRE BACK

BUST LINE

WAISTLINE

HIPLINE

DOUBLED FABRIC

SEW

DISCARD

INNER FABRIC TO BE JOINED WITH FRONT

INNER FABRIC TO BE JOINED WITH BACK

INTERIOR FOLD

BOTTOM FOLD

FRONT FACING

BACK FACING

CENTRE BACK

BACK COLLAR

CENTRE SHOULDER

FRONT COLLAR

COLLAR

Measurements: Size 42, as in the table on p.17.

Ease: "Outerwear".

- Draw the base block of the loose-fitting coat.
- U2-U3 5 cm/1.97" B1-B2 like U2-U3. FRONT OVERLAP.
- D-D2 9 cm/3.54" C1-C2 like D-D2. ENTIRE INVERTED PLEAT.
- E2-E3 4.5 cm/1.77" E2-E4 like E2-E3. FLARE AT THE SIDE.
- D2-D3 15 cm/5.91" - D-D1 1.5 cm/0.59".
- Sew D-L on the back and discard D1-D4-D3-D2-D1.
- Shape the pattern on the inside as in the figure.

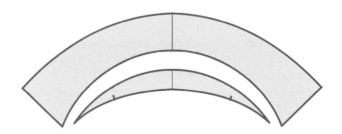

BASE MONTGOMERY COAT BLOCK

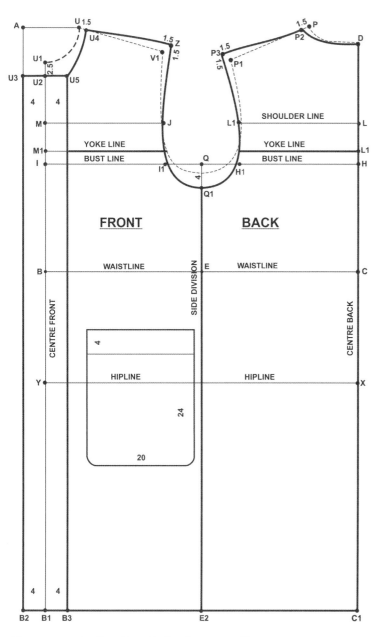

Measurements: Size 42, as in the chart on p. 19.

Ease: Like a cape, 22-24 cm/8.66-9.45".

- Draw the base block of the loose-fitting coat, with an ease of 22-24 cm/8.66-9.45". Draw the extension of the lapels U3-B2, 4 cm/1.57".
- Draw the yoke line M1-L1 with the desired measurements and shape.
- U1-U2 2-2.5 cm/0.79-0.98".
- U3-U5 8 cm/3.15". - Draw the outline U3-B2-B3-U5.
- U-U4 1.5 cm/0.59" - P-P2 1.5 cm/0.59".
- Draw U4-Z and P2-P3 raising it by 1.5 cm/0.59" and lengthening it by 1.5 cm/0.59", according to the design.
- Q-Q1 4 cm/1.57" or according to the design.
- Draw the pocket as preferred (20 x 24 cm/7.87 x 9.45").

HOOD

- Draw a rectangle A-B-C-D, where:
- A-B is the measurement of the contour of the head from the centre of the neckline (43 cm/16.93" or the desired measurement).
- B-C measurement from one temple to the other passing through the nape of the neck (31 cm/12.20" or desired measurement).
- A-E half of A-B.
- Draw E-F.
- C-C1 2.5 cm/0.98".
- D-D1 like A-U2 of the front bodice (9 cm/3.5").
- A-A1 2.5 cm/0.98".
- Draw the guide line A1-D1.
- Draw the back and front neck line with the appropriate shape A1-D1.
- Create two 1.5 cm/0.59" darts on the back.
- D1-D2 like U2-U5 of the bodice (4 cm/1.57").
- C1-C2 2.5 cm/0.98". Connect C2-D2 with a curved shape.
- Create the contour of the back following the shape shown in the figure.

MONTGOMERY COAT SLEEVES

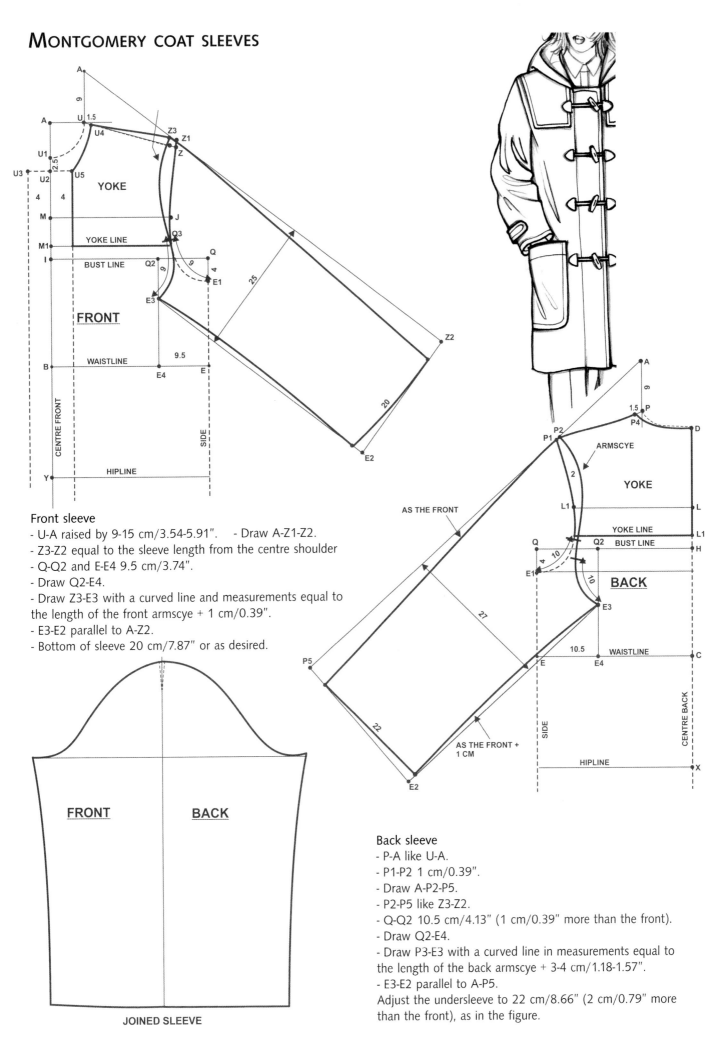

Front sleeve
- U-A raised by 9-15 cm/3.54-5.91".   - Draw A-Z1-Z2.
- Z3-Z2 equal to the sleeve length from the centre shoulder
- Q-Q2 and E-E4 9.5 cm/3.74".
- Draw Q2-E4.
- Draw Z3-E3 with a curved line and measurements equal to the length of the front armscye + 1 cm/0.39".
- E3-E2 parallel to A-Z2.
- Bottom of sleeve 20 cm/7.87" or as desired.

Back sleeve
- P-A like U-A.
- P1-P2 1 cm/0.39".
- Draw A-P2-P5.
- P2-P5 like Z3-Z2.
- Q-Q2 10.5 cm/4.13" (1 cm/0.39" more than the front).
- Draw Q2-E4.
- Draw P3-E3 with a curved line in measurements equal to the length of the back armscye + 3-4 cm/1.18-1.57".
- E3-E2 parallel to A-P5.
Adjust the undersleeve to 22 cm/8.66" (2 cm/0.79" more than the front), as in the figure.

OVERCOAT WITH HORIZONTAL SEAMS

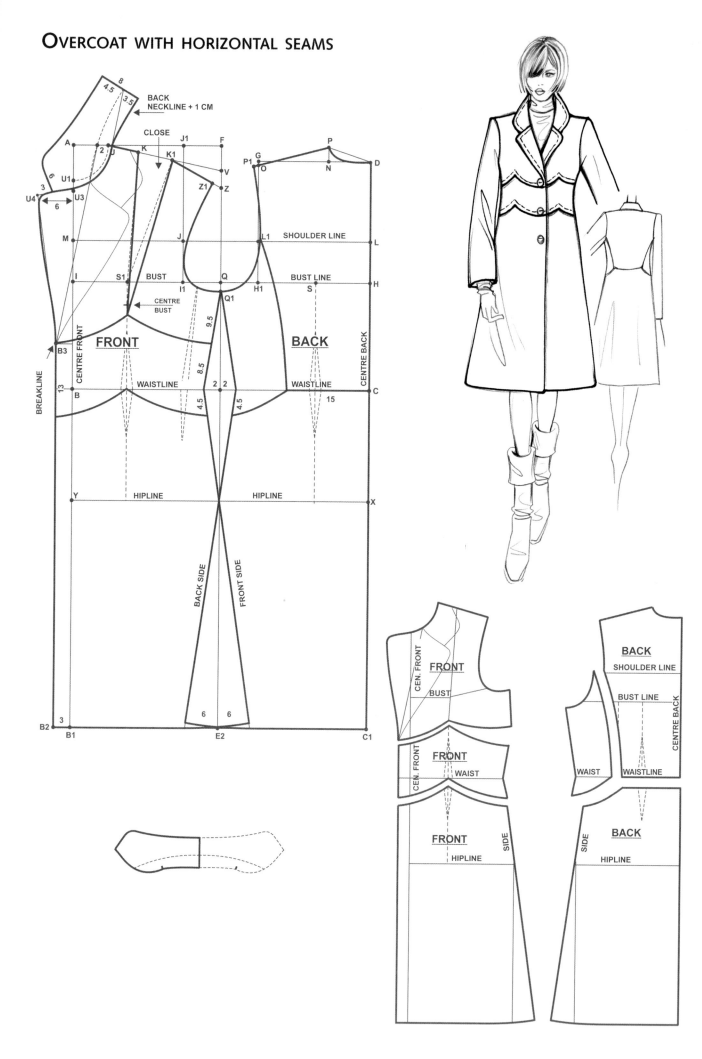

REDINGOTE OVERCOAT

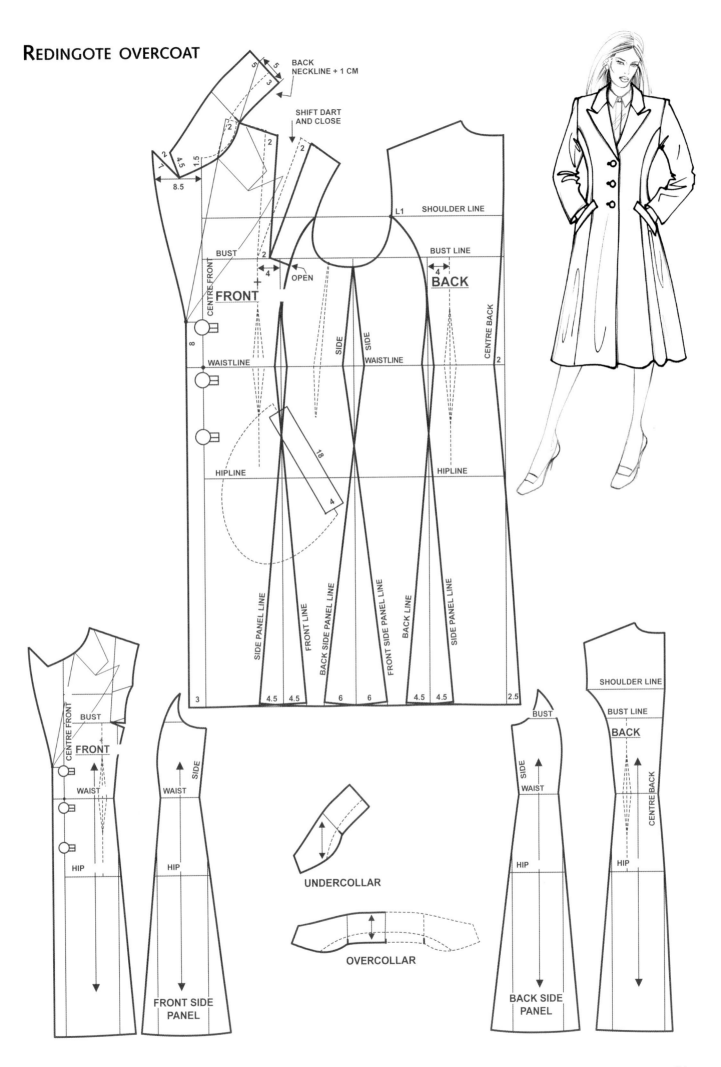

BACK
NECKLINE + 1 CM

SHIFT DART
AND CLOSE

5
5
3

2

2
2

2

1.5
4.5
2
1

8.5

L1   SHOULDER LINE

BUST   2

CENTRE FRONT

4   OPEN

BUST LINE

4

BACK

FRONT

8

SIDE

SIDE

CENTRE BACK

WAISTLINE   WAISTLINE

2

HIPLINE   18   HIPLINE

4

SIDE PANEL LINE

FRONT LINE

BACK SIDE PANEL LINE

FRONT SIDE PANEL LINE

BACK LINE

SIDE PANEL LINE

3   4.5   4.5   6   6   4.5   4.5   2.5

CENTRE FRONT   BUST

FRONT

WAIST

HIP

SIDE

WAIST

HIP

UNDERCOLLAR

OVERCOLLAR

FRONT SIDE
PANEL

BUST

SIDE

WAIST

HIP

SHOULDER LINE

BUST LINE

BACK

CENTRE BACK

HIP

BACK SIDE
PANEL

91

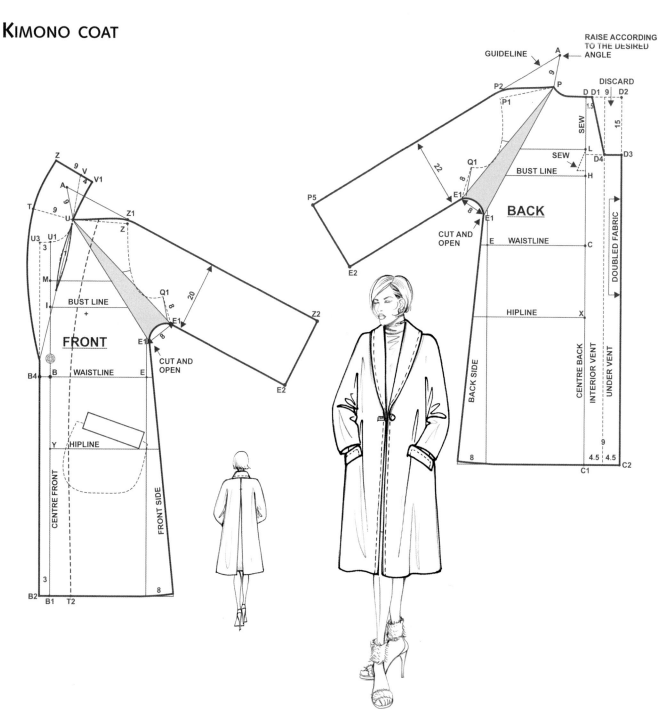

- Draw the base of the overcoat and separate the front from the back.

Back
- From point P, draw a perpendicular line (with a height of 9-12 cm/3.54-4.72").
- From A, passing through P2 at 1-1.5 cm/0.39-0.59" from P1, draw A-P5 with a straight line.
- P2-P5 measuring the length of the sleeve from the point of the shoulder.
- From Q1 drop point E1 by 6-12 cm (here 8 cm/3.15").
- Draw the diagonal line P-E1.
- Draw E1-E2 parallel to P2-P5.
- Draw the cuff P5-E2 and adjust the width of the bottom of the sleeve.
- Cut along the diagonal line E1-P, open according to the design used (E.g.: 8 cm/3.15") and join the separate parts with a curved line.
- Draw the inverted pleat as in the figure.

Front
- From point U, draw a perpendicular line of 9 to 12 cm/3.54 to 4.72", as on the back.
- From A, passing through Z1 1-1.5 cm/0.39-0.59" from Z, draw a straight line connecting A-Z2.
- Z1-Z2 sleeve length from the point of the shoulder as on the back.
- From Q1, drop down from 6-12 cm/2.36-4.72", (8 cm/3.15" as on the back) and draw point E1.
- Draw a diagonal line connecting U-E1.
- Draw E1-E2 parallel to Z1-Z2.
- Draw the bottom Z2-E2 at a right angle to Z1-Z2, adjusting the length of the bottom of the sleeve so that it is 2 cm/0.79"shorter than the back.
- Cut along the diagonal line E1-U, open as on the back according to the needs of the design (E.g.: 8 cm/3.15" like the back) and join the separate parts with a curved line.
- Check the pattern, overlapping the front over the back.
- Draw the shawl collar as in the figure.

KIMONO COAT WITH GUSSET

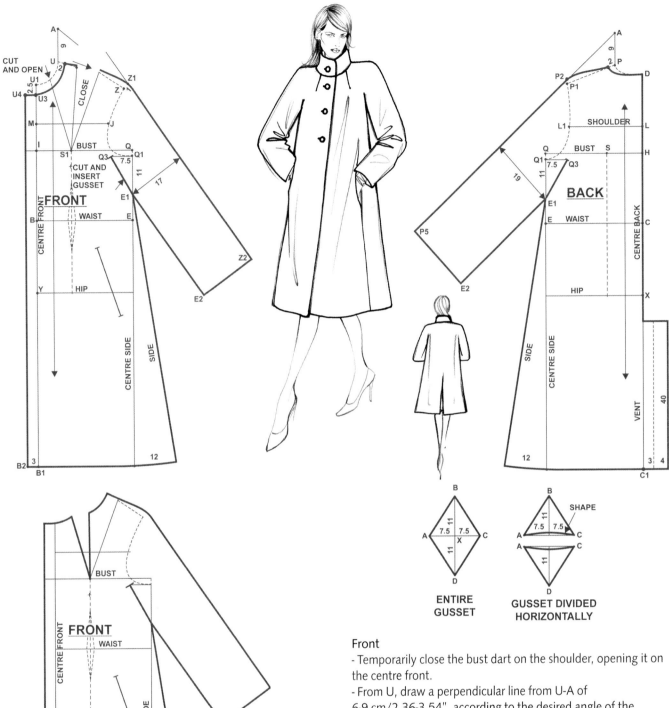

ENTIRE GUSSET

GUSSET DIVIDED HORIZONTALLY

GUSSET
- Draw a diamond A-B-C-D where:
- A-B like Q3-E1 of the front and back of the coat.
- A-X like Q1-Q3 of the front and back of the bodice.
- The gusset may be cut horizontally or vertically, according to the needs of the design.
- Draw the front of the base of the overcoat with adequate darts and ease, flaring as necessary and separate the back from the front.

Front
- Temporarily close the bust dart on the shoulder, opening it on the centre front.
- From U, draw a perpendicular line from U-A of 6-9 cm/2.36-3.54", according to the desired angle of the sleeve.
- From A, passing through Z1 (at 1 cm/0.39" from Z), draw a straight line from A-Z2.
- From Q, drop down 11 cm/4.33" from E1.
- Draw E1-E2 parallel to Z1-Z2.
- Draw the bottom Z2-E2.
- Q1-Q3 7.5 cm/2.95". - Draw E1-Q3 for the gusset.

Back
- From P draw a perpendicular line P-A as on the front according to the desired angle of the sleeve.
- From A, passing through P2 (1 cm/0.39" from P1), draw a straight line from A-P5.
- From Q drop down 11 cm/4.33" from E1.
- Draw E1-E2 parallel to P2-P5.
- Draw the cuff P5-E2. - Q1-Q3 7.5 cm/2.95". - Draw E1-Q3.

Raglan sleeve coat

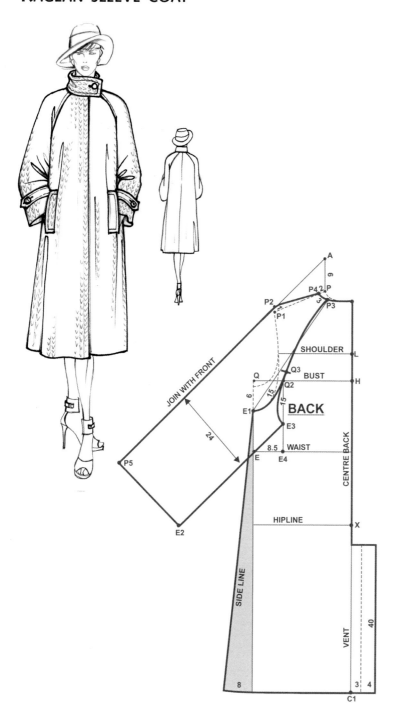

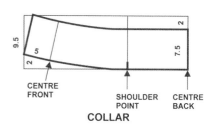

COLLAR

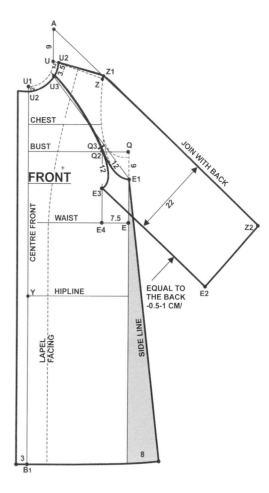

- Draw the overcoat base block with or without darts, separate the back half from the front half and create the desired flare.

Back
- Draw a perpendicular line P-A in the desired measurement according to the angle of the sleeve (9 cm/3.54").
- Draw the straight line A-P2-P5, remaining 1 cm/0.39" away from P1, with P2-P5 equal to the sleeve length taken from the centre shoulder (60 cm/23.62").
- Q-E1 6 cm/2.36", or according to the depth of the desired armscye.
- E-E4 8.5 cm/3.35". - Draw E4-Q2.
- P4-P3 3 cm/1.81" or as desired.
- Draw the guide line P3-E1.
- From E1 towards P3 15 cm/5.91", for the meeting point of the curves. Point Q3.

- Draw a curved line E1-Q3-P3.
- Draw a curved line connecting E3-Q3-P3.

Front
- On half of the front, draw a perpendicular line U-A with a measurement equal to that of the back (9 cm).
- Draw the straight line A-Z1-Z2 remaining 1 cm/0.39" away from Z, with Z1-Z2 equal to the sleeve length (60 cm/23.62") taken from the centre shoulder, as on the back.
- Q-E1 6 cm/2.36" as on the back (here, 6 cm/2.36").
- E-E4 7.5 cm/2.95".
- Draw a line connecting E4-Q2.
- From E1 towards U2, 12 cm/4.72", passing through Q3, the meeting point of the curves.
- U2-U3 3.5 cm/1.38" or as desired.
- Draw E1-Q3-U3 with a curved line.
- Draw E3-Q3-U3 with a curved line.

COAT WITH DROPPED SHOULDERS

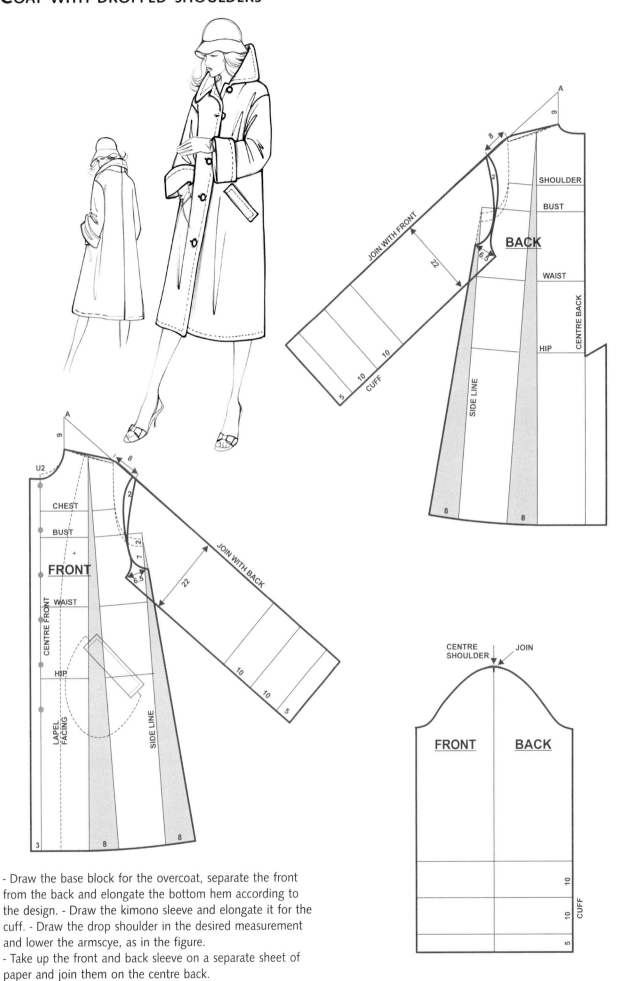

- Draw the base block for the overcoat, separate the front from the back and elongate the bottom hem according to the design. - Draw the kimono sleeve and elongate it for the cuff. - Draw the drop shoulder in the desired measurement and lower the armscye, as in the figure.
- Take up the front and back sleeve on a separate sheet of paper and join them on the centre back.

COAT WITH SADDLE RAGLAN SLEEVES

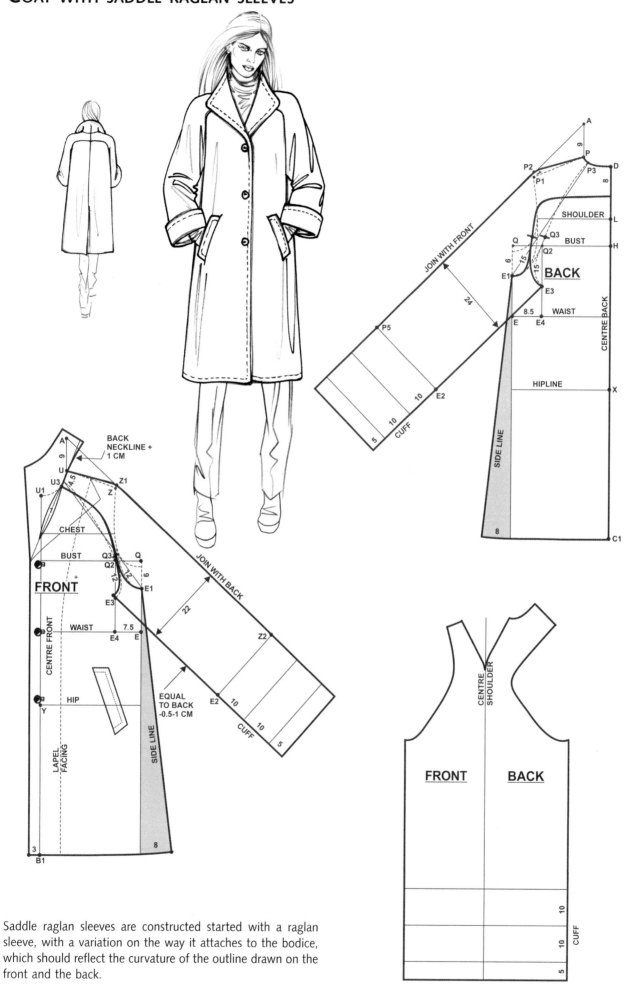

Saddle raglan sleeves are constructed started with a raglan sleeve, with a variation on the way it attaches to the bodice, which should reflect the curvature of the outline drawn on the front and the back.

Overcoat with yoke

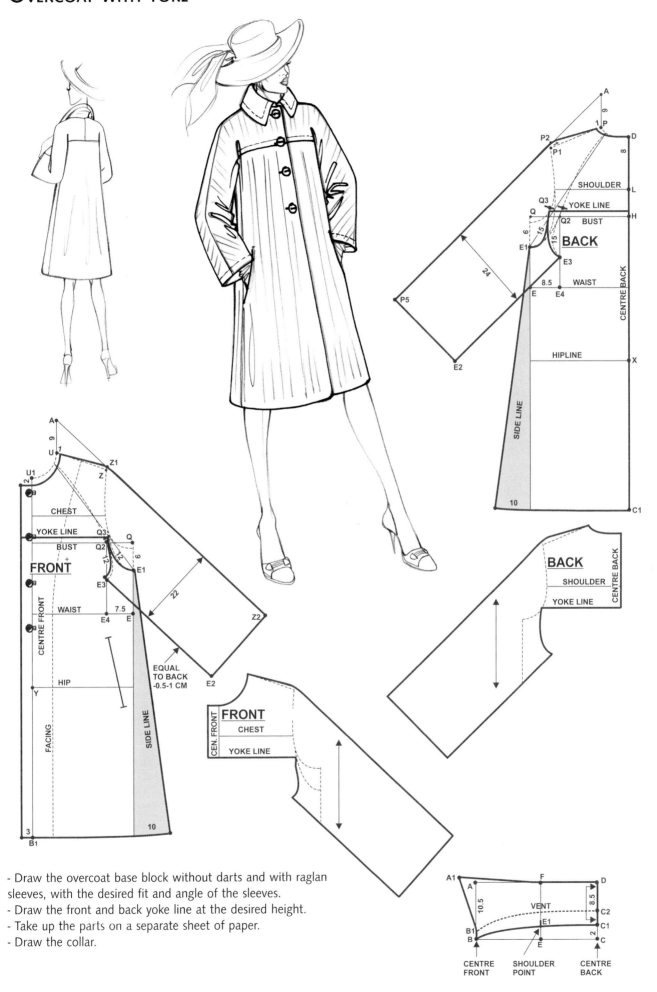

- Draw the overcoat base block without darts and with raglan sleeves, with the desired fit and angle of the sleeves.
- Draw the front and back yoke line at the desired height.
- Take up the parts on a separate sheet of paper.
- Draw the collar.

CREATIVE OVERCOAT

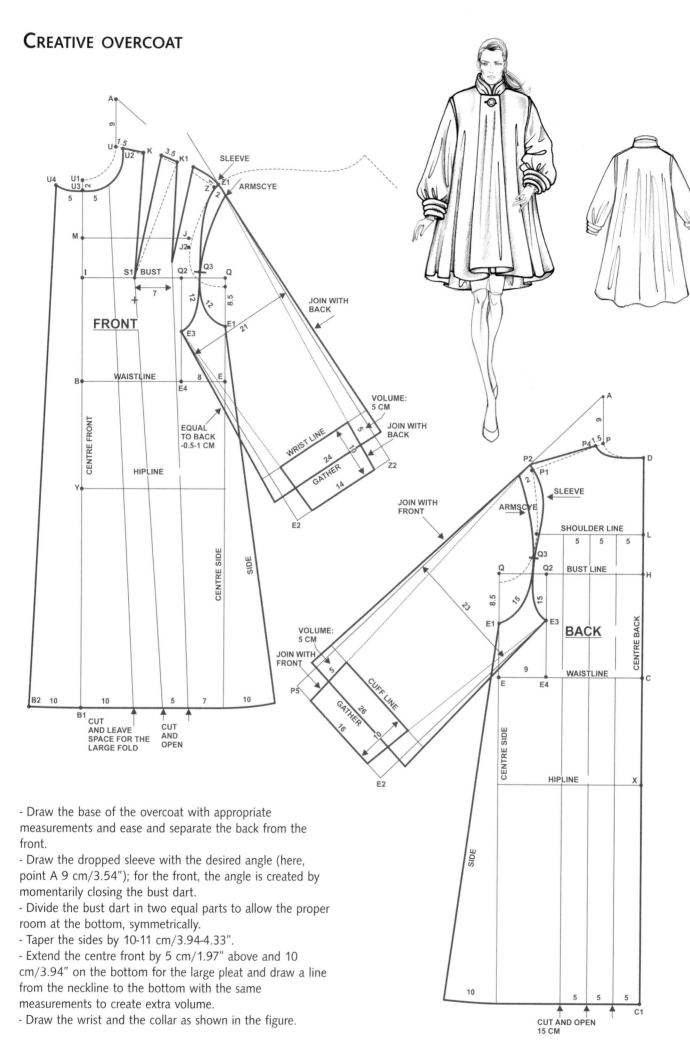

FRONT

SLEEVE
ARMSCYE
BUST
WAISTLINE
CENTRE FRONT
HIPLINE
CENTRE SIDE
SIDE

JOIN WITH BACK

EQUAL TO BACK -0.5-1 CM

VOLUME: 5 CM
JOIN WITH BACK

WRIST LINE
GATHER

CUT AND LEAVE SPACE FOR THE LARGE FOLD

CUT AND OPEN

JOIN WITH FRONT

BACK
SLEEVE
ARMSCYE
SHOULDER LINE
BUST LINE
CENTRE BACK
WAISTLINE
HIPLINE
CENTRE SIDE
SIDE

VOLUME: 5 CM
JOIN WITH FRONT
CUFF LINE
GATHER

CUT AND OPEN 15 CM

- Draw the base of the overcoat with appropriate measurements and ease and separate the back from the front.
- Draw the dropped sleeve with the desired angle (here, point A 9 cm/3.54"); for the front, the angle is created by momentarily closing the bust dart.
- Divide the bust dart in two equal parts to allow the proper room at the bottom, symmetrically.
- Taper the sides by 10-11 cm/3.94-4.33".
- Extend the centre front by 5 cm/1.97" above and 10 cm/3.94" on the bottom for the large pleat and draw a line from the neckline to the bottom with the same measurements to create extra volume.
- Draw the wrist and the collar as shown in the figure.

98

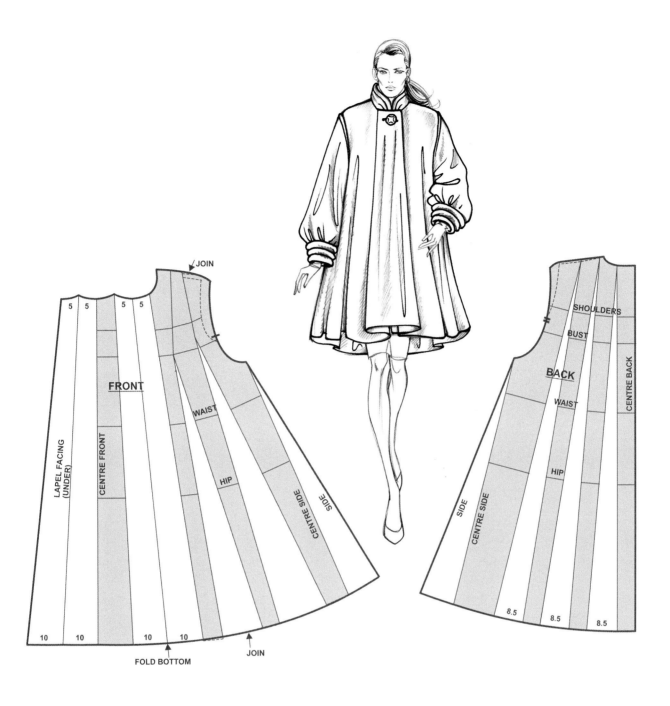

JOIN

5 5 5 5

FRONT

LAPEL FACING (UNDER)

CENTRE FRONT

WAIST

HIP

CENTRE SIDE

SIDE

10 10 10 10

FOLD BOTTOM

JOIN

SHOULDERS

BUST

BACK

CENTRE BACK

WAIST

HIP

SIDE

CENTRE SIDE

8.5 8.5 8.5

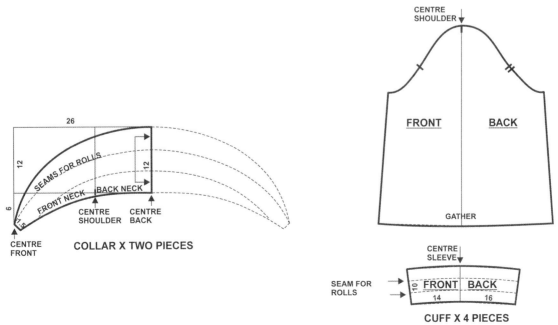

26

12

12

SEAMS FOR ROLLS

FRONT NECK

BACK NECK

6

1.5

CENTRE FRONT

CENTRE SHOULDER

CENTRE BACK

COLLAR X TWO PIECES

CENTRE SHOULDER

FRONT   **BACK**

GATHER

CENTRE SLEEVE

SEAM FOR ROLLS

10

FRONT **BACK**

14 16

CUFF X 4 PIECES

Base mac (trench) block

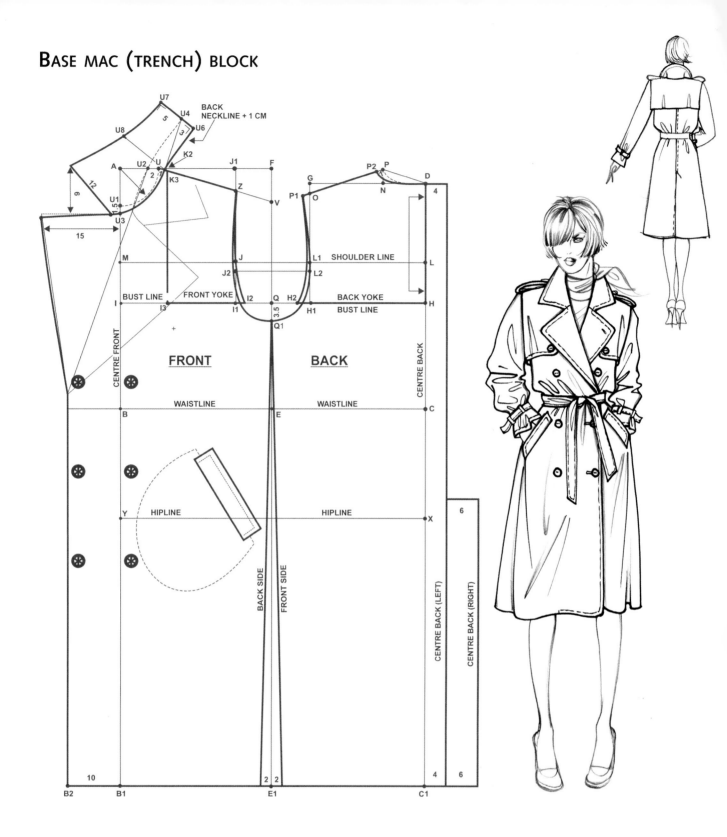

- Draw the base block of the loose-fitting coat without darts, with the "Mac" ease (see the "ease" table), lower the armscye by 3-3.5 cm/1.18-1.38", create the desired length and create a slight flare along the side towards the bottom hem.

Back
- On the left back panel, extend the back centre by 4 cm/1.57" from the top to the bottom.
- For the bottom right panel, add another 5-6 cm/1.97-2.36" for the inverted pleat, from the bottom of the hip.
- P-P2 1 cm/0.39".

- Draw the yoke of the back D-H-H2-P1-P2-D, at the desired height, extending along the armscye (point H2) by 1-1.5 cm/0.39-0.59" for added softness.

Front
- Extend the centre front for the fastening (double-breasted, 10 cm/3.94").
- Draw the lapel with the desired abundance and depth.
- U-K2 like P-P2.
- Draw the collar in the shape and size desired.
- Draw the front yoke K3-I3-I2-Z-K3, extending it along the armscye (point 12) by 1-1.5 cm/0.39-0.59" for softness.
- Draw the pocket as in the design.

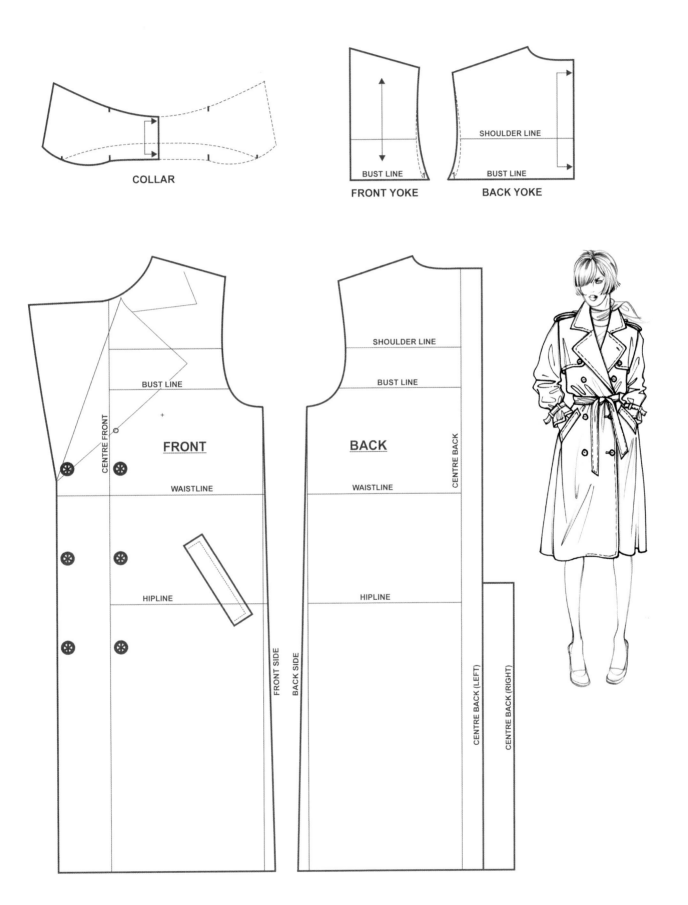

COLLAR

FRONT YOKE

BACK YOKE

SHOULDER LINE

BUST LINE

BUST LINE

SHOULDER LINE

BUST LINE

FRONT

BACK

CENTRE FRONT

BUST LINE

WAISTLINE

HIPLINE

FRONT SIDE

BACK SIDE

CENTRE BACK

WAISTLINE

HIPLINE

CENTRE BACK (LEFT)

CENTRE BACK (RIGHT)

Mac (trench) with raglan sleeves

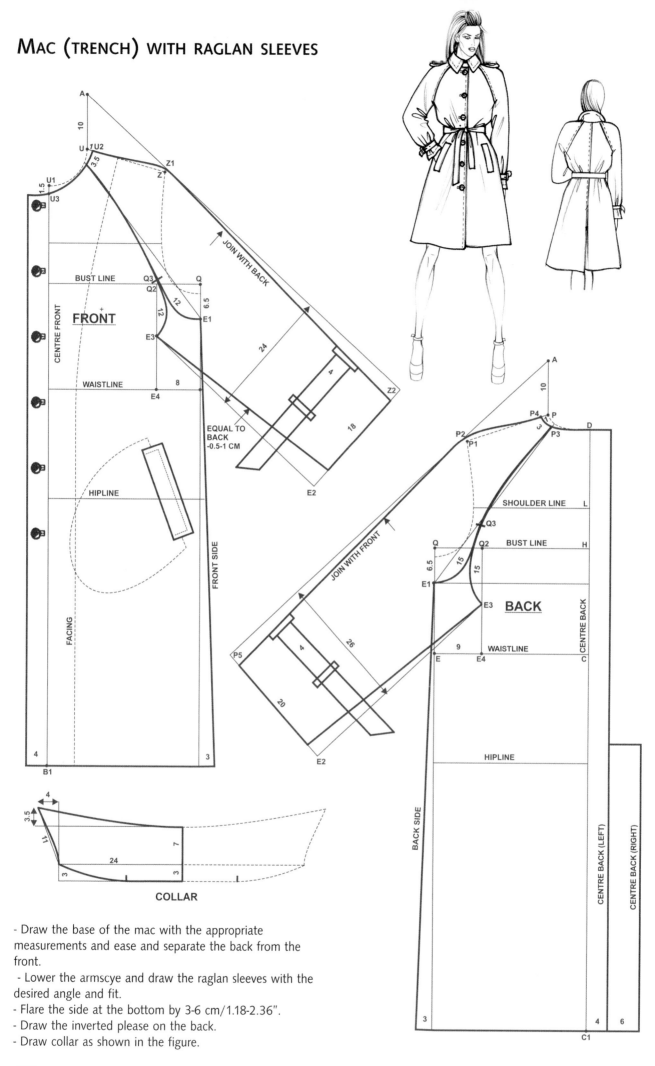

COLLAR

- Draw the base of the mac with the appropriate measurements and ease and separate the back from the front.
- Lower the armscye and draw the raglan sleeves with the desired angle and fit.
- Flare the side at the bottom by 3-6 cm/1.18-2.36".
- Draw the inverted please on the back.
- Draw collar as shown in the figure.

Sporty mac (trench)

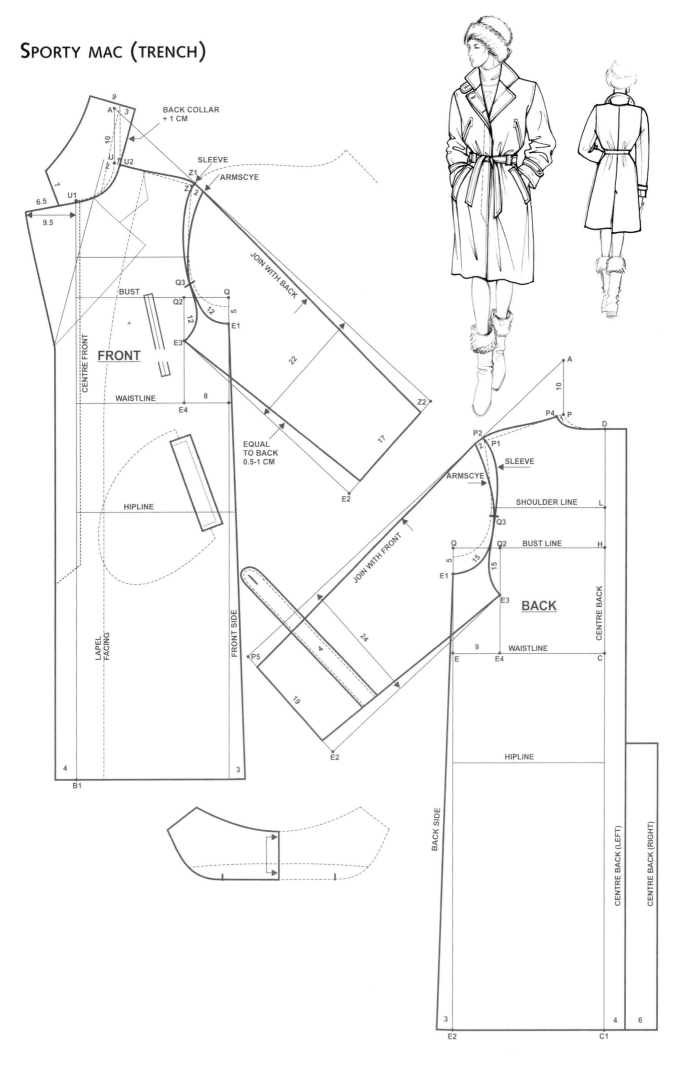

CAPES AND CLOAKS

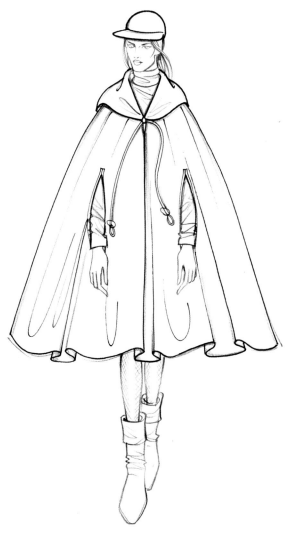

Capes and cloaks 106
Cape lines and forms 107
Base cape block 108
Flared cape. 109
Princess cut cape 110
Cape with a yoke 111
Cape with in-form sleeves 112
Half circle cape. 113
3/4 circle cape 114
Circle cape 115
Double cape. 116
Mexican poncho. 117
Inverness cape 118
Hoods 119
Hood measurements. 119
Base form-fitting hood block 120
Hood with a collar 121
Loose-fitting hood. 122
Removable hood 122
Baggy hood 123
Hood with a scarf fastening 124
Creative hoods 125

CAPES AND CLOAKS

D&G A/W 2009-2010

J.Galliano S/S 2008

Capes (or their longer versions, cloaks) are a heavy garment worn over other clothing to protect from cold weather.

The cape has ancient origins. The Athenians wore long, draped cloaks which were essentially rectangular shawls clasped with pins, cut from pieces of fabric in the same form as they came off the family's loom.

The ancients often wore a cloak-shawl called a himation over the nude body. The Etruscans wore smaller-sized capes, called *lacerna* and *tebenna*, while Roman citizens wore the *pallium*, the *lacerna*, or even the *paennula*, a cloak that is very similar to today's poncho with a hole in the centre for the head and an ample hood. The *burrus*, which was similar to the paenula, was used by farmers, while athletes wore the *endromide*, a purple waterproof cloak. Similarly, the Byzantines wore the *clamide*.

In the 4th century AD in the Roman Empire, generals wore a *paludamentum*, a lavish purple wool cloak, while both male and female citizens wore the *colubium*, a lush, soft, bell-shaped cape with a hole for the head and two openings for the arms.

Over the centuries, the cape has undergone many transformations and taken on many guises: daytime, night-time, long, short, wide, to be worn over the shoulder or wrapped tightly around the body, doubled, overlapping, etc.

After a period of relative stagnation, today women's capes are presented in some designer collections, made of prized wools and in simple shapes.

Burberry S/S 2009

Cape lines and forms

The lines and lengths of capes or cloaks may vary according to the dictates of fashion, where and when they are worn, and the customs of a given country.

Classic cloaks (military style) are constructed from half-circle or full-circle patterns and fall down to the ankle. They generally have a mandarin collar, come with or without a hood and have two openings for the hands (particularly in those which fall below the knee). However, there are numerous other capes with different cuts and lines: princess cut, with a yoke, or inspired by South American or English-style ponchos, etc.

Heavy wool is generally used for capes and ponchos but, as with overcoats, materials vary according to fashion: heavy cloth, brushed fabrics, double heavy wool crepes, camelhair, knickerbocker, tweed, herringbone, etc.

Main types of capes

Princess cape

Princess capes have two vertical seams that begin near the shoulder and drop down on the front and back.

Half circle cape

This cape is roomy along the bottom and is similar to the half circle skirt. It is made by joining the shoulder point of the armscye of the front to that of the back, positioned at a 90° angle.

Circle cape

This type of cape has a very wide bottom and is made like the circle skirt, joining the front to the back on the shoulder line, positioned at 180° (in a straight line).

Inverness cape

This cape is long, down to the knee, with an overlapping, smaller cape on top. It has a flat peter pan collar and it is fastened high up with buttons or with a bow. The small cape covers the arms, while the larger portion of the cape has two openings for the arms to poke through near the armscye or further down.

Poncho

This is a garment typical of Latin America made up of a large square of wool. It is often also used as a blanket, and has a slit opening in the centre for the head.

Mexican poncho

This type of poncho is made with two rectangular pieces, which, when sewn together, form an "L" shape without overlaps. Then one of the ends is joined with the other via a seam or with hooks and buttons.

Poncho

Princess cape

Circle cape

Capelet

Kimono cape with in-form sleeves

Cape with yoke

Inverness cape

Half-circle cape

107

Base cape block

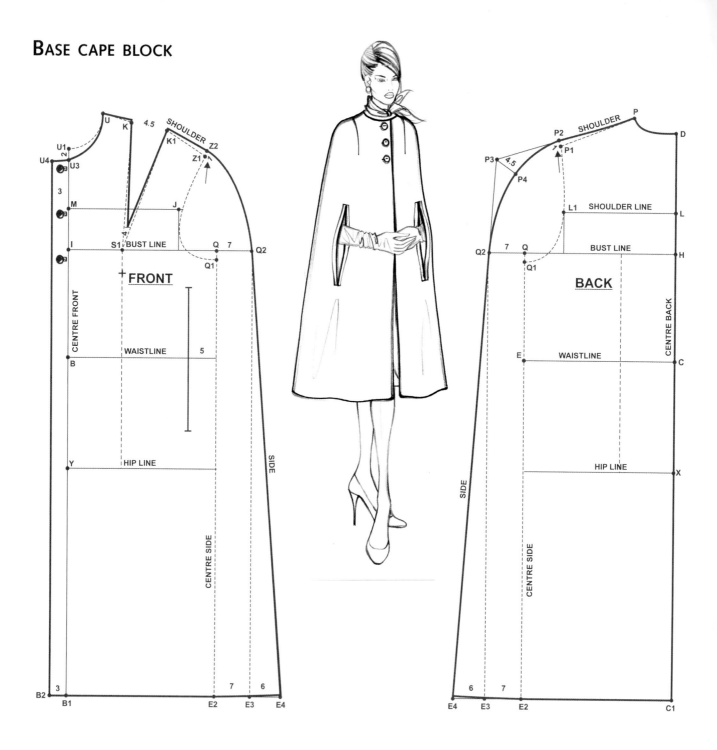

- Draw the base coat block with appropriate measurements and with the "cape" ease and fit. Divide the back from the front along the "centre front" line.

Back

- Extend the bust line towards the outer edge of the side by 1/4 of H-Q (e.g.: 28 : 4 cm = 7 cm).
- Draw Q2-E3.
- Flare the bottom by the desired measurement (e.g.: 6 cm/2.36").
- Draw line Q2-E4.
- Raise point P1 by 0.5-1 cm/0.20-0.39": point P2.
- Elongate the shoulder line P-P2.
- Elongate the side line E4-Q2 until it crosses the shoulder line: point P3.
- From point P3 draw a diagonal line and, at 4.5-5 cm/1.77-1.97" mark point P4.

- Draw a curved line P2-P4-Q2-E4.

Front

- Q-Q2 like Q-Q2 on the back (7 cm/2.76").
- Raise the shoulder point, Z1-Z2, like the back.
- B1-E4 like E4-C1 on the back.
- Draw the bottom hem like the back.
- Draw the side line Z2-Q2-E4 curving as necessary.
- Raise the point of the bust dart by 4 cm/1.57" and reduce its width as necessary (e.g.: 4.5 cm/1.77").
- Extend the centre front by 3 cm/1.18" for the fastening.
- Draw the opening for the arm, 5 cm/1.97" from the side line or as desired, in the desired length (e.g.: 26 cm/10.24"), with its centre on the waistline.
- Place the back over the front to check that the width and shape are equal.

Flared cape

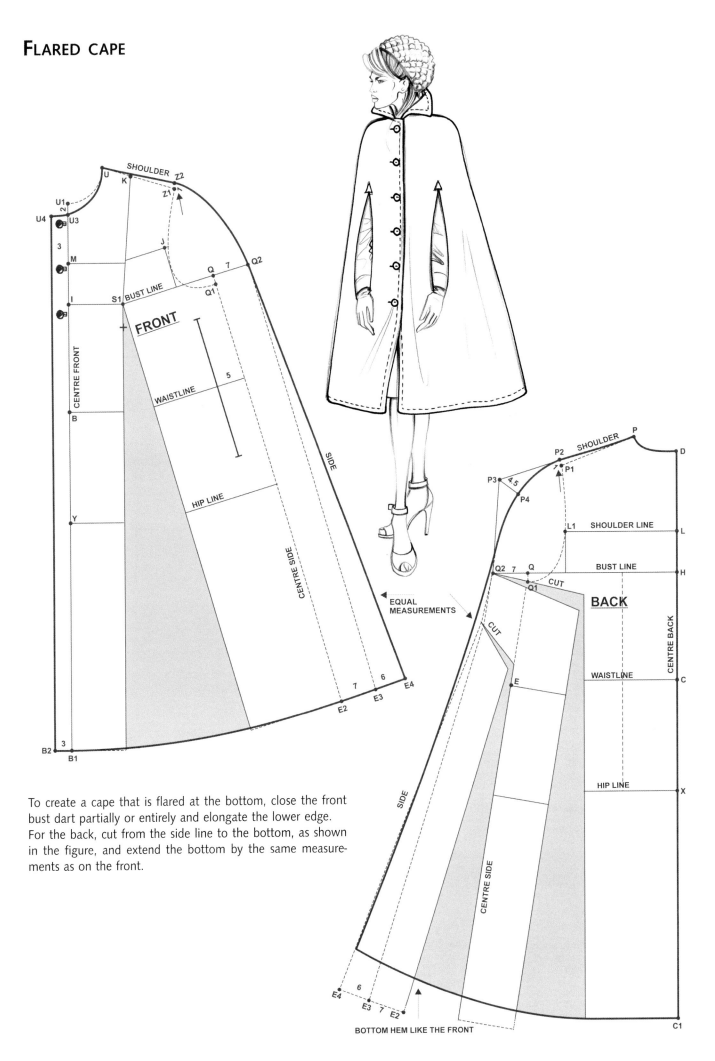

To create a cape that is flared at the bottom, close the front bust dart partially or entirely and elongate the lower edge. For the back, cut from the side line to the bottom, as shown in the figure, and extend the bottom by the same measurements as on the front.

109

PRINCESS CUT CAPE

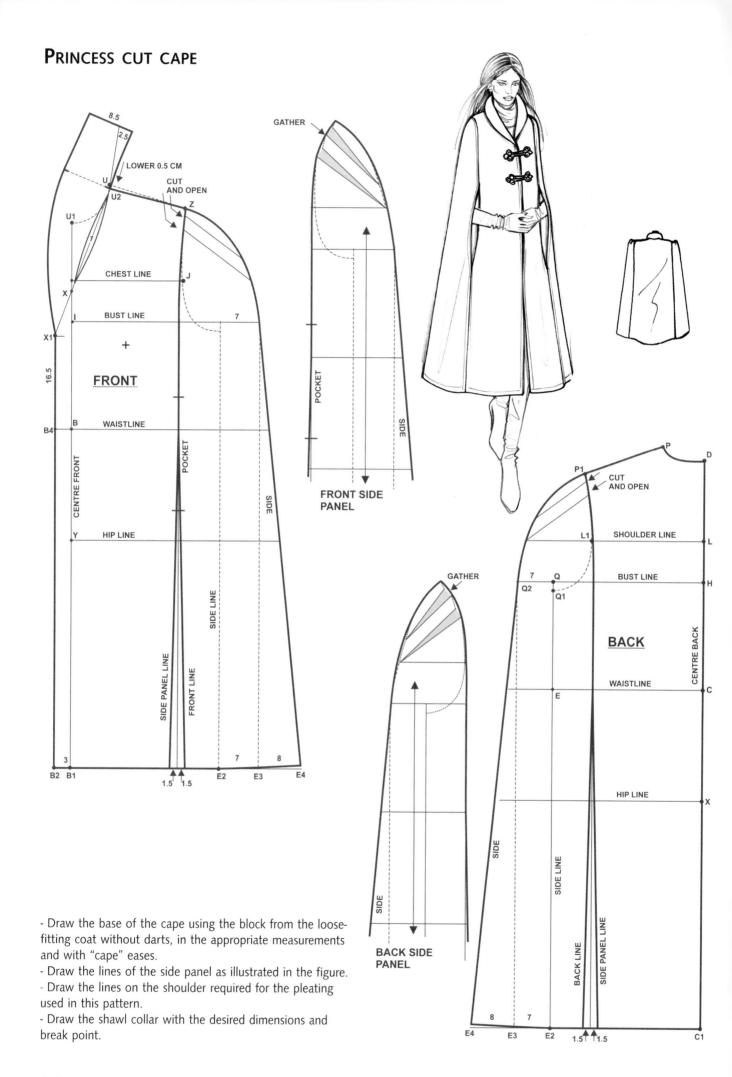

FRONT SIDE PANEL

BACK SIDE PANEL

- Draw the base of the cape using the block from the loose-fitting coat without darts, in the appropriate measurements and with "cape" eases.
- Draw the lines of the side panel as illustrated in the figure.
- Draw the lines on the shoulder required for the pleating used in this pattern.
- Draw the shawl collar with the desired dimensions and break point.

CAPE WITH A YOKE

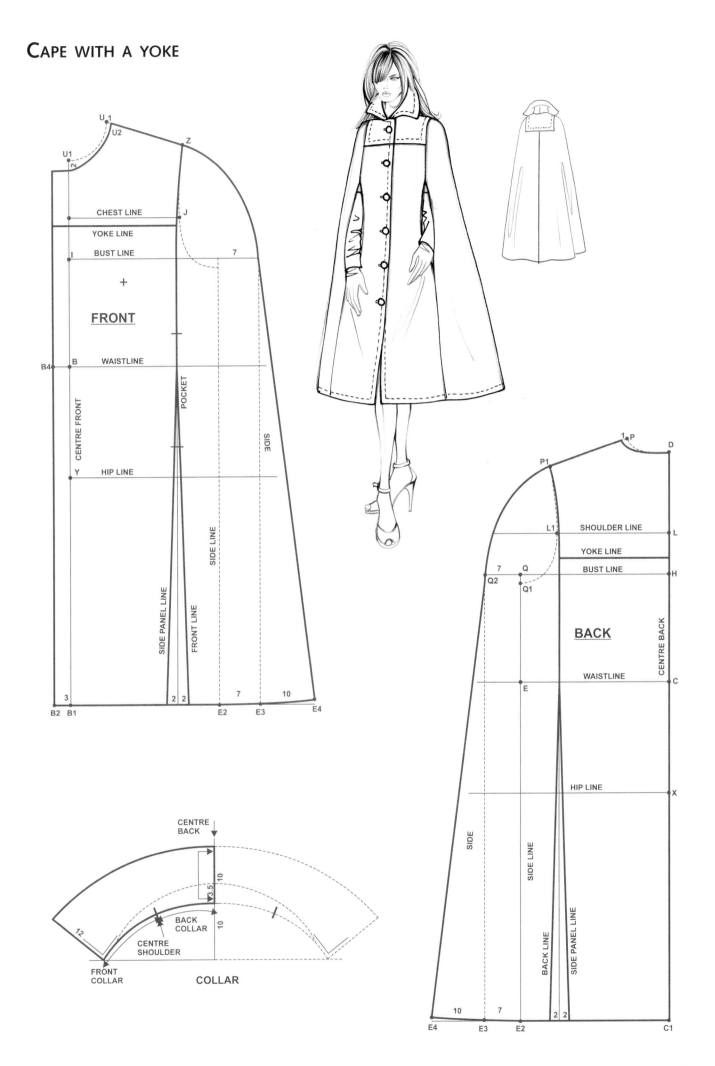

FRONT

CHEST LINE
YOKE LINE
BUST LINE
WAISTLINE
HIP LINE

CENTRE FRONT

POCKET

SIDE PANEL LINE
FRONT LINE
SIDE LINE
SIDE

U 1
U2
U1
Z
J
I
+
B4
B
Y
3
B2 B1
2 2
7
E2
7
E3
10
E4

BACK

SHOULDER LINE
YOKE LINE
BUST LINE
WAISTLINE
HIP LINE

CENTRE BACK

SIDE
SIDE LINE
BACK LINE
SIDE PANEL LINE

1 P
D
P1
L1
L
Q2
7
Q
Q1
H
E
C
X
10
E4
7
E3
E2
2 2
C1

COLLAR

CENTRE
BACK
BACK
COLLAR
CENTRE
SHOULDER
FRONT
COLLAR
10
3.5
10
12

CAPE WITH IN-FORM SLEEVES

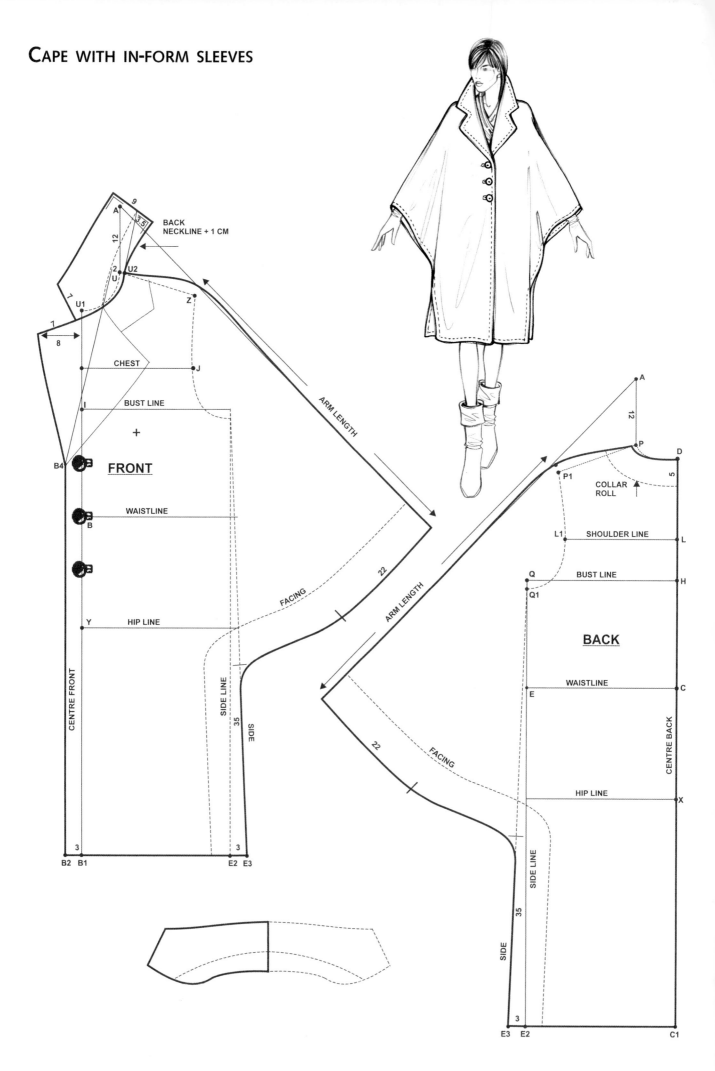

FRONT

BACK NECKLINE + 1 CM

CHEST

BUST LINE

WAISTLINE

HIP LINE

CENTRE FRONT

SIDE LINE

SIDE

FACING

ARM LENGTH

BACK

COLLAR ROLL

SHOULDER LINE

BUST LINE

WAISTLINE

HIP LINE

CENTRE BACK

SIDE LINE

SIDE

FACING

ARM LENGTH

Half-circle cape

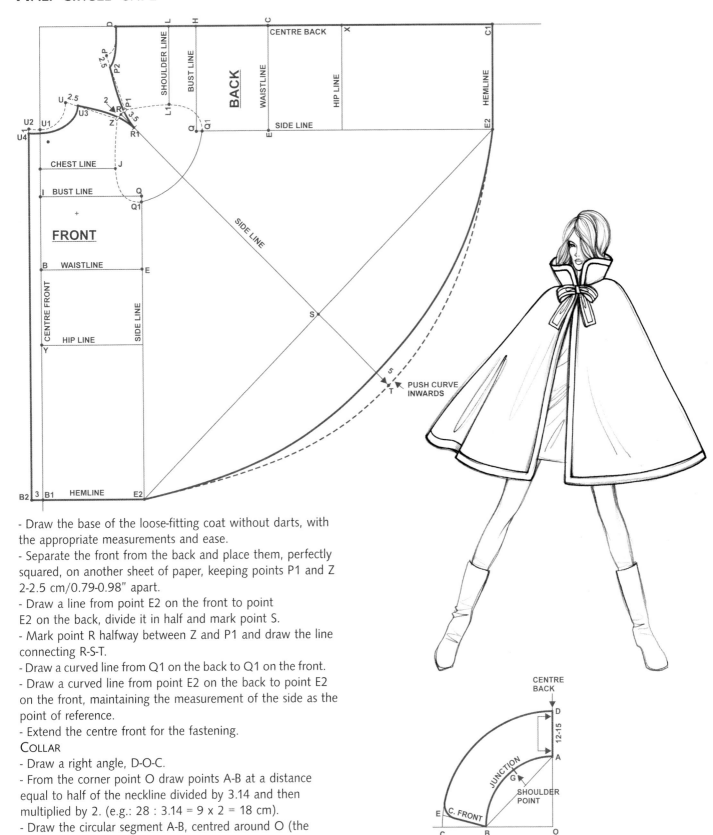

- Draw the base of the loose-fitting coat without darts, with the appropriate measurements and ease.
- Separate the front from the back and place them, perfectly squared, on another sheet of paper, keeping points P1 and Z 2-2.5 cm/0.79-0.98" apart.
- Draw a line from point E2 on the front to point E2 on the back, divide it in half and mark point S.
- Mark point R halfway between Z and P1 and draw the line connecting R-S-T.
- Draw a curved line from Q1 on the back to Q1 on the front.
- Draw a curved line from point E2 on the back to point E2 on the front, maintaining the measurement of the side as the point of reference.
- Extend the centre front for the fastening.

Collar
- Draw a right angle, D-O-C.
- From the corner point O draw points A-B at a distance equal to half of the neckline divided by 3.14 and then multiplied by 2. (e.g.: 28 : 3.14 = 9 x 2 = 18 cm).
- Draw the circular segment A-B, centred around O (the segment should be equal to half of the neckline 28 cm/11.02"). SEAM LINE.
- Draw the circular segment D-C centred around O, with A-D equal to the desired collar height (12-15 cm/4.72-5.91"). EDGE LINE.
- A-G same length as the back neckline D-P2.
- On line A-D write CENTRE BACK.
- On line B-C write CENTRE FRONT.
- C-E 3 cm/1.81".
- Draw B-E and round the corners as desired.

COLLAR

Note: This cape pattern may be completed in three different ways: 1) In one single piece, if the fabric will allow, laying the pattern out with the centre back on doubled fabric; 2) With one single seam on the centre back; 3) With a seam on the centre back and two on the sides.

3/4 CIRCLE CAPE

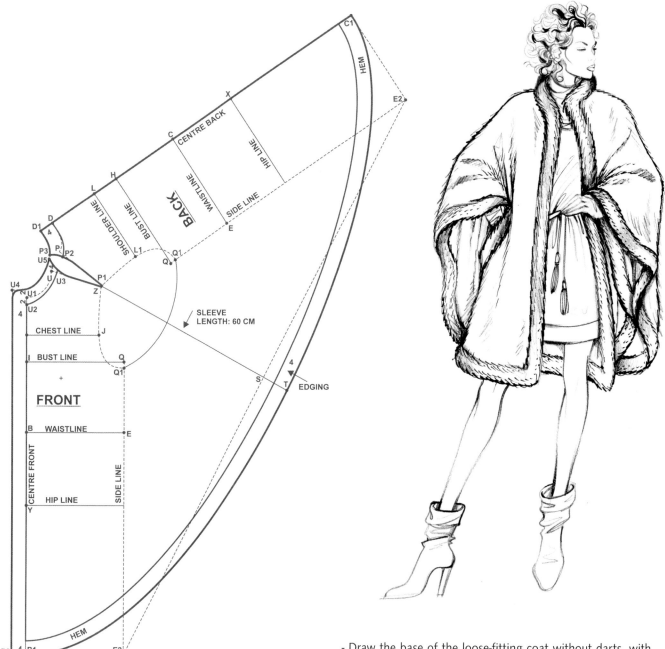

- Draw the base of the loose-fitting coat without darts, with the appropriate measurements and ease.
- Separate the front from the back and place them on another sheet of paper, keeping points P1 on the back and Z on the front joined, and points P on the back and U3 on the front separated by 6 cm/2.36".
- Draw a line from E2 on the front to E2 on the back, divide it in half and mark point S.
- Draw the line Z/P1-T, passing through S, with a measurement equal to the sleeve length or just a bit more (58-62 cm/22.83-24.41").
- Draw a curved line from Q1 on the back to Q1 on the front.
- Draw a curved line from E2 on the back to E2 on the front.
- Extend the centre front for the fastening or for the edging.
- Draw the high collar to be joined with the edging.
- Draw bottom edging.

CIRCLE CAPE

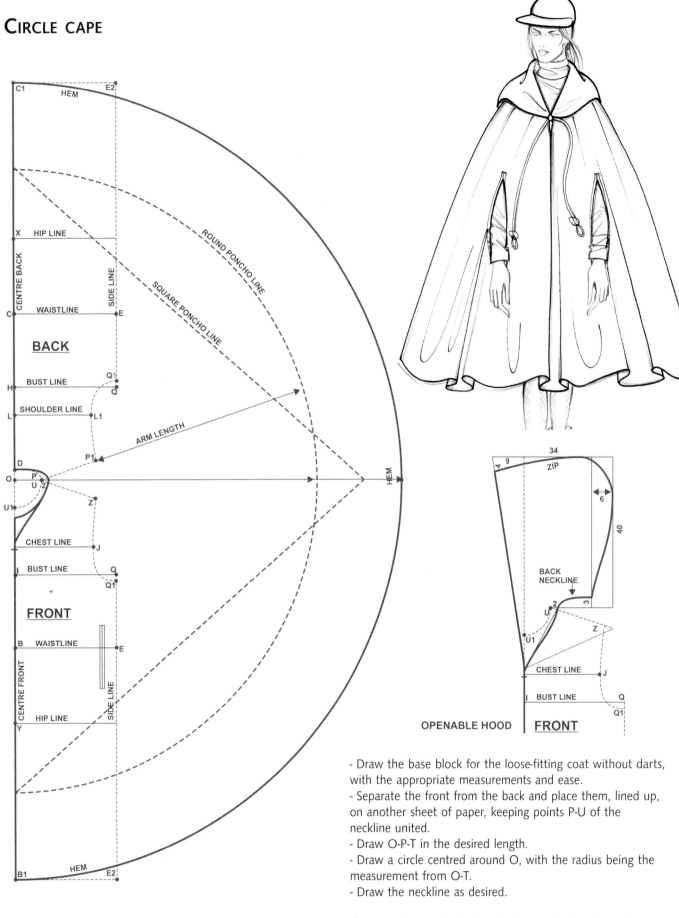

- Draw the base block for the loose-fitting coat without darts, with the appropriate measurements and ease.
- Separate the front from the back and place them, lined up, on another sheet of paper, keeping points P-U of the neckline united.
- Draw O-P-T in the desired length.
- Draw a circle centred around O, with the radius being the measurement from O-T.
- Draw the neckline as desired.

COLLAR: Construct the hood collar on the front, as shown in the figure.

Note: This cape may be made from a single piece of doubled fabric, if the material will allow for it, or it can have two seams (one on each side), or have four seams (on the sides, centre back and centre front).

DOUBLE CAPE

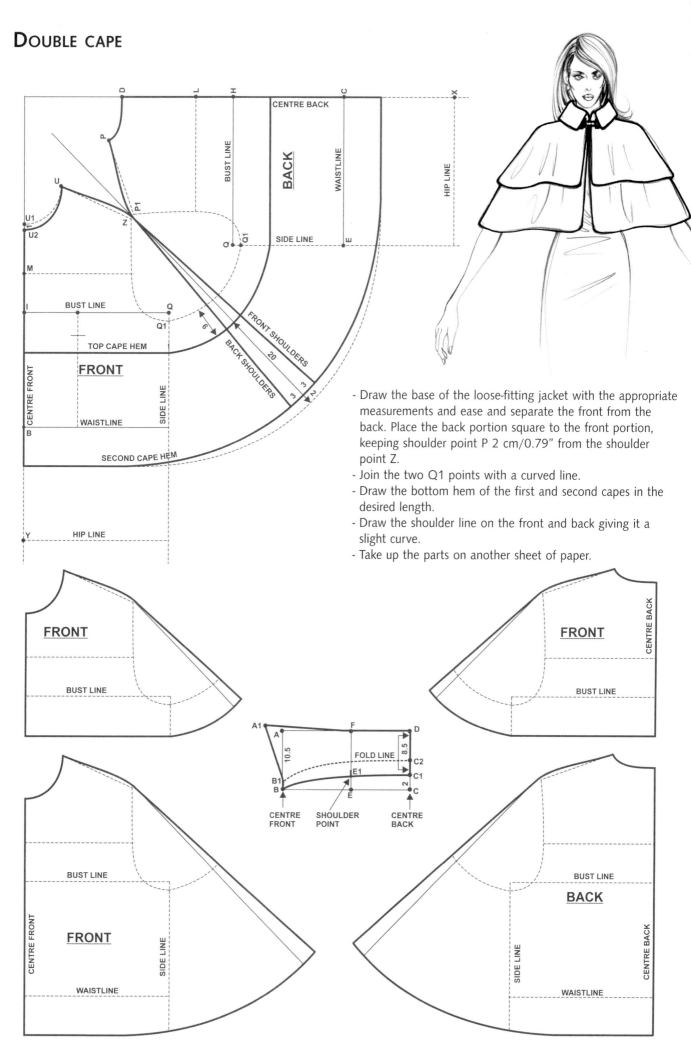

- Draw the base of the loose-fitting jacket with the appropriate measurements and ease and separate the front from the back. Place the back portion square to the front portion, keeping shoulder point P 2 cm/0.79" from the shoulder point Z.
- Join the two Q1 points with a curved line.
- Draw the bottom hem of the first and second capes in the desired length.
- Draw the shoulder line on the front and back giving it a slight curve.
- Take up the parts on another sheet of paper.

MEXICAN PONCHO

This type of poncho is constructed by placing the entire front section square to the entire back section, plus a front placket on the opposite part, always at right angles, keeping shoulder points Z and P1 2 cm/0.79" apart.
- Mark the pattern as illustrated in the figure, in the desired length.

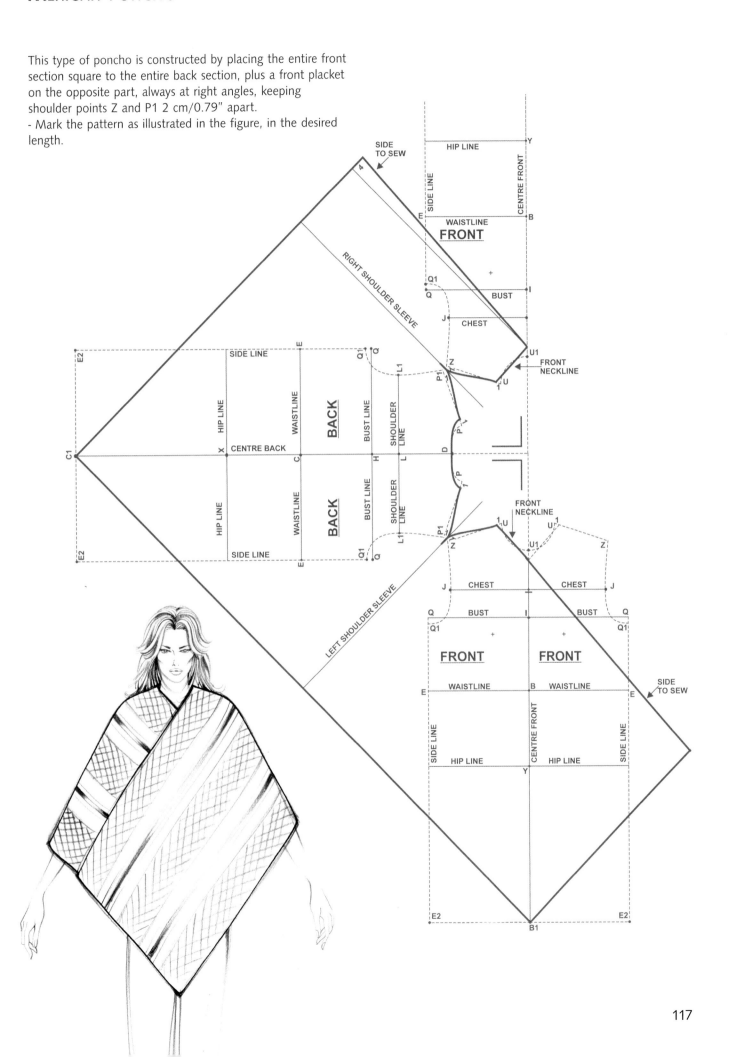

INVERNESS CAPE

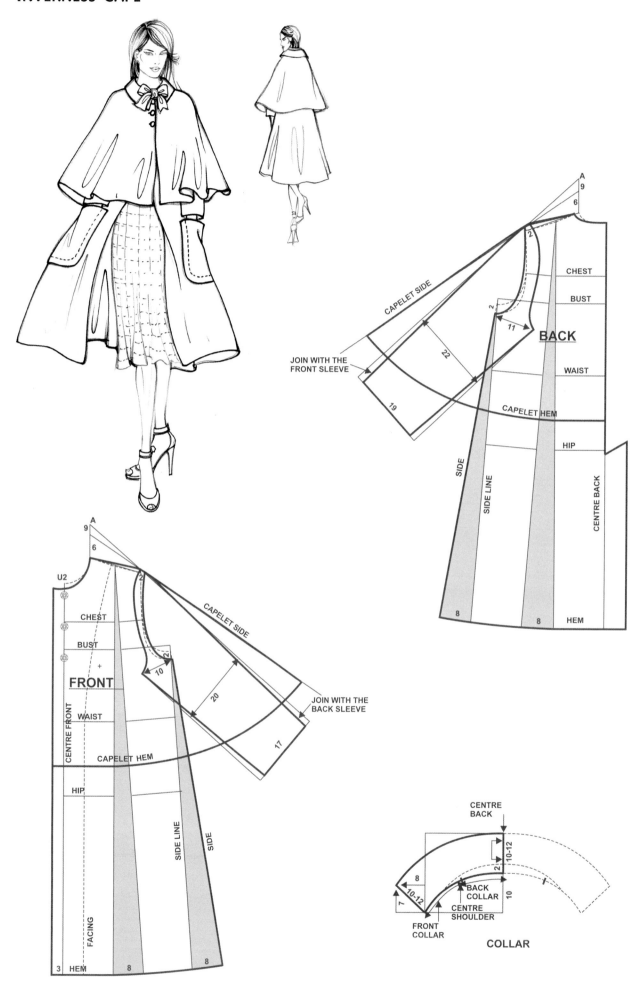

BACK

A
9
6
2

CHEST
BUST
2
11
22
CAPELET SIDE
JOIN WITH THE
FRONT SLEEVE
19
WAIST
CAPELET HEM
HIP
SIDE
SIDE LINE
CENTRE BACK
8   8   HEM

FRONT

A
9
6
U2
CHEST
BUST
2
10
CAPELET SIDE
20
JOIN WITH THE
BACK SLEEVE
17
+
CENTRE FRONT
WAIST
CAPELET HEM
HIP
SIDE LINE
SIDE
FACING
3   HEM   8   8

COLLAR

CENTRE
BACK
10-12
8
2
10
1
7   10-12
BACK
COLLAR
CENTRE
SHOULDER
FRONT
COLLAR

Hoods

Introduction

A hood is a head covering that is mostly conical in shape or rounded. It extends from the nape of the neck and its purpose is to protect the head, the neck and part of the face from rain and the cold. However, some hoods are purely stylistic, following the trends at the time.

The hood may be constructed separately or it may be integral to the garment: a tracksuit, hoodie, wind jacket, winter jacket, coat, cape, etc.

Hoods may be closely fitted to the head, soft or very loose-fitting. They may come in different shapes and connect to diverse necklines – or even have a neckline that extends up to the chin.

The fabric used for the hood usually is the same as the rest of the garment.

The material should be waterproof if it is used to protect from rain, in heavy wool for overcoats and capes, or in other types of fabric for fashionable garments.

Fendi A/W 2009-2010

Lacoste A/W 2009-2010

HOOD TYPES

Close-fitting *With a collar* *Loose-fitting* *Baggy* *Removable* *With a scarf tie*

Hood measurements

The measurements to take for the hood are: **head circumference, head height and a horizontal measurement.** When measuring, it is necessary to have the subject hold his or her head in a normal, erect and perfectly vertical position with the hair down and without any bulky accessories.

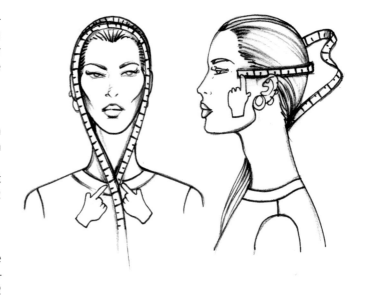

Head circumference and height measurement

Place the measuring tape at the centre base of the neck, then pass it around the head at the highest point and back down to the starting point.

You will add a few centimetres or inches to this measurement for ease, varying from 4 cm/1.57" for fitted hoods, to 12 cm/4.72" for baggy hoods (e.g.: 70 + 4 = 74 cm).

Horizontal measurement

Measure from one temple to the other, passing around the back of the head. You will add a few centimetres to this measurement for ease, from 4 cm/1.57" to 10 cm/3.94" (e.g. 42 + 4 = 46 cm).

BASE FORM-FITTING HOOD BLOCK

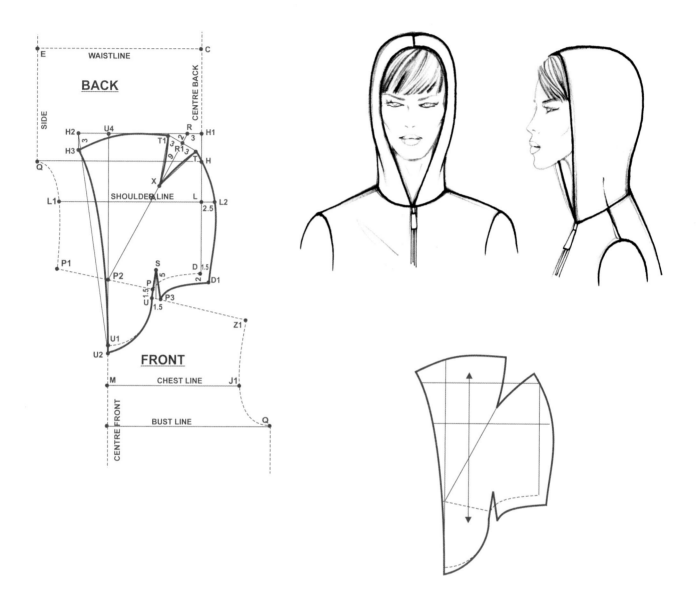

To construct a hood that is closely fitted, you must create a dart on the back of the peak of the head and on the neckline where the hood meets the shoulder.

- Place the garment's back pattern portion perpendicular and opposite to that of the front, keeping points U on the front and P on the back separated by 1.5-2 cm/0.59-0.79", as illustrated in the figure.
- Elongate the centre front line, from point U1 to point U4, with a measurement equal to 1/2 of the head height plus ease. (e.g.: 70 + 6 = 76 : 2 = 38 cm).
- Draw the horizontal line H1-U4-H2, with its length equal to 1/2 of the head's horizontal measurement plus ease (e.g.: 42 + 4 = 46 : 2 = 23 cm).
- H2-H3 3 cm/1.18".

- Draw the curved line H3-U2.
- H1-R 3 cm/1.18".
- Draw R-P2.
- R-R1 2 cm/0.79".
- Draw the dart T-X-T1, with a width of 4-6 cm/1.57-2.36" and a length of 9 cm/3.54".
- Draw the curved line H3-T1.
- Drop the back neckline D-P by 2 cm/0.79" and shift it towards the centre back by 1.5 cm/0.59" for the dart: points D1-P3.
- L-L2 2-3 cm/0.79-1.18". Draw curved line T-L2-D1.
- Draw the curved line D1-P3 equal to that of the back neckline.
- Draw the dart U-S-P3 with a width of 1.5-2 cm/0.59-0.79" and a depth of 5 cm/1.97".

HOOD WITH A COLLAR

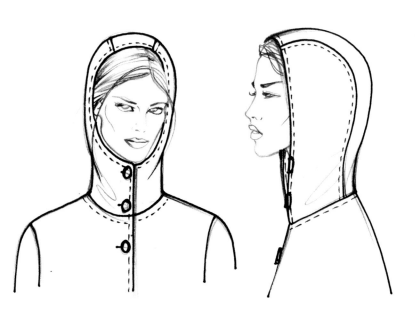

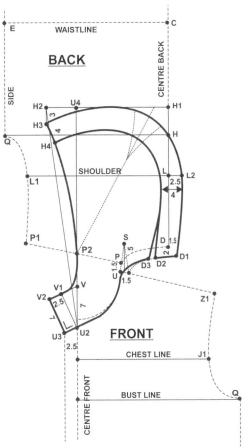

- Draw the base of the form-fitting hood with the appropriate measurements and ease, on the base with the extension for the fastening.
- H2-H3 3 cm/1.18".
- H3-H4 4-4.5 cm/1.57-1.77".
- D1-D2 like H3-H4.
- Draw the curved line H4-D2, parallel to H3-D1.
- Draw the neckline and bring the dart together in the seam of the band: D2-D3.
- U2-V 6.5-7.5 cm/2.56-2.95".
- Draw V-V2 parallel to the neckline.
- U2-U3 2.5 cm/0.98". Extension for fastening.
- V1-V2 like U2-U3.
- Draw U3-V2 square with V-V2 and U2-U3.

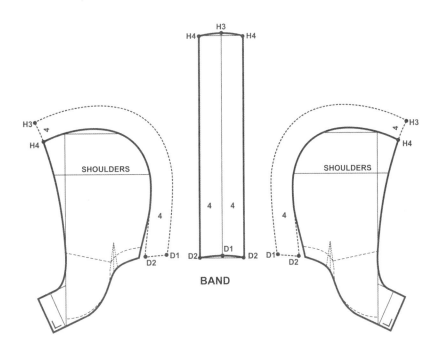

BAND

LOOSE-FITTING HOOD

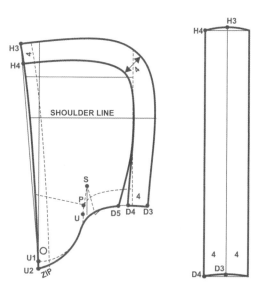

For the loose-fitting hood, begin from the base of the garment which the hood will be attached to, positioning the front over the back, perpendicularly along the shoulder.

- Place the back pattern portion of the garment perpendicular and opposite to the front, keeping points U on the front and P on the back separated by 1.5-2 cm/0.59-0.79", as illustrated in the figure.
- Elongate the centre front line, from point U1 to point U4, with a measurement equal to 1/2 of the head height plus ease. (e.g.: 70 + 10 = 80 : 2 = 40 cm).
- U4-H2 3-3.5 cm/1.18-1.38".
- Draw the horizontal line H2-U4-H4, with its length being equal to 1/2 of the horizontal head measurement plus the

ease of the hood (e.g.: 42 + 8 = 50 : 2 = 25 cm).
- D-D1 3 cm/1.18".
- Draw the horizontal line D1-D2 like H1-H4.
- Draw the vertical line H4-D2.
- D2-D3 1.5 cm/0.59".
- H2-H3 1-1.5 cm/0.39-0.59".
- Drop the back neckline D-P by 3 cm/1.18"and shift it towards the centre back by 1.5-2 cm/0.59-0.79" for the dart.
- Draw the curved line D3-P3, equal to that of the back neckline + 1 cm/0.39".
- Draw the dart U-S-P3 with a width of 1.5-2 cm/0.59-0.79", and a depth of 5 cm/1.97".
- Draw the curved line of the back H3-L2-D3.
- Draw the line on the front, U2-H3.

REMOVABLE HOOD

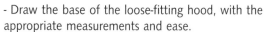

- Draw the base of the loose-fitting hood, with the appropriate measurements and ease.
- Draw the curved line H4-D4 at a distance that is equal to 1/2 of the width of the band.
- Connect the front and back neckline U2-D5, discarding the dart in the band's seam.
- Draw the band with a length equal to the measurement of the hood's external edge and with a width equal to double the distance between H3-H4 and D3-D4.

BAGGY HOOD

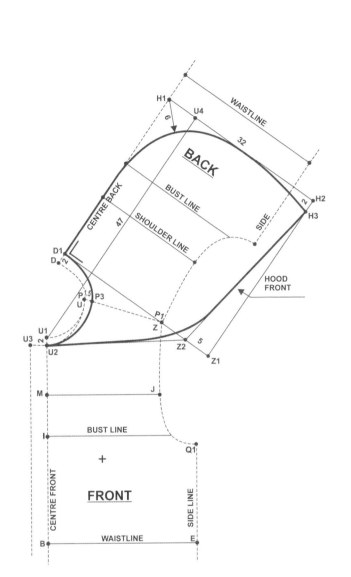

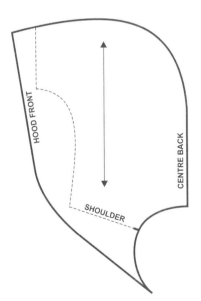

The baggy hood is constructed starting from the base of the garment to which the hood will be attached: coat, cape, etc.

- Place the garment's back bodice portion on that of the front, keeping them joined on the shoulder line as illustrated in the figure.
- Adjust the front and back neckline as necessary.
- From U1 to U4, measure 1/2 of the head height from the neck point, plus an ease of 24-28 cm/9.45-11.02",
depending on how baggy you would like the hood to be (e.g.: 70 + 24 = 94 : 2 = 47 cm).
- Draw H1-U4-H2, parallel to the waist line of the back bodice, with a length equal to 1/2 of the horizontal head measurement + hood ease 18-24 cm/7.09-9.45" (e.g.: 42 + 22 = 64 : 2 = 32 cm).
- D1-Z1 like H1-H2.
- Draw H2-Z1.
- H2-H3 1-2 cm/0.39-0.78".
- Z1-Z2 4-6 cm/1.57-2.36".
- Join Z2 to U2 on the front neckline.
- Connect H3-U2 with a curved line. FRONT HOOD.
- Connect D1-H3 with a curved line. BACK HOOD.

HOOD WITH A SCARF FASTENING

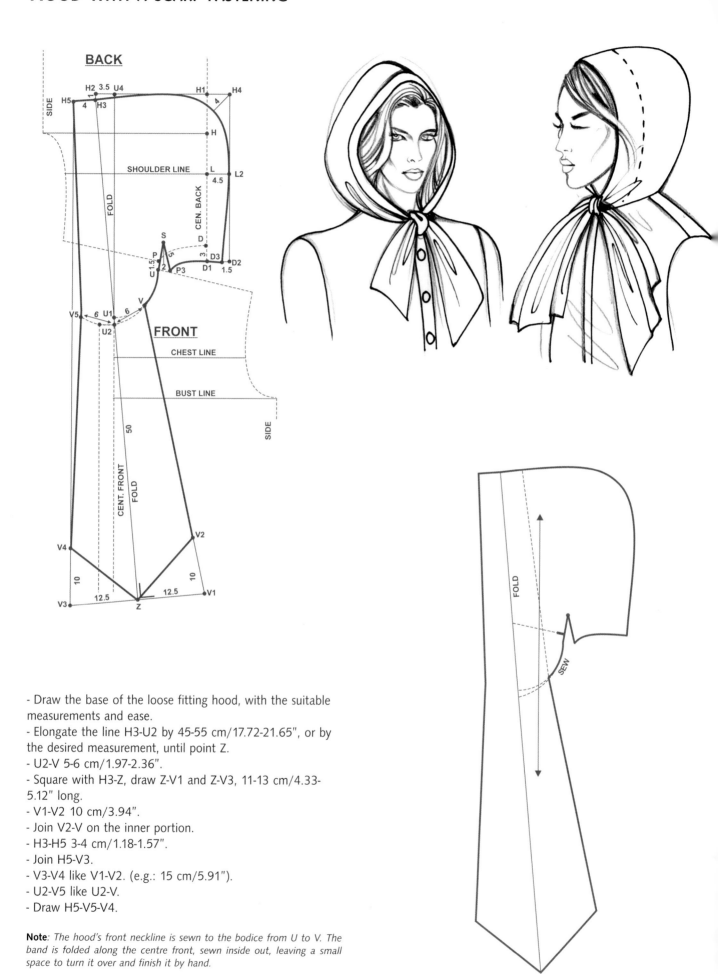

- Draw the base of the loose fitting hood, with the suitable measurements and ease.
- Elongate the line H3-U2 by 45-55 cm/17.72-21.65", or by the desired measurement, until point Z.
- U2-V 5-6 cm/1.97-2.36".
- Square with H3-Z, draw Z-V1 and Z-V3, 11-13 cm/4.33-5.12" long.
- V1-V2 10 cm/3.94".
- Join V2-V on the inner portion.
- H3-H5 3-4 cm/1.18-1.57".
- Join H5-V3.
- V3-V4 like V1-V2. (e.g.: 15 cm/5.91").
- U2-V5 like U2-V.
- Draw H5-V5-V4.

Note: *The hood's front neckline is sewn to the bodice from U to V. The band is folded along the centre front, sewn inside out, leaving a small space to turn it over and finish it by hand.*

SHOULDER

BUST

BACK

SIDE

UNDER

WAIST

DETACHABLE HOOD

4

2

CENTRE BACK

SIDE

LENGTH
+ BACK BODICE
+ HOOD HEIGHT
+ EXTRA VOLUME

13

HOOD

40

38-40

47

FACING

BUST

FACING

CENTRE FRONT

WAIST

FRONT

HIP LINE

SIDE LINE

BUST

CENTRE FRONT

WAIST

CREATIVE HOODS

30-34

30-34

4

4

CHEST LINE

BUST LINE

CENT. FRONT

FACING

FRONT

SIDE

8

FRONT

BACK

CENT. FRONT

FACING

RIGHT ANGLE

25   12   20

45

27

4.5   4

BUST

CENT. FRONT

SIDE

WAIST

63

63

HIP

FRONT   SIDE

MEN'S JACKETS AND OVERCOATS

Lines for men's coats 128
Proportion analysis 129
Base men's coat block. 130
Double-breasted coat 132
Double-breasted coat with peak lapels. . . 133
Seam margins for men's coats 134
Base sleeves for men's coats 135
Base loose-fitting overcoat. 136
Loose-fitting overcoat and sleeve 137
Base Mac (trench). 138
Inset sleeve for macs (trenches) 139
Raglan overcoat 140
Double-breasted raglan coat 141
Montgomery 142
Montgomery sleeve 143
Clergyman's coat 144
Overcoat with a deep armscye 145
Base padded heavy jacket 146
Base sleeve for padded jackets. 147
Parka 148
Technical foundations 149
Seam margins for raglan sleeves 152

LINES FOR MEN'S COATS

The lines and lengths of coats and other outerwear also vary according to the dictates of fashion and when and where they will be worn.

On the back, coats may have a centre vent or box pleat.

The fabric used for outerwear depends on the type of garment and fashion at the time.

The fabrics most commonly used for coats are bouclé, heavy cloth, velour, brushed fabric, heavy double wool crepes, camelhair, knickerbocker, tweed, herringbone, etc. They are often paired with sportier materials, such as leather inserts.

The main types of coats and overcoats

Classic overcoat

Classic overcoats, which come in typical menswear lines, may be single- or double-breasted.

The single-breasted closure may be smooth and without seams, with the breakpoint of the lapels at the bust line or lower down, near the waist. It may have one, two or three buttons.

The garment may feature cross-wise seams or motifs, vertical seams, side panels at the waist or be redingote shaped. It may be flared at the bottom edge or be amphora shaped and narrower along the bottom. The sleeves may be fitted, raglan, kimono or with a dropped armscye. The garment may be collarless, come with a collar and lapels or have a collar that is very broad along the shoulders.

The double-breasted version may feature six buttons, with the lapel's breakpoint below the bust, or it may come with four buttons, with the breakpoint at the waist. It may feature vertical seams, side panels or have a redingote shape.

The Loden overcoat

The loden overcoat, which gets its name from the type of fabric it is made of, was originally a garment used for labour. In the 1960s, it was transformed into a menswear item, and then subsequently offered as a women's coat. Originally in bottle green and made of pure brushed wool, this type of coat stands out for its slight trapezoid shape and shoulders with flaps over the armscye to cover the seams.

The flap and the sleeve's stitching and attachment leave open space at the underarms for breathability and to allow perspiration to escape, in addition to providing better ease of movement.

On the back, there is generally an inverted pleat fixed with a fly or a triangle-shaped piece of leather.

Car coat

The car coat is a type of outercoat whose length is from 3/4 (hitting at the thighs) to 7/8 and 9/10 above the knee. It comes in all the cuts and lines as a classic overcoat and even comes in the same materials.

Topcoat

The topcoat is a light item of outerwear made in various medium-weight fabrics to be worn mid-season.

This type of garment existed as early as the 18th century, though it has undergone countless changes and transformations since then.

Macintosh or trench coat

The Macintosh or trench coat is an item of outerwear for men or women, made in waterproof fabric. It comes in various lines, according to current fashions, but it is always relatively loose-fitting. It is worn as protection from the rain.

Single-breasted coat   Double-breasted coat   Single-button coat

Raglan overcoat   Loden   Montgomery

Loose-fitting coat   Mac (trench)

PROPORTION ANALYSIS

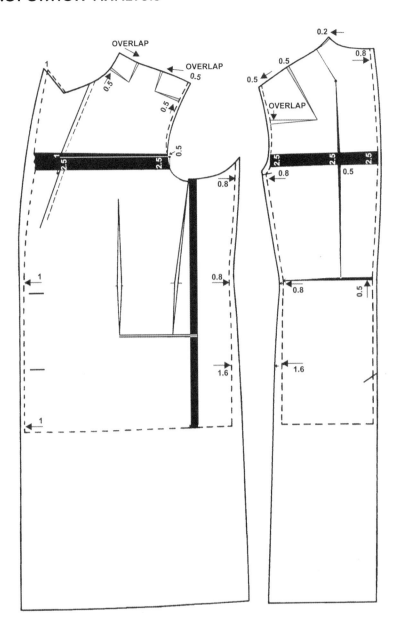
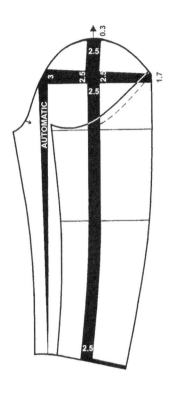

The illustration above clearly demonstrates the general differences that set the base of the jacket apart from the base of an overcoat. It highlights the fact that an overcoat does not require the purely proportional methodology seen on the jacket.

A purely-proportioned pattern obtained only by increasing the measurement of the chest or taking the measurements directly from the jacket will not produce the correct distribution between the sectors, nor will it be correctly adapted to the wearer's shape.

Thus it is necessary to take the following into consideration:

1) Keep in mind the greater needs of the armscye and the alteration of its measurements due to the sleeves of the jacket.

2) Consider the need to increase the curve of the shoulder due to the effect deriving from the jacket's collar.

3) The need to lengthen and add rounded volume to the rises to make the garment easier to put on, in addition to having to cover a more robust chest, derived from the doubling and overlapping of the thickness of the jacket and the overcoat. For these reasons, it is necessary to analyse which type of logic to use when making the coat.

Back: - Increase the length at the armscye level; - parallel enlargement of the neckline and the side sector; - increase in the rounded shape of the shoulders. The back thus increases by a total of 2.1 cm/0.83" in width and 2.5 cm/0.98" in height.

Front: The front, in addition to being expanded at the level of the armscye by 2.5 cm/0.98" just like the back, is to be increased by a total of 2.5 cm/0.98" in width. This is completed with two steps. In addition, the front profile is increased by 1 cm/0.39", plus the other devices illustrated in the figure.

For this reason, the width of the front chest potentially increases by 1.5 cm/0.59"; the armscye by 2.5 cm/0.98"; the back by 2.1 cm/0.83", for a total of 6.1 cm/2.40". The distribution must be well-planned with the appropriately rational vertical and horizontal increases.

Sleeve: The increases on the sleeve are examined by considering the two overlapping pieces, moving the pieces while respecting the horizontal axis of the armscye and the elbow. The central opening must be equal to the increase in the armscye of the bodice; and the increase must, in turn, be equal to the lowering carried out on the overcoat, with two variations: the rear piece rotates for a difference of 0.8 cm/0.31" on the sleeve crown, while the front piece rotates forward for a play on lengths and aesthetic effects on the front shoulder.

BASE MEN'S COAT BLOCK

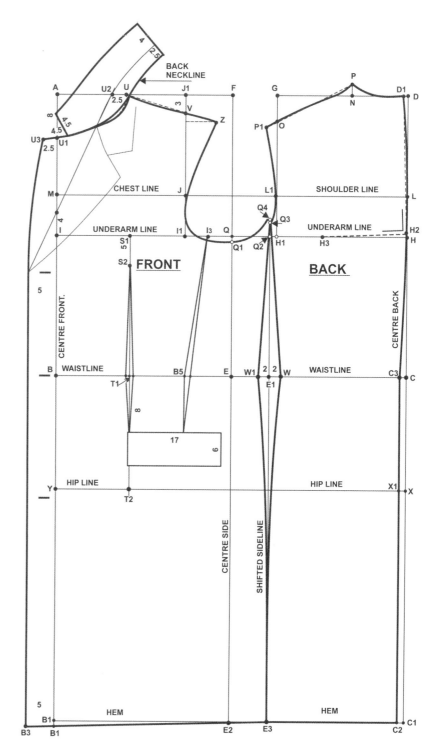

Measurements: (without ease)
- Chest circumference 96 cm/37.80"
- Waist circumference 88 cm/34.65"
- Hip circumference 96 cm/37.80"
- Neck circumference 42 cm/16.54"
- Waist length 47 cm/18.50"
- Shoulder width 44 cm/17.32"

- Draw a right angle A-B-C, where:
- A-B waist length +coat ease.
(e.g.: 47 + 3 = 50 cm).
- B-C Chest semicircumference+ ease.
(e.g.: 96 + 32 = 128 : 2 = 64 cm).
- C-D like A-B.
- D-C1 Coat length (e.g.: 112 cm/44.09").
- Join D-C1 and write CENTRE BACK.
- B-B1 like C-C1.
- Join A-B1 and write CENTRE FRONT. - B1-C1 like B-C.
- Join B1-C1 and write HEM LINE.
- B-E half of B-C.
- B1-E2 like B-E.
- A-F like B-E.
- Join F-E2 and write CENTRE SIDE.
- D-H half of D-C + 0.5 cm/0.20" (e.g.: 50 : 2 = 25 + 0.5 = 25.5 cm).
- H-I parallel to B-C write ARMPIT LEVEL.

- E2-E3 7 cm/2.76".
- Q-Q2 like E2-E3.
- Join Q2-E3 and write SHIFTED SIDE.
- B-Y and C-X side height (e.g.: 20 cm/7.87").
- Draw Y-X and write HIP LINE.
- D-G half of shoulder width + ease.
(e.g.: 44 + 3.5 = 47.5 : 2 = 23.75 cm).
- H-L 1/4 of D-H (e.g.: 25.5 : 4 = 6.37 cm).
- Draw L-M. SHOULDER LINE AND CHEST LINE.
- H-H1 like D-G (e.g.: 23.75 cm/9.34").
- Draw G-H1.
- I1-I1 like D-G-0.5 cm/0.20" on the back.
(e.g.: 23.75 – 0.5 = 23.25 cm).
- Draw I1-J1 parallel to G-H1.

130

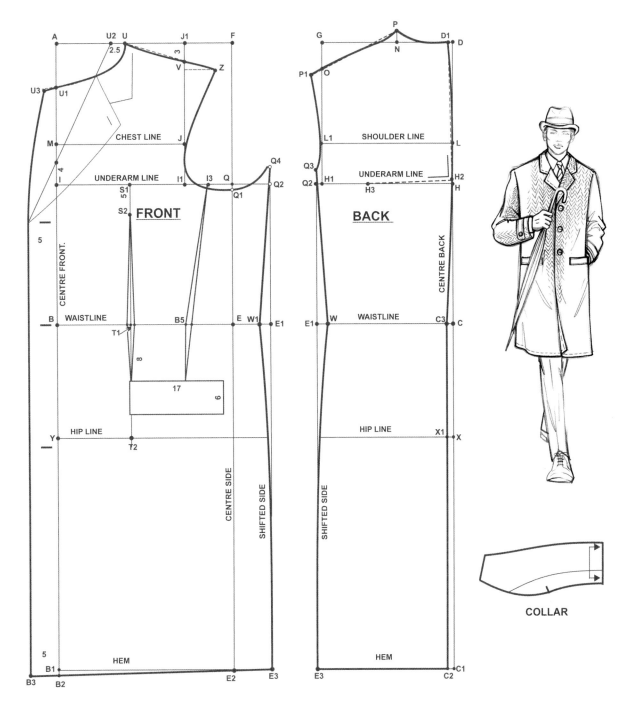

FRONT

BACK

COLLAR

Back
- H-H3 16 cm/6.30".
- H-H2 0.6 cm/0.24". - Create the corner H3-H2-D1.
- H2-D1 like H-D.
- D1-N 1/3 of D-G + 1 cm/0.39" (e.g.: 23.75 : 3 = 7.9 + 1 = 8.9 cm).
- N-P 2.5 cm/0.98".
- Draw D1-P, connecting the points with a curved line.
- G-O 4.5 cm/1.77".
- P-P1 Shoulder length + 2 cm/0.79" (e.g.: 16 + 2 = 18 cm).
- Draw P-P1 with a curved line, passing through O.
- Q2-Q3 3 cm/1.18".
- Draw armscye P1-L1-Q3, smoothly.
- E1-W 1.5-3 cm/0.59-1.18".
- C-C3 1.2-1.7 cm/0.47-0.67".
- C1-C2 like C-C3.
- Draw the centre back line D1-L-H-C3-X1-C2.
- Draw the side line Q3-W-E3.

Front
- A-U 12.5 cm/4.92". (half of A-J1 + 0.5 cm/0.20").

- A-U1 7.5-8 cm/2.95-3.15".
- U-U2 2.5 cm/0.98".
- Draw the breakpoint at the desired height.
- U1-U3 2-2.5 cm/0.79-0.98".
- I-S1 13.5 cm/5.31".
- I1-I3 4.5 cm/1.77".
- B-B5 like I-I1 (23.2 cm/9.13").
- Draw the 1-1.5 cm/0.39-0.59" waist darts.
- J1-V 3.5 cm/1.38".
- U-Z like P-P1 on the back, minus 1 cm/0.39" (17 cm).
- Draw U-Z, shaped as necessary, passing through V.
- Q-Q1 1-2 cm/0.39-0.79".
- Q2-Q4 3.5 cm/1.38".
- Smoothly draw armscye Z-J-Q1-Q4.
- E1-W1 like E1-W.
- Draw the side line Q4-W1-E3.
- B1-B2 0.5-1 cm/0.20-0.39".
- B2-B3 5 cm/1.97" extension for the fastening.
- Draw the shaped lapel.
- Draw the hem E3-B3.

DOUBLE-BREASTED COAT

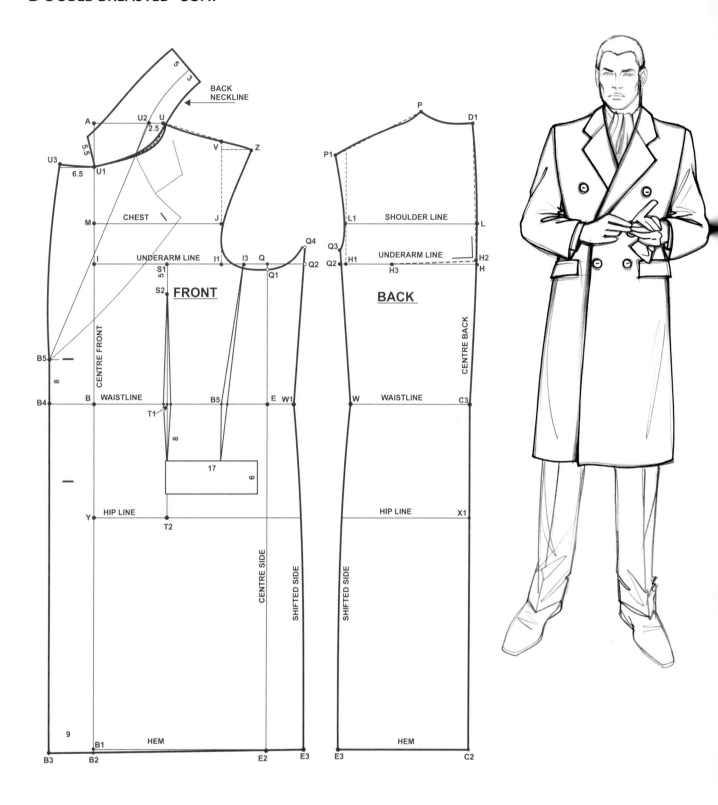

BACK NECKLINE

FRONT

BACK

CHEST

SHOULDER LINE

UNDERARM LINE

WAISTLINE

HIP LINE

HEM

CENTRE FRONT

CENTRE BACK

CENTRE SIDE

SHIFTED SIDE

- Draw the base coat block with the appropriate measurements and ease, in the total length desired.
- Extend the overlap of the centre front B1-B3 and B-B4 by 9 cm/3.54".
- B4-B5 6-8 cm/2.36-3.15".
- Draw the break point from U2 to B5.
- U1-U3 6.5-7 cm/2.56-2.76".
- Join B3-B5-U3 as in the figure.

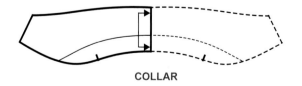

COLLAR

DOUBLE-BREASTED COAT WITH PEAK LAPELS

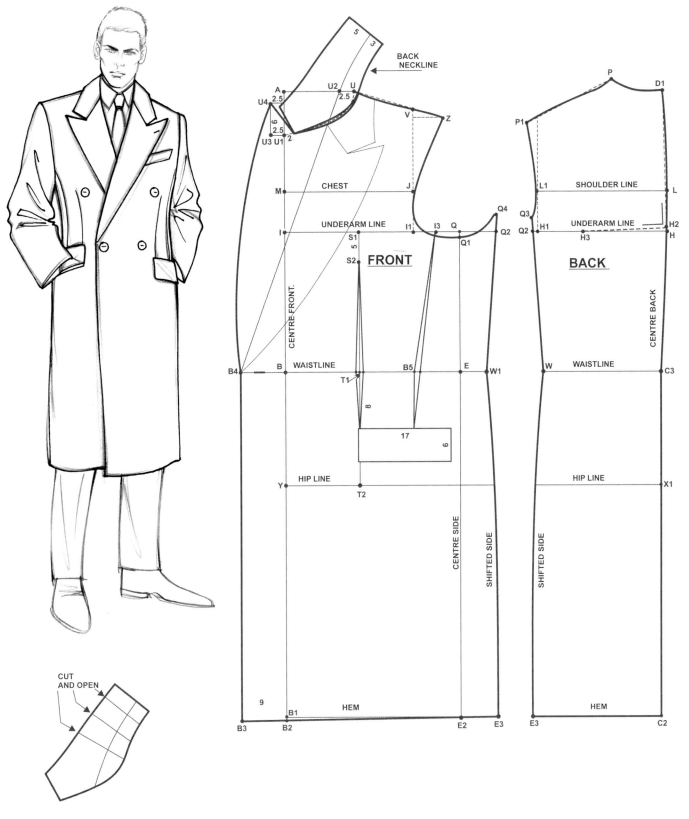

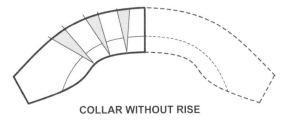

COLLAR WITHOUT RISE

- Draw the base for the double-breasted coat with appropriate measurements and ease and in the desired total length, with the overlap of the centre front by 9 cm/3.54".
- Draw the break point from U2 to B4 at the desired height.
- U1-U3 2.5-3 cm/0.98-1.18".
- U3-U4 6 cm/2.36" (or as desired).
- Join B3-B4-U4 like in the figure.

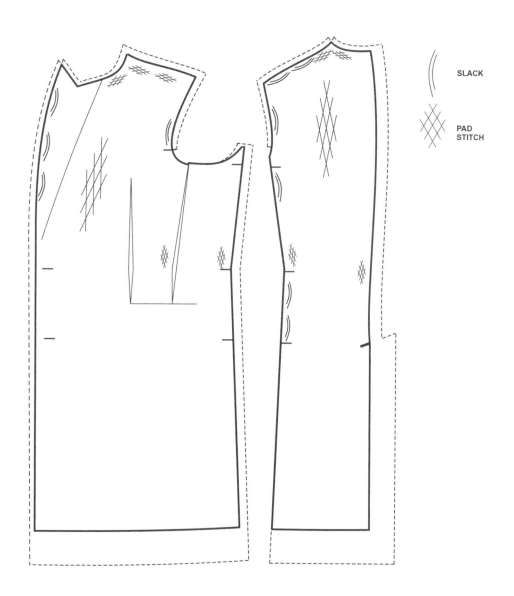

SLACK

PAD
STITCH

Note for the margins: Remember that the margins are parallel to the seam lines; the margins on the back shoulder, which are optional, require that you sew below the demarcation line by 0.6 cm/0.24".

COLLAR

After having temporarily placed the back of the coat over the front so that the two shoulder points meet, this collar requires that the measurements and shape are followed exactly in order to make it easier to adjust the part of the garment that surrounds the collar.

The collar will require shrinking only on the back curve of the neckline and, should you wish to cut through the break point, it may also be ok without any processing.

The break point, duly shifted by 2 cm/0.79" from K towards K1, will allow you to impose all the rotations required on the neckline through the seams and the relative expansions carried out, as shown in the figure.

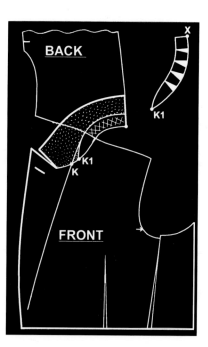

Base sleeves for men's coats

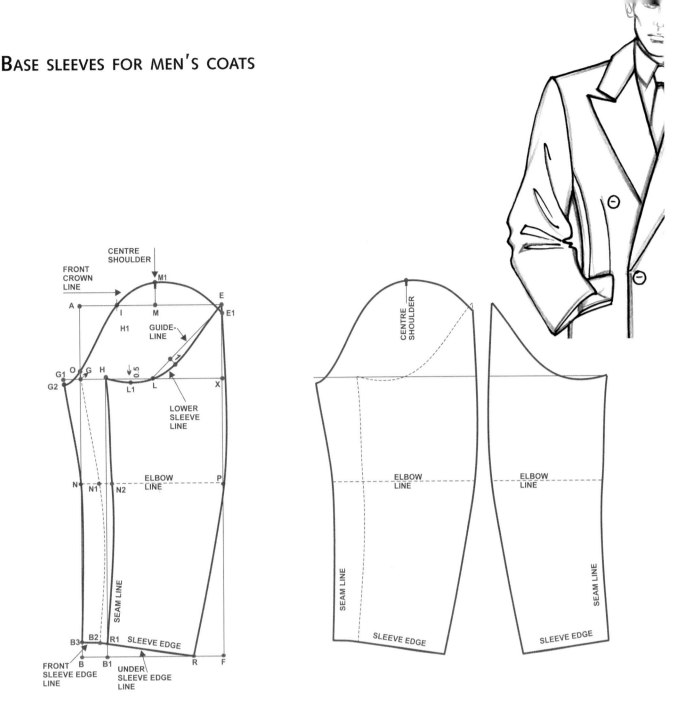

On the left side of a sheet of pattern paper, draw a rectangle A -B -E -F, where:
- A-E like the bodice sector I1-H1+1/2 sector + 2 cm/0.79". (e.g.: 15.8 + 7.9 = 23.7 + 2 = 25.7 cm).
- A-B sleeve length measurement (e.g.: 62 cm).
- A-G like the measurement of L1-P1+ 0.5 cm/0.20" of the back bodice base. (e.g.: 12.5 + 0.5 = 13 cm).
- Draw G-X parallel to A-E.
- A-N half of A-B (e.g. 62 : 2 =31). ELBOW LINE.
- A-M 1/2 of A-E + 1 cm/0.39". (e.g.: 25.7 : 2 = 12.85 + 1 = 13.85 cm). CENTRE SHOULDER.
- M-M1 1/3 A-G. (e.g.: 13 : 3 = 4.35 cm).
- A-I 1/4 A-E. (e.g.: 25.7 : 4 = 6.42 cm).
- G-H 3.5 cm/1.38".
- G-G1 2.7 cm/1.06".
- G1-G2 1 cm/0.39".
- E-E1 1 cm/0.39".
- X-L half of G-X. (e.g.: 25.7 : 2 = 12.85 cm).

- Draw the guide line E-L.
- L-L1 half of H-L.
- G-O 1.5 cm/0.59".
- Smoothly draw the front sleeve crown E1-M1-I-O-G2.
- Smoothly draw the back sleeve crown E-L-L1-H.
- B-B1 4.5 cm/1.77".
- B-B3 2.5 cm/0.98".
- B3-B2 and N-N1 2.5 cm/0.98".
- R-F 5.5 cm/2.17".
- R-R1 16 cm/6.30" (according to the desired length).
- Connect R-P-E and R1-N2-H with a curved line.
- Connect B3-N-G2 with a curved line.
- Copy the undersleeve E-P-R-R1-N2-H-L1-L-E and place it on E1-F on the front.
Check the measurements of the total sleeve crown, which should be greater than the measurement for the armscye by a variable number, according to the type of fabric used.

BASE LOOSE-FITTING OVERCOAT

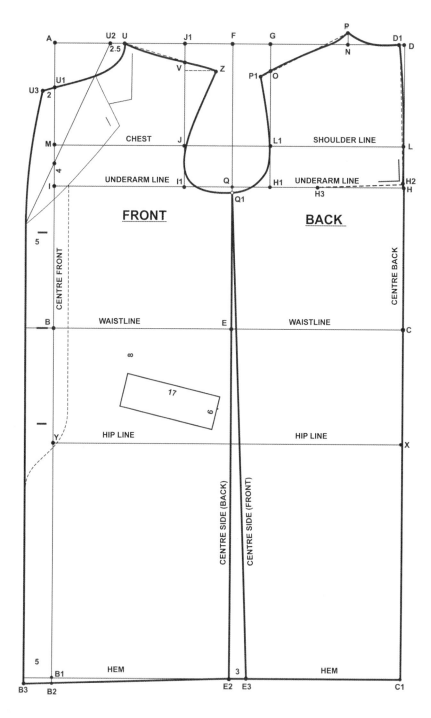

- Draw a right angle A-B-C, where:
- A-B waist length + loose-fitting coat ease.
(e.g.: 47 + 3 = 50 cm).
- B-C Chest semicircumference + loose-fitting
coat ease. (e.g.: 96 + 36 = 132 : 2 = 66 cm).
- C-D like A-B.
- D-C1 overcoat length. (e.g.: 112
cm/44.09").
- Join D-C1 and write CENTRE BACK.
- B-B1 like C-Cl.
- Join A-B1 and write CENTRE FRONT.
- B1-C1 like B-C.
- Join B1-C1 and write HEM LINE.
- B-E half of B-C.
- B1-E2 like B-E.
- A-F like B-E.
- Join F-E2 and write CENTRE SIDE.
- D-H half of D-C + 0.5 cm/0.20".
(e.g.: 50 : 2 = 25 + 0.5 = 25.5 cm).
- H-I parallel to B-C write ARMPIT LEVEL.
- B-Y and C-X side height. (e.g.: 20 cm/7.87").
- Draw Y-X and write HIP LINE.
- D-G half of shoulder width + ease.
(e.g.: 44 + 4 = 48 : 2 = 24 cm).
- H-L 1/4 of D-H (e.g.: 25.5 : 4 = 6.37 cm).
- Draw L-M. SHOULDER LINE AND CHEST
LINE.
- H-H1 like D-G (e.g.: 24 cm/9.45").
- Draw G-H1.
- I-I1 like D-G - 0.5 cm/0.20" of the back.
(e.g.: 24 – 0.5 = 23.5 cm).
- Draw I1-J1 parallel to G-H1.

Back
- H-H3 16.5 cm/6.49".
- H-H2 0.6 cm/0.24".
- Create the corner H3-H2-D1.
- H2-D1 like H-D.
- Dl-N 1/3 of D-G + 1.5 cm/0.59".
(e.g.: 24 : 3 = 8 + 1.5= 9.5 cm).
- N-P 2.7 cm/1.06".
- Draw a curved line, D1-P.
- G-O 4.5 cm/1.77".
- P-P1 Shoulder length + 2 cm/0.79".
(e.g.: 16 + 2 = 18 cm).
- Draw P-P1 with a curved line, passing
through O.
- Q-Q1 1-2 cm/0.39-0.79".
- Draw the back armscye P1-L1-Q1.

Front
- A-U 12.5 cm/4.92" (half of A-J + 0.5 cm/0.20").
- A-U1 7.5-8 cm. - U-U2 2.5 cm/0.98".
- Draw the break point.
- U1-U3 2-2.5 cm/0.79-0.98".
- J1-V 3.5 cm/1.38".
- U-Z like P-P1 of the back minus 1 cm/0.39".
- Draw a shaped line U-Z passing through V.
- Q-Q1 like the back (1-2 cm/0.39-0.79").
- Draw the front armscye Z-J-Q1.
- E2-E3 2.5-3.5 cm/0.98-1.38".
- Draw the front side Q1-E3.
- B1-B2 0.5-1 cm/0.20-0.39".
- B2-B3 5 cm/1.97" extension for the fastening.
- Draw the lapel with a curve.
- Draw the hem E3-B3.

LOOSE-FITTING OVERCOAT AND SLEEVE

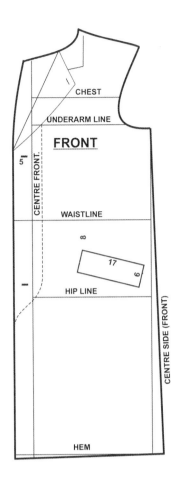

FRONT

CHEST

UNDERARM LINE

CENTRE FRONT.

5

WAISTLINE

8

17

9

HIP LINE

CENTRE SIDE (FRONT)

HEM

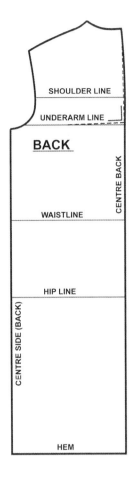

BACK

SHOULDER LINE

UNDERARM LINE

CENTRE BACK

WAISTLINE

HIP LINE

CENTRE SIDE (BACK)

HEM

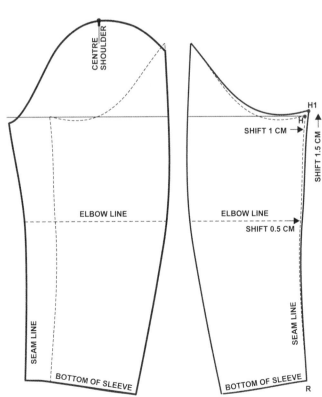

CENTRE SHOULDER

H1

H

SHIFT 1 CM

SHIFT 1.5 CM

ELBOW LINE

ELBOW LINE

SHIFT 0.5 CM

SEAM LINE

SEAM LINE

BOTTOM OF SLEEVE

BOTTOM OF SLEEVE

R

Sleeve

To construct the sleeve for the chesterfield overcoat (a loose-fitting overcoat), use the same sleeve as on the classic overcoat. You'll need to move point H1 on the undersleeve, raising it by 1.5 cm/0.59" and expanding it by 1 cm/0.39".
- Connect H1-R.

Base mac (trench)

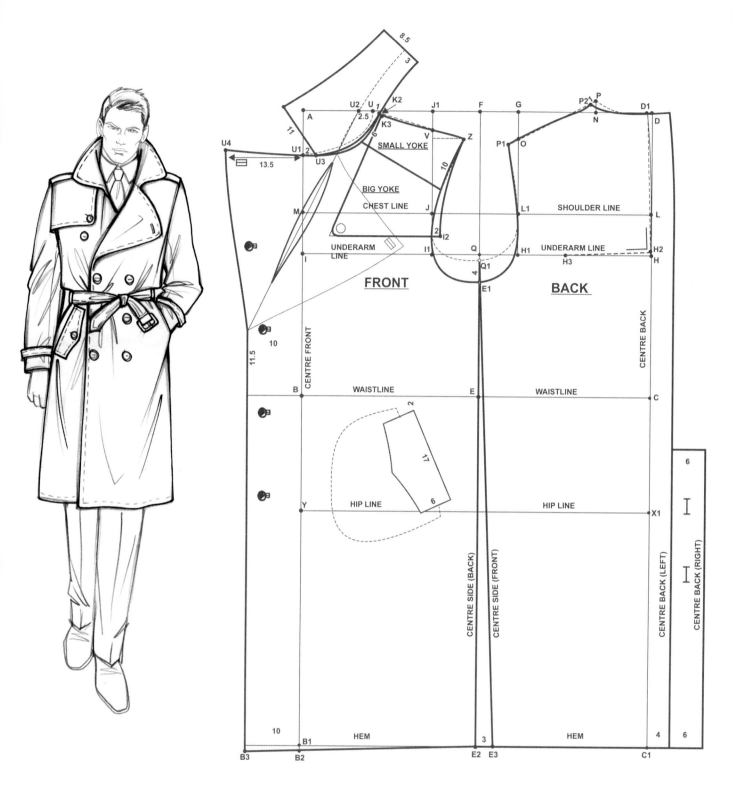

- Draw base of the loose-fitting coat, with the "dusters, mac and capes" ease (see the ease chart).
- Lower the armscye by 3-4 cm/1.18-1.57", create the desired length and create a slight flare on the side at the bottom.

Back
- For the back left side, extend the centre back by 4 cm/1.57" from top to bottom.
- For the back right side, add another 5-6 cm/1.97-2.36" for the inverted pleat, from the bottom to the hip.
- P-P2 1 cm/0.39".

Front
Extend the centre front for the overlapping closure (10 cm/3.94" for a double-breast).
- Draw the lapel in the desired width and depth.
- U-K2 like P-P2.
- Draw the collar in the desired shape and size.
- Draw the front yoke K3-13-I2-Z-K3, extending it over the armscye (point I2) by 1.5-2 cm/0.59-0.79" for freedom of movement.
- Draw the pocket according to the pattern.

INSET SLEEVE FOR MACS (TRENCHES)

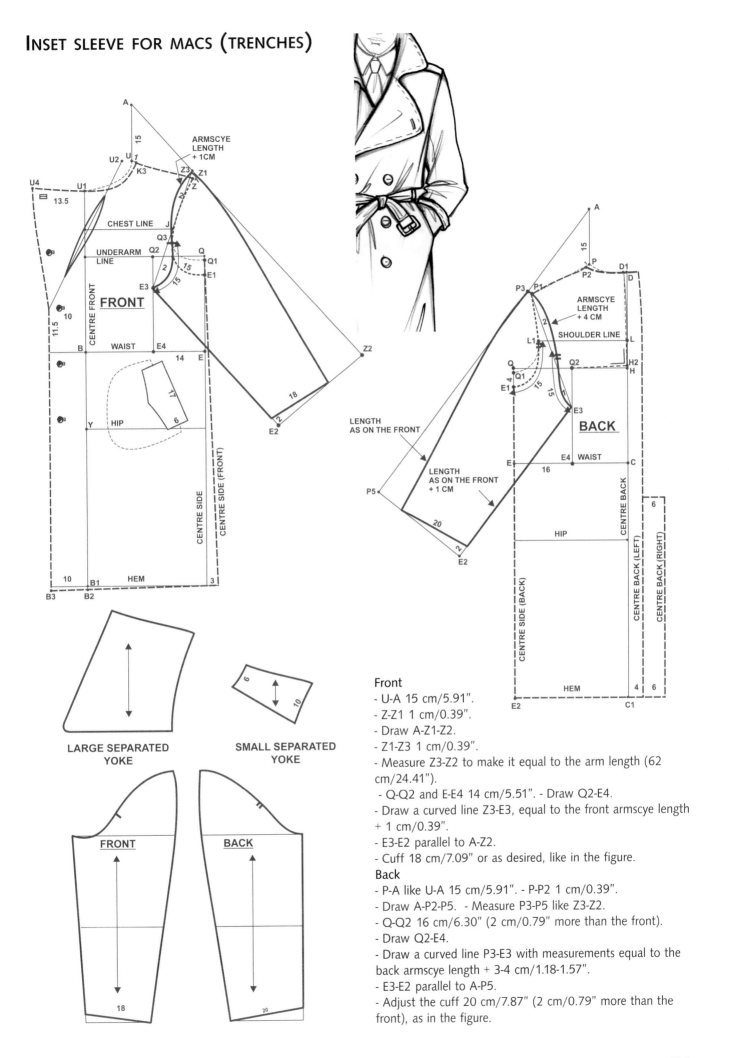

Front
- U-A 15 cm/5.91".
- Z-Z1 1 cm/0.39".
- Draw A-Z1-Z2.
- Z1-Z3 1 cm/0.39".
- Measure Z3-Z2 to make it equal to the arm length (62 cm/24.41").
- Q-Q2 and E-E4 14 cm/5.51". - Draw Q2-E4.
- Draw a curved line Z3-E3, equal to the front armscye length + 1 cm/0.39".
- E3-E2 parallel to A-Z2.
- Cuff 18 cm/7.09" or as desired, like in the figure.

Back
- P-A like U-A 15 cm/5.91". - P-P2 1 cm/0.39".
- Draw A-P2-P5. - Measure P3-P5 like Z3-Z2.
- Q-Q2 16 cm/6.30" (2 cm/0.79" more than the front).
- Draw Q2-E4.
- Draw a curved line P3-E3 with measurements equal to the back armscye length + 3-4 cm/1.18-1.57".
- E3-E2 parallel to A-P5.
- Adjust the cuff 20 cm/7.87" (2 cm/0.79" more than the front), as in the figure.

RAGLAN OVERCOAT

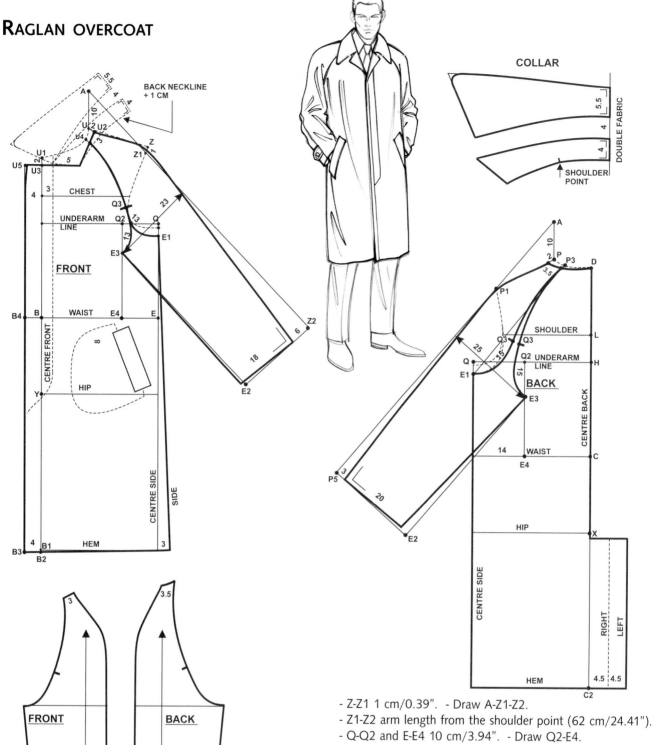

- Z-Z1 1 cm/0.39". - Draw A-Z1-Z2.
- Z1-Z2 arm length from the shoulder point (62 cm/24.41").
- Q-Q2 and E-E4 10 cm/3.94". - Draw Q2-E4.
- U-U4 3 cm/1.18".   - E1-Q3 13 cm/5.12".
- Q3-E3 like Q3-E1.
- Draw a shaped line E1-Q3-U4 and E3-Q3-E4.
- Draw the length and width desired for the sleeve.
Back
- P-A like U-A. Draw A-P1-P5 like A-Z2.
- Q-Q2 14 cm/5.51" (back sleeve width 2 cm/0.79" more than the front).
- Draw Q2-E4.
- P-P3 3.5 cm/1.38". - Q3- E1 15 cm/5.91".
- Q3-E3 like Q3-E1.
- Draw shaped lines P3-Q3-E1 and P3-Q3-E3.
- Draw the sleeve length like the front, but with 2 cm/0.79" greater in width than the front, as shown in the figure.
- Adjust the bottom of the sleeve (the cuff).
- Take up the parts and place them on the straight of the grain.

- Draw the base coat block with appropriate ease and with the desired collar and length.
- Lower the armscye by the desired amount (3-7 cm/1.18-2.76").
Front
- U-A 10 cm/3.94" (or a different amount, according to the angle desired).

DOUBLE-BREASTED RAGLAN COAT

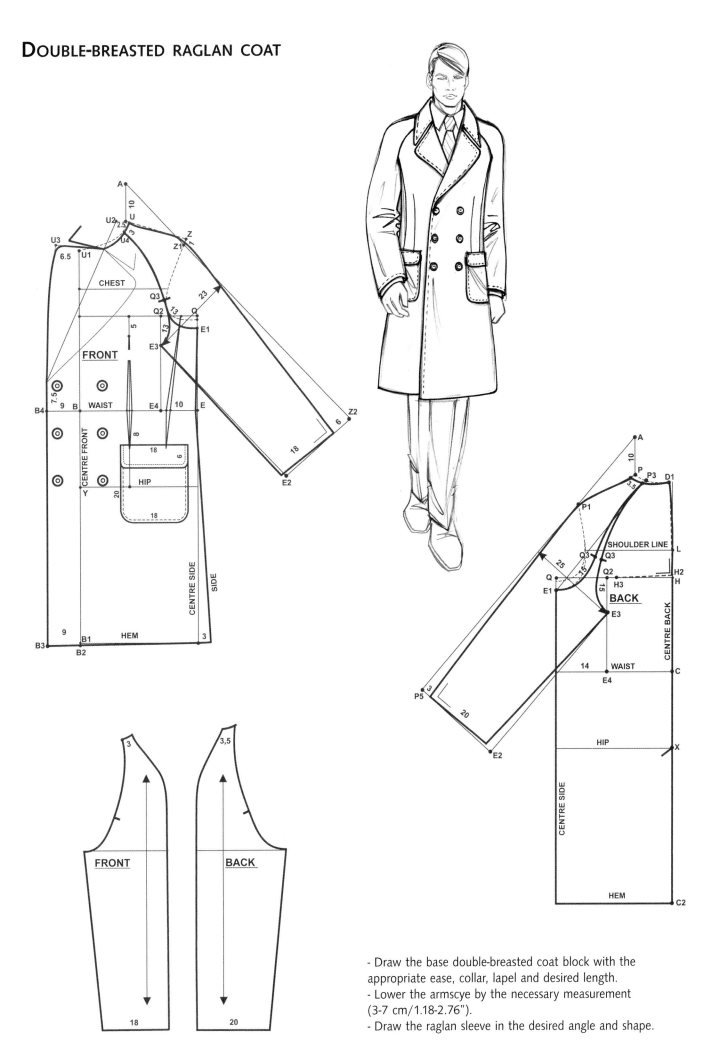

- Draw the base double-breasted coat block with the appropriate ease, collar, lapel and desired length.
- Lower the armscye by the necessary measurement (3-7 cm/1.18-2.76").
- Draw the raglan sleeve in the desired angle and shape.

MONTGOMERY

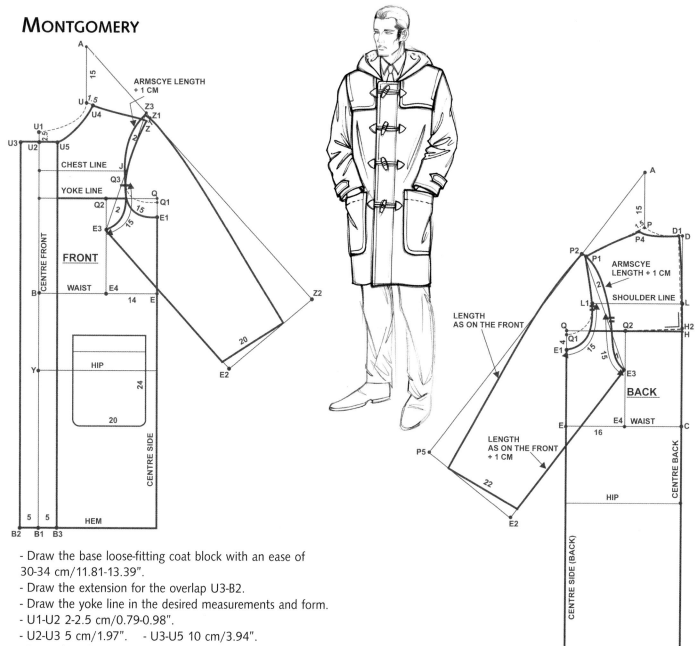

- Draw the base loose-fitting coat block with an ease of 30-34 cm/11.81-13.39".
- Draw the extension for the overlap U3-B2.
- Draw the yoke line in the desired measurements and form.
- U1-U2 2-2.5 cm/0.79-0.98".
- U2-U3 5 cm/1.97".   - U3-U5 10 cm/3.94".
- Draw the edge U3-B2-B3-U5.
- U-U4 1.5 cm/0.59". - P-P3 on the back 1.5 cm/0.59".
- Draw U4-Z and P3-P2.
- Q-E1 4 cm/1.57" or as in the pattern.
- Draw the pocket as desired.

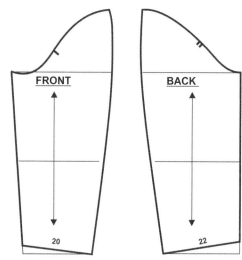

SLEEVE WITH CENTRE SEAM

SLEEVE
Front
- Raise U-A by 12-15 cm/4.72-5.91".
- Z-Z1 1 cm/0.39". - Z1-Z3 1 cm/0.39".
- Draw A-Z1-Z2.
- Z3-Z2 equal to the sleeve length from the centre shoulder.
- Q-Q2 and E-E4 9.5 cm/3.74".
- Draw Q2-E4.
- Draw a curved line Z3-E3 with measurements equal to the front armscye length + 1 cm/0.39".
- E3-E2 parallel to A-Z2.
- Adjust the bottom of the sleeve by 20 cm/7.87" or as desired.
Back
- P-A like U-A. -P2-P1 1 cm/0.39". – Draw A-P2-P5. - P2-P5 like Z1-Z2 - Q-Q2 11.5 cm/4.53" (2 cm/0.79" more than the front).
- Draw Q2-E4.
- Draw a curved line P2-E3, equal to the back armscye length + 3-4 cm/1.18-1.57".
- E3-E2 parallel to A-P5.
Adjust the cuff to 22 cm/8.66" (2 cm/0.79" more than the front), as in the figure.

Montgomery sleeve

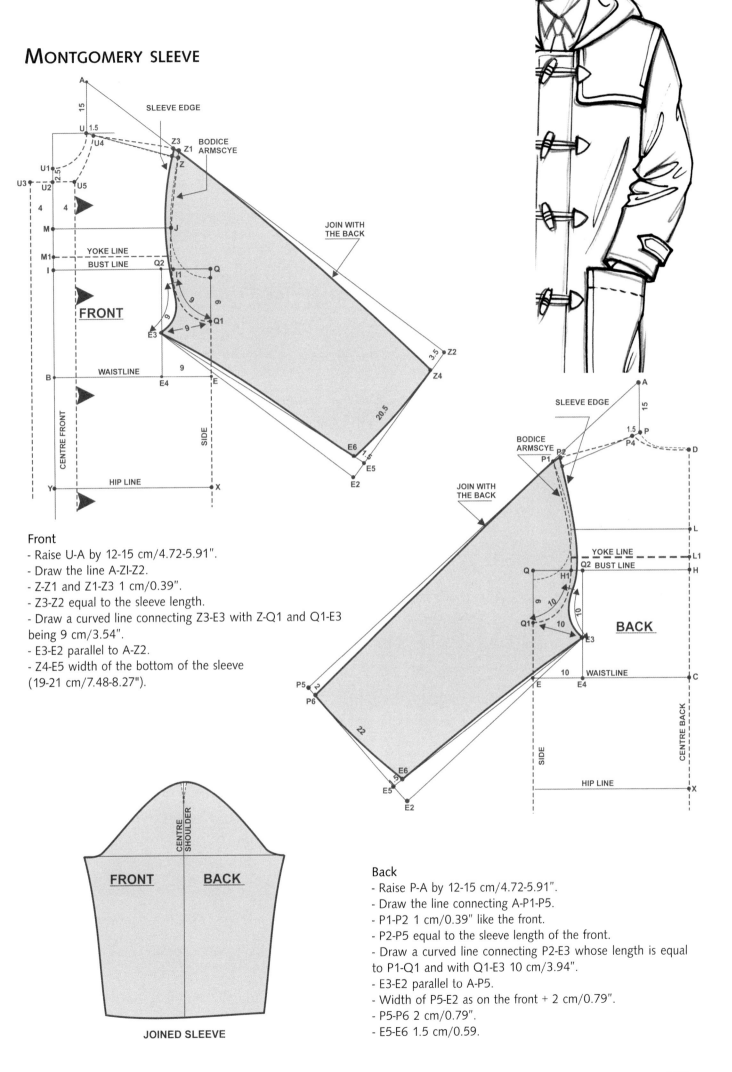

Front

- Raise U-A by 12-15 cm/4.72-5.91".
- Draw the line A-ZI-Z2.
- Z-Z1 and Z1-Z3 1 cm/0.39".
- Z3-Z2 equal to the sleeve length.
- Draw a curved line connecting Z3-E3 with Z-Q1 and Q1-E3 being 9 cm/3.54".
- E3-E2 parallel to A-Z2.
- Z4-E5 width of the bottom of the sleeve (19-21 cm/7.48-8.27").

Back

- Raise P-A by 12-15 cm/4.72-5.91".
- Draw the line connecting A-P1-P5.
- P1-P2 1 cm/0.39" like the front.
- P2-P5 equal to the sleeve length of the front.
- Draw a curved line connecting P2-E3 whose length is equal to P1-Q1 and with Q1-E3 10 cm/3.94".
- E3-E2 parallel to A-P5.
- Width of P5-E2 as on the front + 2 cm/0.79".
- P5-P6 2 cm/0.79".
- E5-E6 1.5 cm/0.59.

JOINED SLEEVE

143

CLERGYMAN'S COAT

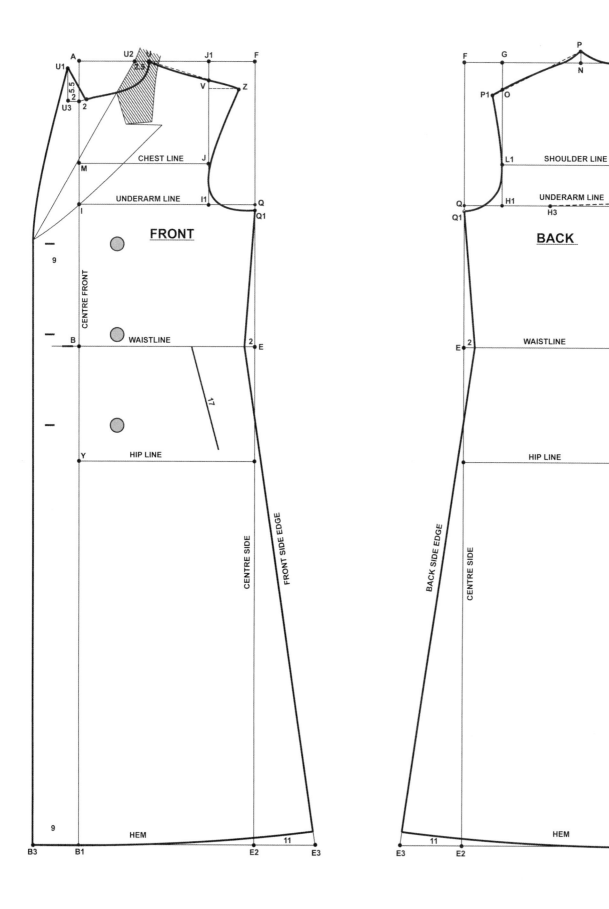

FRONT

BACK

CHEST LINE

UNDERARM LINE

WAISTLINE

HIP LINE

HEM

SHOULDER LINE

UNDERARM LINE

WAISTLINE

HIP LINE

HEM

CENTRE FRONT

CENTRE SIDE

FRONT SIDE EDGE

CENTRE BACK

CENTRE SIDE

BACK SIDE EDGE

OVERCOAT WITH A DEEP ARMSCYE

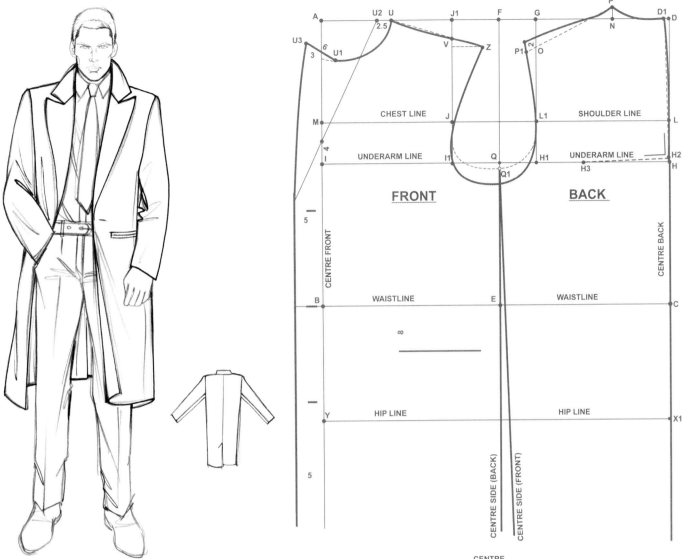

- Draw the base of the chesterfield overcoat (the loose-fitting overcoat) in the appropriate measurements and ease.
- Lower the armscye by the desired measurement.
- Raise the back shoulder point by 1.5-2 cm/0.59-0.79".

Sleeve with central seam

- Draw a rectangle A-B-E-F where:
- A-B sleeve length + 2 cm/0.79". (e.g.: 60 + 2 = 62 cm).
- A-E like the bodice sector measurement + 1/2 of the sector + ease of 2.5 cm/0.98".
- (e.g.: sector 16 + 8 = 24 + 2.5 = 26.5 cm).
- A-G like L1-P1 of the bodice + 2 cm/0.79" (18 cm/7.09").
- Draw G-X.
- Join G-E with a diagonal line.
- A-N half of A-B+2.
- Join N-P.
- A-L half of A-E.
- Draw L-L1.
- L2 half of G-E.
- Draw E-G on the back like in the figure.
- Draw E-G on the front like in the figure.
- B1-C1 sleeve width.
- B1-B2 2-2.5 cm/0.79-0.98". Adjust the width of the bottom.
- Take up the front and back sleeve and draw the entire sleeve as shown in the figure.

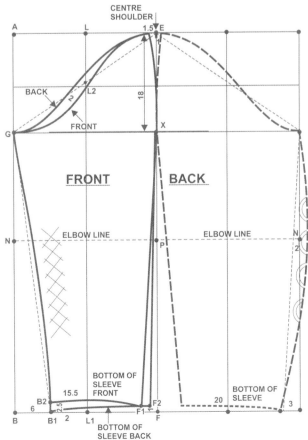

BASE PADDED HEAVY JACKET

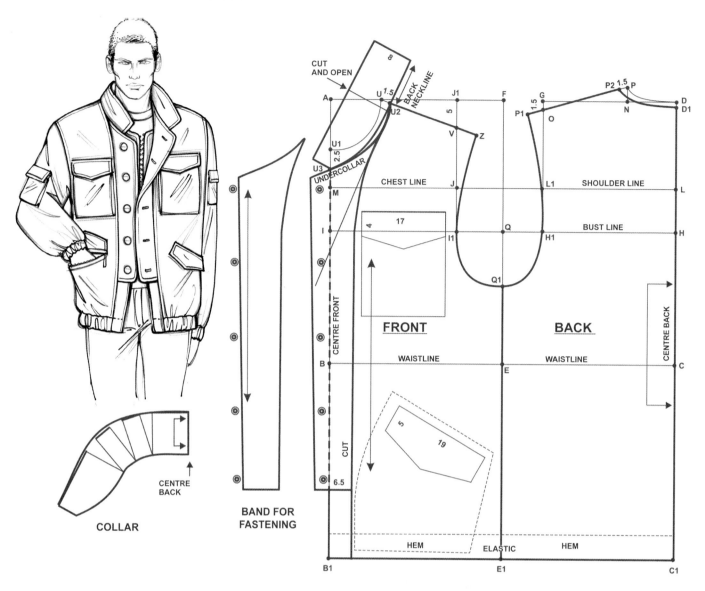

Padded jackets should have the appropriate ease according to the type of fabric used and the thickness of the padding used, in addition to the ease which allows the subject to wear a heavy sweater or dungarees underneath.

To construct this base, you must use the ease listed in the chart from the previous chapters: for the chest and hip circum-ference, 30 cm/11.81"; for the front and back waist length, 3 cm/1.18"; for the sector, 6 cm/2.36", etc.

However, it is always advisable to check all the measurements, including that of the armscye with respect to the sleeve crown and to test the sample garment before continuing on to the successive phases.

Size: 48 (men)
- Draw a rectangle A-B-C-D where:
- A-B equal to the front waist length + 3 cm/1.18" for ease (e.g.: 44 + 3 = 47 cm).
- B-C equal to the semicircumference of the chest + 1/2 ease 15 cm/5.91" (e.g.: 96 + 30 = 126 : 2 = 63 cm).
- B-E Half of B-C.
- Draw F-E (centre side).
- B-B1 elongation of the jacket as desired (28-35 cm/11.02-13.78").
- Draw B1-C1. (hem line).
- A-U 1/6 shoulder width (including 10 cm/3.94" for ease) (e.g.: 44 + 10 = 54 : 6 = 9 cm).
- Draw the arch U-U1 with a compass.
- C-D back waist length + 3 cm/1.18" ease (47 cm/18.50").
- C-H half of C-D (21.5 cm/8.46").
- Draw H-I (bust line).

- H-L 1/3 of H-D (e.g.: 21.5 : 3 = 7.2 cm).
- Draw L-M (chest and shoulder line).
- D-G 1/2 back shoulder width + 4.5-6 cm/1.77-2.36" for ease (e.g.: 44 + 4.5 = 48.5 : 2 = 24.2). (or 2/5 of B-C -1 cm/0.39")
- H-H1 like D-G 24.2 cm/9.53".
- Draw G-L1-H1.
- I-I1 like H-H1 minus 1.5 cm/0.59". (e.g.: 24.2 - 1 = 23.2 cm).
- Draw I1-J-J1.
- G-O 1.5 cm/0.59". - D-D1 1 cm/0.39".
- D-N 1/3 D-G (9 cm/3.54"). - N-P 2.5 cm/0.98".
- P-P1 shoulder length + 3-4.5 cm/1.18-1.77", according to the fabric's padding (e.g.: 15 + 4 = 19 cm).
- P-P2 1.5 cm/0.59". - Draw P2-P1.
- J1-V 5 cm/1.97".
- U-U2 1.5 cm/0.59". - U-U3 2.5 cm/0.98".
- U2-Z like P-P1. - Draw U2-Z with the measurement of P2-P1.
- Q-Q1 8-10 cm/3.15-3.94".

BASE SLEEVE FOR PADDED JACKETS

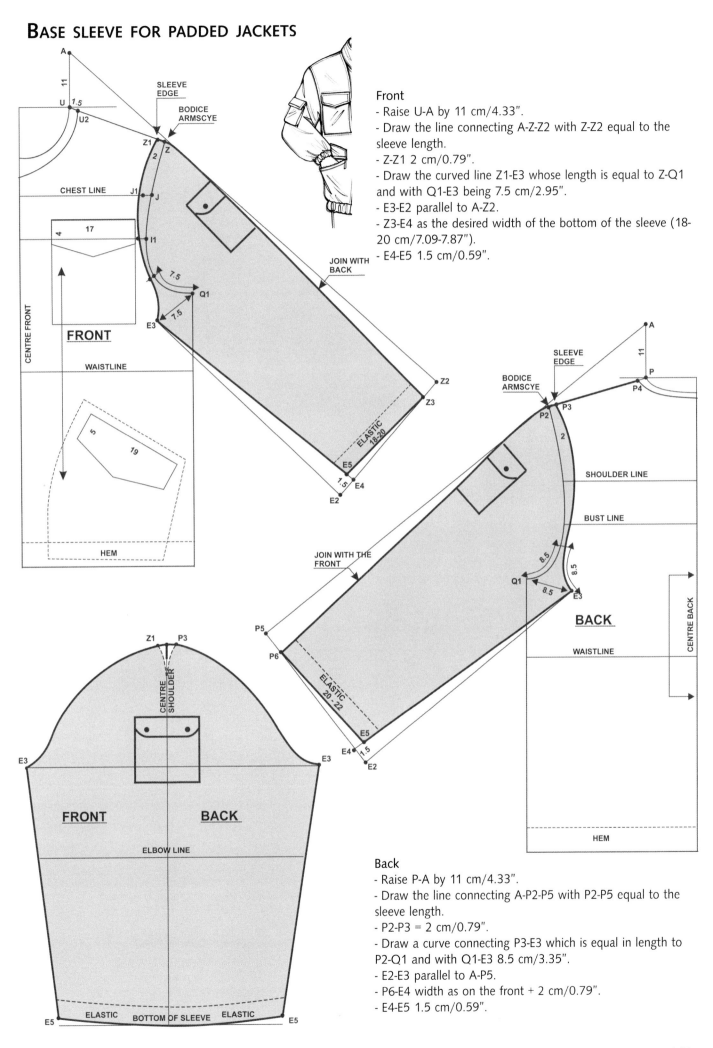

Front
- Raise U-A by 11 cm/4.33".
- Draw the line connecting A-Z-Z2 with Z-Z2 equal to the sleeve length.
- Z-Z1 2 cm/0.79".
- Draw the curved line Z1-E3 whose length is equal to Z-Q1 and with Q1-E3 being 7.5 cm/2.95".
- E3-E2 parallel to A-Z2.
- Z3-E4 as the desired width of the bottom of the sleeve (18-20 cm/7.09-7.87").
- E4-E5 1.5 cm/0.59".

Back
- Raise P-A by 11 cm/4.33".
- Draw the line connecting A-P2-P5 with P2-P5 equal to the sleeve length.
- P2-P3 = 2 cm/0.79".
- Draw a curve connecting P3-E3 which is equal in length to P2-Q1 and with Q1-E3 8.5 cm/3.35".
- E2-E3 parallel to A-P5.
- P6-E4 width as on the front + 2 cm/0.79".
- E4-E5 1.5 cm/0.59".

147

PARKA

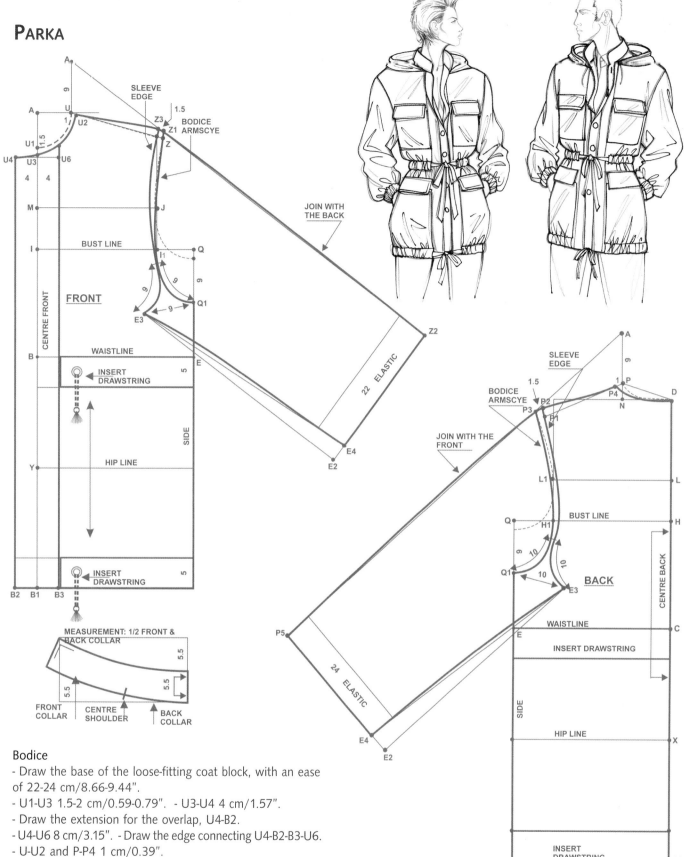

Bodice
- Draw the base of the loose-fitting coat block, with an ease of 22-24 cm/8.66-9.44".
- U1-U3 1.5-2 cm/0.59-0.79". - U3-U4 4 cm/1.57".
- Draw the extension for the overlap, U4-B2.
- U4-U6 8 cm/3.15". - Draw the edge connecting U4-B2-B3-U6.
- U-U2 and P-P4 1 cm/0.39".
- Draw U2-Z3 and P4-P3, raising them by 1.5 cm/0.59" and elongating by 1.5 cm/0.59", according to the pattern.
- Q-Q1 9 cm/3.54" or according to the pattern.
- Draw the pockets as desired (20 x 24 cm and 17x19 cm – 7.87x9.45" and 6.69x7.48").

Front sleeve
- Raise U-A by 9-11 cm/3.54-4.33". - Draw A-Z3-Z2.
- Z3-Z2 equal to the sleeve length.
- Z1-Z3 1-1.5 cm/0.39-0.59". - Draw a curved line Z3-E3 whose length is equal to Z1-Q1 and with Q1-E3 9 cm/3.54".

- E3-E2 parallel to A-Z2. - Z2-E4 width of the bottom of the sleeve as desired (20-22 cm/7.87-8.66").

Back sleeve
- Raise P-A by 9-11 cm/3.54-4.33". - Draw a line connecting A-P3-P5. - P3-P5 equal to the front sleeve length.
- P2-P3 1 cm/0.39" as on the front.
- Draw the curved line P2-E3 whose length is equal to P3-Q1 and with Q1-E3 10 cm/3.94".
- E3-E2 parallel to A-P5. - P5-E4 width as on the front + 2 cm/0.79".

TECHNICAL FOUNDATIONS

PRACTICAL THREE-PIECE SUIT CONSTRUCTION

Starting with a regular pattern, take the following steps to correctly create a three-piece sleeve:

Bodice
- A-A1 on the back 1.6 cm/0.63".
- B-B1 of the front 1.6 cm/0.63".

Sleeve
The sleeve, whose ideal centre is marked by point A and, more precisely, from the point that normally coincides with the seam running down the standard shoulder, is split vertically until the elbow. From there, it is split with a curved line towards the bottom, oriented along half of the width.
- A-A1 1.6 cm/0.63" (like B-B1 on the front).
- A1-A2 0.5 cm/0.20".
- B-B1 1.6 cm/0.63" (like A-A1 on the back).
- B1-B2 0.5 cm/0.20".
- X-X1 2.2 cm/0.87".
- K-K1 0.5 cm/0.20" (opening).
- C-C1 3 cm/1.18". - D-D1 3 cm/1.18"

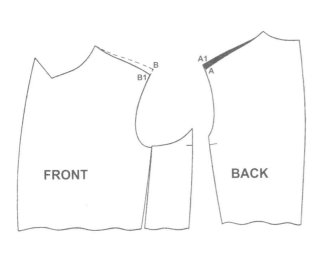

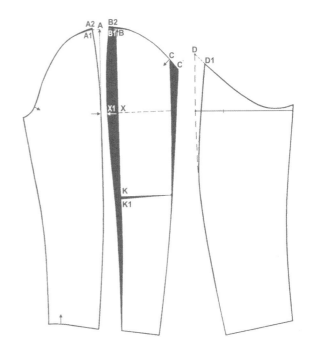

FUR COLLARS

When a classic-cut overcoat is given a fur collar, you mustn't proceed to testing the garment without having appropriately prepared for it.

A fur collar, when turned over due to its thickness, thickens the neckline and thus may potentially cause defects or ugly results.

For this reason, it is necessary to expand the place of attachment and give the collar itself a larger size. These two loosening effects combined can also be obtained by pressing the garment along the entire curve of the neckline. However, it is preferable to carry out the preventative actions as illustrated in the figure, keeping in mind that, in any case, the base of the neckline will need to be altered.

In regards to the appropriate modifications, for an average fur, you should calculate the following increases:
- 0.3 cm/0.12" for the opening in the centre back sector.
- 0.6 cm/0.24" laterally.
- 0.3 cm/0.12" on the front.

The placements are illustrated below.

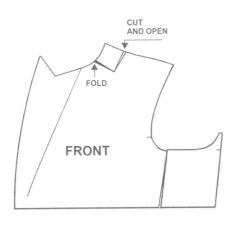

Adding the half-belt to the coat

Beginning with the straight, loose-fitting (chesterfield) overcoat, you can easily make adjustments to create a classic overcoat with a half-belt.

Of course, the resulting model will require certain working processes due to its very nature, but it will without a doubt be a highly functional model with nice features.

The transformations to make are clearly illustrated in the figure, where the dotted lines refer to the straight, sack-shaped pattern. In particular:

- B-B1 1.2 cm/0.47". Continue on a parallel line down to the bottom edge.

The resulting line must be corrected from the armscye to the bottom and for this reason you must make a pivot point on the lateral dotted line to open at the waist by the necessary measurement.

-Subsequently, compress 4 cm/1.57" along the side in parallel.

- Drop the points where the waist and hip meet by 0.5 cm/0.20".

- Elongate the bottom hem by the resulting measurement

After carefully arranging the two darts and after increasing the armscye in the underarm area, extend the front to compensate for that which was removed from the back and for that which will be required for the seams. That is:

- P-P1 6.4 cm/2.52". - At the waist: 5.6 cm/2.20". - At the hips: 6.4 cm/2.52".

- Raise the meeting point of the armscye by 0.7 cm/0.28".

- From the resulting point, move up again by 2.5 cm/0.98" to adjust for the overlapping of the sides.

Enlarging the sleeve

Sometimes a garment may require greater ease of movement in the sleeve, beyond what is normally expected. The process shown in the figure is particularly effective because it gives the item the harmonious movement desired, both for the elevation of the sleeve crown and for the forward movement of the arm. The process requires two openings with pivots of equal measures, after having temporarily overlapped the two parts by 1.2 cm/0.47". The two openings allow you to raise the piece at the same time.

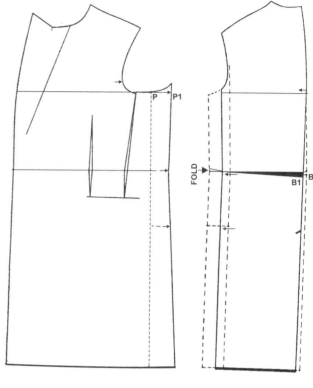

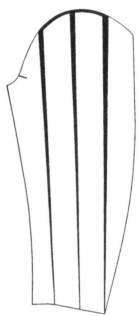

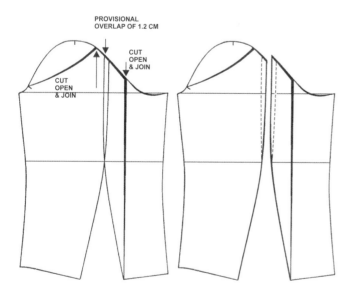

Sleeve with vertical effects

Fashion trends often feature sleeves in graceful dimensions located on well-defined verticals, which at times are altered for stylistic reasons.

The figure depicts the details of the process and how it essentially becomes automatic, deriving from the shifting of the pieces.

The shift measurements aren't shown as they depend on the fabric. In almost all cases, however, they should be moderate. An opening of 0.5 cm/0.20" is certainly enough, keeping in mind that you must signal the demarcation points on the fabric for every single opening. This is done so that you may then gather the greater looseness on them and re-establish the stability of the sleeve.

Increasing the arm height for raglan sleeves

This is a technical adjustment which may also be used for set-in sleeves. It corrects any possible undesired effects which may result from wearing the overcoat with a belt.

Even if not tightened excessively, a belt always gathers the width of a coat and forces it from a natural draping point to mostly converge at the waist. That means that the long, vertical lines involved (the sides for example), are effectively shortened.

A part of the length may come from the bottom, but it is obvious that one part, if we follow geometric logic, comes from the upper part - even more so if the armscye is particularly roomy.

The lengthening that comes from above acts perpendicularly and effects the sleeve. As a result, it causes a lowering and the elongation of the armscye, giving it an oval shape while blocking the movement of the sleeve.

For this reason, especially where the raglan sleeve pattern allows or requires the use of a belt, it is often necessary to modify the armscye with a riser which makes up for any possible defects.

Obviously the amount it to be shifted is calculated on a case by case basis, so not knowing exactly what the lift and the degree of tension imposed by the wearer's belt will be, we will try to be generous. In any case, the amount to be shifted must be of an equal measurement on the back and on the front.

Various widths at the bottom of split sleeves

The sleeves drop delicately from the position of the shoulders, which makes it difficult to establish the width of the cuff without respecting the movement of the meeting points of the single pieces of the sleeve.

This is true for the raglan sleeves and it is true for fitted sleeves with a deep armscye also.

Figure 1 and figure 2 show the process for gathering the bottom cuff. You will note that this variant directly involves a seam on the under arm, to which variations of the basic model are applied.

Figure 1 illustrates the process for tightening the bottom:

- Create a vertical cut A-B on the back and on the elbow line and overlap the bottom, opening along the under-arm elbow. To aesthetically adjust the parts and balance all the effects, move the external seam, elongating the back cuff and decreasing that in the front.

Figure 2 illustrates the process which is the inverse of the elongation of the bottom:

- Create a vertical cut A-B on the back and on the elbow line. Open along the cuff, overlapping the elbow line on the under arm to increase the breadth along the hem.

In this case, aesthetical adjustments are unnecessary on the external seam.

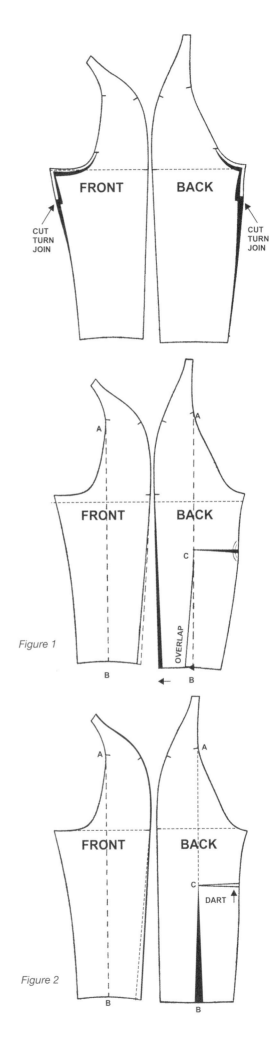

Figure 1

Figure 2

151

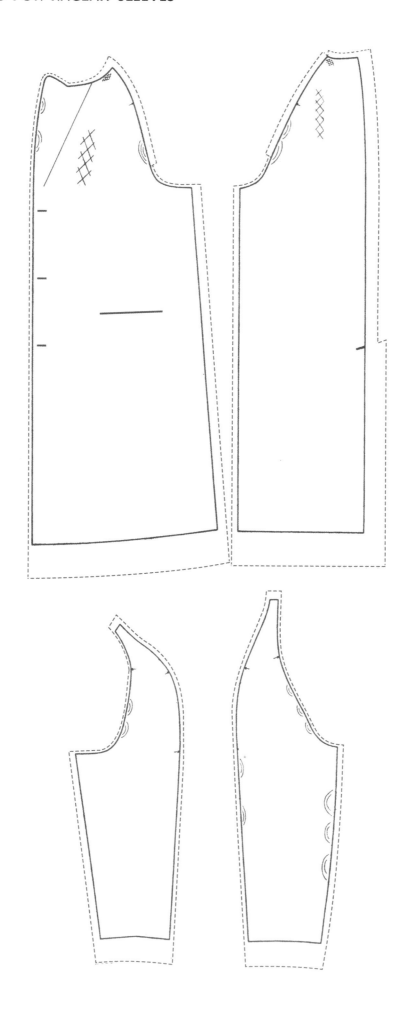

CORRECTIONS

Correcting finished garments 154
Slight abnormalities 154
Correcting the collar 156
Correcting the sides 156
Sleeve peak defects 157
Armscye defects 158
Front and back sleeve width 159
Correcting jacket defects 160
Correcting jacket neckline defects 162
Correcting overcoats 163
Abnormal body shapes 164

CORRECTING FINISHED GARMENTS

INTRODUCTION

When testing a garment, a good seamstress must take three things into consideration: 1) techniquel; 2) artistic qualities, or "good taste" 3) psychology.

Technical defects must be found and eliminated, which is done by shifting, removing or adding differently sized pieces of fabric. In this case, the seamstress must understand if the defects are caused by an imperfect cut, a defect in the way the fabric falls, poor construction or an imprecise application of linings and paddings.

Artistic requirements must go hand in hand with technical elements: a perfectly-made garment must also be artistic and in good taste.

The psychological aspect refers to the client's desires, as he or she may request capricious alterations which at times contrast with your perfectly-executed work. When unable to reconcile the client's unusual demands with the garment's technical and aesthetic demands, the seamstress must tactfully explain and persuade the client, justifying her responses.

The main causes of defects are:

1) Lack or deviation of the way garment drapes and the balance of the body.

2) Forces acting upon the fabric and which change its shape, creating folds which are mostly slanted.

3) Inertia due to excess fabric which creates longitudinal and, at times, even horizontal folds.

The most common force that may have a negative effect on a garment is the weight of the fabric itself. It may in fact produce deformations and cause the garment fall incorrectly.

These forces compete with each other if they converge on one point; they are divergent if they depart from one point but act in different directions; they are conspiring if they are parallel; and contrary if they move in opposite directions. The inertia or state of rest does not change unless acted upon by an outside force.

How to check the draping

While fabric mainly falls from the shoulders in menswear, for womenswear, the garment must be draped over the shoulders and the bust, points which are almost always balanced.

To get a clear, practical idea about draping, place a piece of fabric over the woman's body. The weft and warp lines must form straight lines in the most prominent points of the shoulder and the bust.

If you do not find these straight lines and the corresponding right angles of the vertical thread with the horizontal one, the garment will not drape correctly due to the wearer's flaws.

At this point, it is worth nothing that the irregularity of the shoulders on the horizontal line due to height and thickness will be reflected on the bust and the hips.

Thus, if the right shoulder is lower than the left, the right bust and hip will be lower than the left.

It is not uncommon to find that a lack of attention when making the slack points before cutting and the related meeting points (or perpendicular points) will produce notable changes of position and thus noticeable defects in the way the item drapes.

The rules for precision in this simple, yet delicate, process are: 1) Put a few pins along the marks to ensure the fabric, which is folded over in two, remains stable; 2) Sew with a threaded straight needle (never a curved one) on the flat surface of the table, (not on your lap), without placing your hands under the fabric, starting from above (never below) and without pressing with the other hand, which may shift the placement of one piece of fabric over the other, especially when using velvet, silk, etc.

SLIGHT ABNORMALITIES

We'll begin our look at the correction of finished garments by presenting the most common defects which result from easily concealable, slight physical irregularities. With the examples shown here, you can see the simple, practical system to introduce more graceful elements, or simply those with a normal appearance, to garments worn by women with varied body shapes.

1) Figure with a normal waist.

2) Figure with a short waist and high hips: correct by lowering the waistline or by adding a motif or using the appropriate pattern.

3) Figure with a long waist and short hips: correct by raising the waistline.

1) Figure with narrow shoulders and wide hips:
Correct by widening the shoulders of the shirt or dress and narrowing the sides of the skirt towards the front, through small pleats.

2) Wide shoulders and narrow hips:
Correct by shifting the sleeve attachment inwards and widening the hips with pockets or similar shapes.

3) Short:
To make a short-statured person seem slimmer and longer, make sure that the characterising lines of the garment are mostly vertical and choose a fabric in a pattern that is also vertical.

4) Too slim:
To give extremely slim figures a bit more volume, make sure that the garment has horizontal elements and choose a fabric with a horizontal pattern.

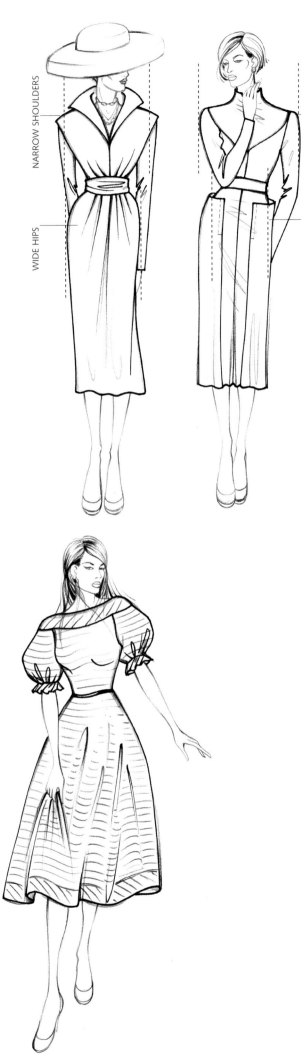

155

CORRECTING THE COLLAR

This defect is caused by the collar being excessively snug and there being too much fabric along the length of the bodice near the neckline. We outline two ways to correct this below.

1) During the last test of the garment, note that under the attachment point of the collar there are horizontal creases which start halfway on the back end towards the shoulder. To eliminate the defect, it is necessary to take the garment up again, gather the folds with pins, remove the collar and un-stitch the shoulder and part of the sleeve. Place a sheet of paper on top and draw, using the tracing wheel, the new neckline and proper shoulder as shown in the illustration.

2) Unstitch the collar and shoulder and shorten the back section near the collar by 1.5 cm/0.59" while elongating the neckline by 0.5 cm/0.20" to 1 cm/0.39", as necessary. The dotted line in the illustration indicates the modification to make.

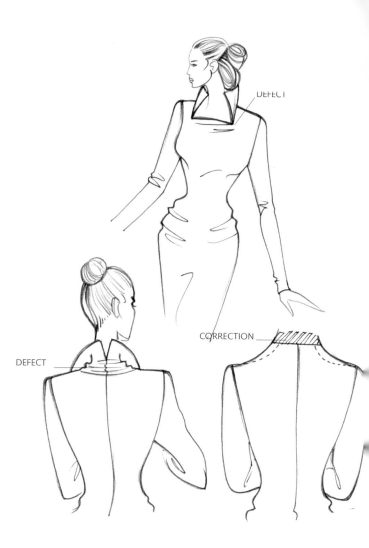

CORRECTING THE SIDES

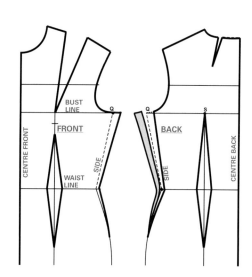

The division of the side with respect to the total circumference of the bust mainly depends on the shape of the wearer's figure. If the seam line along the side is shifted too far forward, you will need to consider three possible defects:

1) Incorrect position of the side seam.
2) The back is too big and the front is correct.
3) The front is too small and the back is correct.

On the figure, the side seam should be centred along the side or slightly shifted towards the back. It should be perfectly vertical.

If the seam on the upper portion is pulling towards the front, it's necessary to move point Q towards the back in the amount necessary to straighten the line.

Shifting towards the back of the side at point Q isn't a common correction, but it may be necessary for some figures, for example, for robust people with prominent busts, or for small figures with broad chests and backs but who are very small underneath the arms.

SLEEVE PEAK DEFECTS

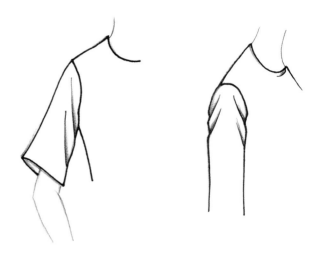

SLEEVE PEAK IS TOO LOW

If the peak of the sleeve is too low, the sleeve will pull downward at the edge of the shoulder and diagonal creases will form in both directions. For short sleeves, the lower edge of the front will tend to move away from the arm. In addition, if it pulls away too much, it will affect the under part of the arm and create a sleeve which appears too loose.

When the defect isn't very pronounced and is visible mostly only in the upper part, the problem can generally be resolved by extending the crown in the highest point. If, however, the peak of the crown doesn't have enough of a margin, it is also often necessary to take up the part under the arm again.

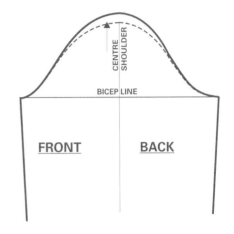

SLEEVE PEAK IS TOO HIGH

This is the opposite defect as the previous one, caused by too high of a sleeve crown. It may be manifested in various ways depending on the width and type of sleeve (wide, tight or fitted). In general, this type of excess may create one or more horizontal folds which constrict and press on the upper part of the arm when raised or moved forward. The defect may not always be visible, especially when the arm is lowered. During the fitting test, however, it is useful to evaluate the situation and decide whether to intervene or not. Keep in mind that sleeves with crowns that are too high and too tight often tend to rip more easily in the recess below the arm.

To correct this defect, you'll need to lower the peak of the sleeve and connect the old line with the new one. You'll also need to consider that the length of the sleeve which is absorbed into the upper portion needs to be added along the cuff, thus increasing the length of the armscye.

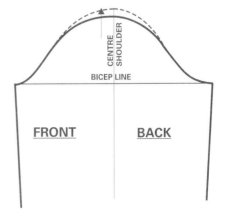

Armscye defects

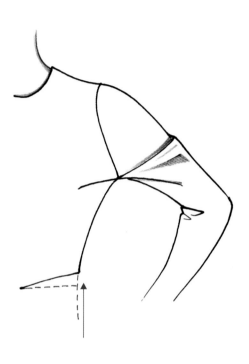

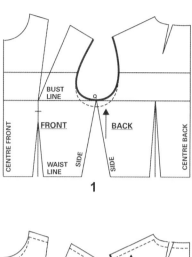

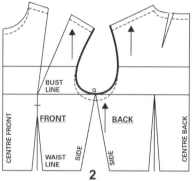

Armscye which is too deep

This defect is found when the armscye is expanded, sinking it too deeply into the side seams of the bodice. As it is a serious defect, it often requires substantial modifications.

The entire garment pulls when the arm is moved, creating tight folds on the upper part of the sleeve. The sleeve is, in turn, very uncomfortable and limits movement. The base of figure 1 illustrates the necessary correction: the armscye must be raised. However, when the seam allowances are not wide enough, the only way to resolve this problem is to cut the entire upper part of the bodice anew, raising it from the shoulders (based on figure 2). This correction, possible or not, is always a difficult modification to make.

Whenever the armscye is lowered, it is necessary to carefully check the length of the side in order to avoid shortening it too much, to the point which after having sewn the sleeve, it pulls when raising the arm. It is worth mentioning that this defect may sometimes be missed in loose-fitting garments and overcoats (if it isn't too excessive). This is because when the sleeve

is raised, the entire garment moves freely enough then returns back to position.

However, the situation changes entirely when the bodice is a bit tighter or snug at the waist or when worn with a tight belt. In fact, the armscye might rip or the seams might fray along the underarm.

Armscye which is too small

We rarely think of a small armscye as a defect as we tend to believe it may always be enlarged. However, complications relating to its adaptation may arise when the sleeve is attached and finished. In this case, it isn't very easy to correct a tight armscye, as it is hard to adapt the sleeve to an enlarged armscye once the wrist has already been finished and the seam margins trimmed: the sleeve, for example, may pull under the arm as a consequence of the modification.

FRONT AND BACK SLEEVE WIDTH

During the test, it's necessary to properly check the sides of the sleeves to make sure they fall straight, without folds or unnecessary volumes, aside from lines created by movement. It is worth mentioning a few defects:
1) Volume along the front of the sleeve.
2) Volume along the back of the sleeve.

VOLUME ALONG THE FRONT OF THE SLEEVE

This defect is visible through the soft folds which form along the front part of the sleeve.
Correct as follows:
- Remove the seam along the armscye and raise it at point "I".
- Raise the front part by 0.5 cm/0.20" or more, until the sleeve falls perfectly vertical.
This correction will flatten and create a deeper indentation on the front of the sleeve's armscye.

VOLUME ALONG THE BACK OF THE SLEEVE

When soft folds are created on the back of the sleeve, almost down to the elbow, correct as follows:
- Raise the back portion. Doing so will hollow out more of the crown and flatten the sleeve.
- Remove the seam of the armscye approximately 8 cm/3.15" above and below point E before proceeding with the rest of the correction. As point E is lowered, it shortens the back line and thus raises it. Before sewing, check that the sleeve is comfortable with the arm raised. In general, the sleeve pulls more along the back line and the back of the bodice.

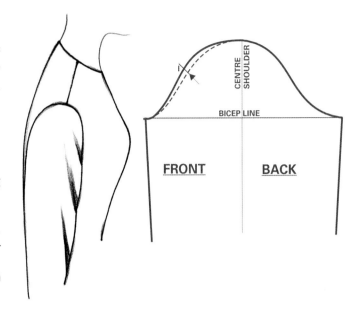

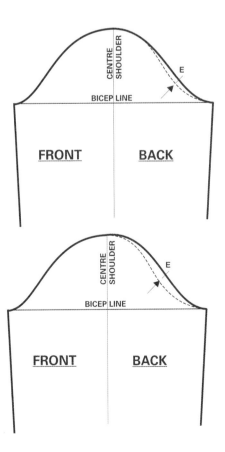

CORRECTING JACKET DEFECTS

JACKET DEFECTS ON THE SIDES ABOVE THE WAIST
DUE TO IMPROPER CUTS
To correct: Pin the folds, remove the seam of the sleeve and undersleeve. Place the pattern over the jacket, laid flat, and give it the new contour, as shown in the illustration.

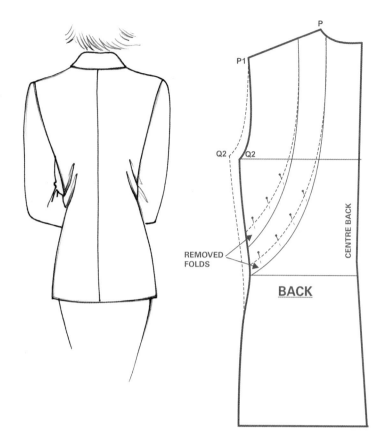

JACKET WITH THE LEFT SHOULDER LOWER THAN THE RIGHT
With a lower left shoulder, the entire bodice is angled towards the left. As a consequence, the collar is shifted towards the left shoulder, as is the seam on the centre back, creating oblique folds which extend from the waist to the shoulder blade.

To correct: Remove the seams on the shoulder, the collar, the cuff, the side, the centre back seam and the sleeve
Back: From the centre back seam, move point D inward by 1 cm/0.39", straightening out the seams until the waist. From D1, take up the neckline; lower the 2nd point of the shoulder, P1, by 1.5 cm/0.59". Join P2 and P3 to determine the shoulder seam. Lower the seam line under the arm by 1.5 cm/0.59" and move it out by 1 cm/0.39"; join Q3 with the new waist point, W1. Lower the bottom hem in the same measurement used to correct the upper.

Front: Lower the shoulder at point U on the neckline by 1 cm/0.39"; extend outward from this point by 1.5 cm/0.59", U5. From the shoulder drop down 1.5 cm/0.59" onto the armscye and move inward by 1.5 cm/0.59", point Z2. On the underarm seam line, drop down by 1.5 cm/0.59" and shift back by 1 cm/0.39"; join Q3 and Z2 and create a new shoulder seam, new armscye and new waist point. Expand the bottom front as already done on the back. Carry out the same lowering on the front half to create the new neckline, the new break point and the lapel. The abnormality due to the deviation of the spine is reflected on the left side, where you will notice a deficiency which is corrected by moving the seam line inwards in proportion to the defect. On the right side, however, you must bring the seam line outwards.

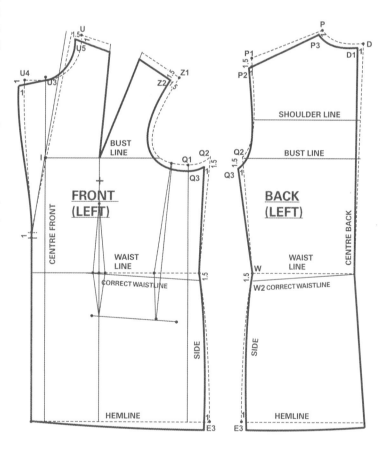

Finished jacket with a lower right shoulder

A finished jacket with a low right shoulder will have folds above the waist and the underarm area, towards the shoulder blade and towards the seam with the front half. The same folds will be seen on the front underarm area, while from the waist down everything appears normal.

In addition to the low shoulder defect, uneven shoulders may present a tight shoulder and a prominent side. Because it is the right shoulder which is low, the entire bodice is angled towards the right, producing the same folds as mentioned above, caused by the two halves being uneven.

To eliminate this defect, proceed as follows:
- With the subject wearing the jacket, pin the folds on the back and the front.

- Once the subject removes the jacket, place a sheet of paper over the front and, making sure that the pinned part won't move over the surface of the table, use the tracing wheel to create a contour around the outline and create the correction. Then, once you've removed the pins, place the correct pattern over the jacket, creating the appropriate outlines on the fabric. As shown in the illustration of the back, lower Q by 4 cm/1.57" along the underarm line, and from D by 8 cm/3.15" on the centre back. Joining D2-Q5, you will create a line where the fold was, which starts from 2 cm/0.79" and ends at zero at D2.

It is understood that in this case the fold is 2 cm/0.79" wide, but it could be a different number, even three, according to the defect. The same steps should be taken to correct the front.

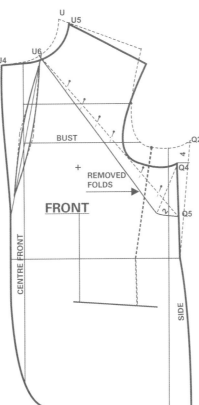

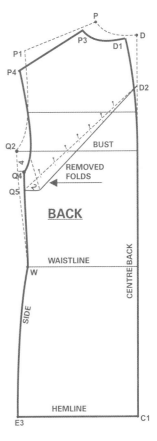

Finished jacket with horizontal folds on the back

The finished jacket has a few horizontal folds on the back, which are caused by a tight underarm area towards the armscye and a greater length on the centre back.

To correct: Remove the seam on the collar, shoulder, the part of the sleeve towards the underarm, the centre back seam and the side panel. Take up the excess fabric on the centre back with pins and elongate along the seam of the side panel.

By doing so, you will eliminate the excess length and tightness.

161

CORRECTING JACKET NECKLINE DEFECTS

JACKET MIS-SIZED ON THE FRONT AND BACK NECKLINE

This defect is also found on subjects who don't have a curve in their backs.

To correct: On the completed jacket, you can see that the line of the back of the neck is poorly positioned. If there is an excess of fabric, after removing the seams on the collar and the shoulder, correct by shifting the part upwards until the defect is eliminated.

If there is a shortage of fabric, remove the seam, including that of the underarm and the side. Place the paper pattern on the front and back of the jacket, laying it on a flat surface. Complete the correction, bringing the amount of fabric necessary to eliminate the defect to the top. The jacket will be shorter as the increase in fabric towards the top will be made at the detriment of the bottom.

You will notice that the paper pattern provides for the modification, raising it by 1 cm/0.39" on the neckline and the shoulder and by 0.5 cm/0.20" along the front of the shoulder.

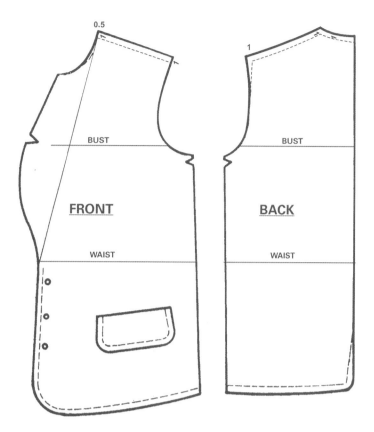

FINISHED JACKET WHICH LACKS STRUCTURE ON THE FRONT NECKLINE AND WHICH HAS DIAGONAL FOLDS, due to an incorrect cut or too tight of a collar.

To correct: Remove the seam of the collar, the shoulder and the sleeve. Take up the excess fabric with pins. Remove 2 cm/0.79" of the material along the shoulder and increase by 1.5 cm/0.59" towards the neckline. Moving most of the fabric towards the armscye, remove the amount that has been added to the neckline at the end of the shoulder and eliminate the diagonal folds. The wrinkles around the underarm area will disappear with the new armscye.

Once you have removed the above defect, the problem of the front neckline remains. This should be remedied with a small insert, which is covered by the lapel and thus invisible. In the same figure, you will note that the lapels do not lay flat. Correct this defect by raising the shoulder and then lowering it only towards the neckline.

When the diagonal folds on the front extend towards the back, proceed with the correction by lowering the shoulder on the back. When the diagonal folds are found on the back neckline, fix them by straightening the upper part of the back centre seam through the appropriate use of a hot press.

CORRECTING OVERCOATS

TAILORED OVERCOATS CEÑIDO, LONG IN THE WAIST AND
WITH FOLDS IN THE BACK

To correct: Gather the folds with pins, forming one single
fold.
- Place a sheet of paper under the overcoat and mark the
correction to be made on the paper.
- Remove the seams on the sleeve, the collar, the side and
the centre back.
- After removing the pins, place the correct pattern over the
coat and mark the corrections to be made on the fabric.
If this defect is seen on a normal subject, it will be enough
to remove the seams and shift the extra fabric towards the
shoulder.

OVERCOAT WITH THE OUTER LAYER FINISHED, MIS-SIZED AT
THE CENTRE-FRONT NECKLINE AND THE SHOULDER, AND
WHICH CROSSES OVER AT THE FRONT HEM (defects caused by
incorrect cut or from the client's abnormal body shape).

If the overcoat isn't cut perfectly perpendicular according to
the posture and confirmation of the subject, the two sides
of the front will overlap along the bottom front when but-
toned.
To correct: Remove the seam along the neckline, the shoulder, the sleeve and the sides and allow the necessary amount of fabric to drop down at the collar point and the shoulder seam until the garment falls as it should. If there isn't
enough fabric at the neckline and the shoulder, raise the
front and bring the normal length back to the bottom using
the seam allowances.

ABNORMAL BODY SHAPES

A LOOK AT THE RESULTING ALTERATIONS

Subject with a wide (compressed) lower body
This subject's leg is pushed towards the rib cage, which decreases his or her height in the same amount as the displacement. The shoulders maintain a natural tilt, while the circumference of the waist is increased due to the compression which takes place (caused by the lowering of the rib cage).

Subject with a wide (compressed) upper body
This subject has shoulders as high as the measurement of the compression, that is, stocky. This decreases the height of the subject, while causing the scapular head to protrude.

Subjects with a thin build
Minimal measurements for all circumferences, portions or sectors of width and length compared to the chest and to his or her height.

Subjects with a stocky build
Larger measurements for all circumferences, portions or sectors of width and length compared to the chest and to his or her height.

Subjects with a heavy build
These subjects have fat tissue throughout the body and have larger measurements for all circumferences, portions or sectors of width and length compared to the chest in proportion to height. The peak of the bust increases by 1/3 in excess of the front of the chest; the curve of the back increases equally to the excess of the back minus 1/3 of the excess of the neck measurement.

Subject with a large waist
This subject's belly (at its widest part) is increased by 1/3 of the excess found at the waist.

Subject with a narrow waist
This subject's belly (at its widest part) is decreased by 1/3 of the difference found at the waist.

Subject with a small chest
The peak of the chest is decreased in an amount equal to the difference found on the front chest area; increase the peak of the belly and a reduce the chest in a corresponding measurement.

Subject with small arms
The chest appears more elliptical; reduce the chest on the lateral section in a measurement equal to the reduction of the arm diameter.

Subject with small hips
Reduced peak of the buttock corresponding to half of the difference in the hip.

Subject with large arms
This subject's chest appears less elliptical; increase the chest on the lateral sector in equal measurement to the excess found on the diameter of the arm.

Subject with an athletic chest
This subject has an increased chest measurement in that the front part of the chest is exceptionally large. The peak of the chest is increased in an equal measurement while the effect of the peak of the belly is reduced in a measurement equal to the peak of the chest.

Subject with protruding shoulder blades
This subject has a deepened groove of the centre back due to the excess of the peaks of the shoulder blades. The back chest sector increases by half of the excess of the peak of the shoulder blades, while the chest increases in a corresponding measurement.

Subject with a protruding chest
This subject has an increased chest circumference depending on how excessive the front chest sector is. The peak of the chest increases by two times the excess of the front chest sector, while the effect of the peak of the belly is reduced.

Subject with protruding shoulders
This subject has almost no groove in the centre of the back and the chest increases according to how excessive the rear chest section is. The spinal curve increases by 5 times the excess of the back chest sector.

Subject with large back muscles
Increase the chest by the excess amount on the back.

Subject with abnormally sized hips.
First case: the subject has prominent buttocks; the peak of the side of the hips is reduced by half of the increase on the buttock.
Second case: the subject has scarcer buttocks; the peak of the side of the hips increases by half of the reduction on the buttock.

Subject with low shoulders
The back sector will be shorter by a measurement equal to the amount the shoulders are lowered; decrease the front sector in a measurement equal to the amount the shoulders are lowered; decrease the chest 2 times the amount the shoulders are lowered; increase the back thoracic sector for the subsequently protruding shoulder blade; decrease the waist in a measurement equal to the amount the shoulder is lowered; increase the chest by the amount the shoulder blade protrudes.

Subject with athletic shoulders
This back section is increased by a measurement equal to the increased height of the shoulders; the front section is increased by a measurement equal to the increased height of the shoulders; increase the chest by twice the shoulder height; decrease the effect of the protruding shoulder blade.

Subject with athletic neck
Alter the angle of the shoulder by half of the excess found on the diameter of the neck; reduce the curve of the back in a measurement equal to the excess found on the diameter of the neck.

Subject with a forward-placed arm
The protrusion of the humerus is increased by a measurement equal to the forward placement of the arm; reduce the angle of the shoulder by half of the forward-placement of the humerus; reduce the effect of the protruding shoulder blade; increase the back thoracic sector equal to the forward placement of the arm; reduce the front thoracic sector equal to the forward placement of the arm; reduce the peak of the chest by half of the forward placement of the arm; reduce the chest by the same amount as the peak of the chest; increase the effect of the peak of the stomach by the same amount that the peak of the chest was reduced; increase the curve of the back by the same amount that the chest was reduced.

Subject with a rear-placed arm
This subject will have a pronounced groove in the centre of the back, while the protrusion of the shoulder blade will be reduced; reduce the angle of the shoulder by half of the amount which the arm is moved back; reduce the back thoracic sector by a measurement equal to the amount which the arm is moved back; increase the front thoracic sector by an amount equal to the rear placement of the arm; increase the peak of the chest by half of the amount which the arm is moved back; reduce the curve of the back by half of the amount which the arm is moved back; the chest requires no alterations; reduce the curve of the stomach by the same amount as the chest peak.

Subject with a hunched back
The curve of the back is increased in a measurement equal to the curvature; increase the back thoracic sector by 1/4 of the curvature; reduce the front thoracic sector by 1/4 of the curvature.

Subject with a hollow back
The curve of the back is reduced by an amount equal to the displacement; increase the front thoracic sector by 1/4 of the displacement; reduce the back thoracic sector by 1/4 of the displacement; reduce the effect of the protruding shoulder blade; reduce the angle of the shoulder by 1/8 of the displacement.

Subject with an inverted waist
The peak of the stomach protrudes by a measurement equal to the displacement; increase the front thoracic sector by half of the displacement; reduce the rear thoracic sector by 1/4 of the displacement; increase the chest by 1/4 of displacement; reduce the effect of the curve of the back by a measurement equal to the displacement; reduce the angle of the shoulder by 1/8 of the displacement.

Subject with a shifted waist
This subject has one low shoulder with a corresponding contracted thorax, and one high shoulder with a corresponding expanded waist.

Subject with wide hips
This subject has buttocks which are half of the excess of the hips.

Subject with inverted hips
This subject has a reduced peak of the buttock equal to the displacement.

Subject with curved hips
This subject has an increased peak of the buttocks equal to the curvature.

Subject with shifted hips
This subject has a low side and a high side displaced in equal measure; reduce the peak on the low side, increase the peak on the high side.

PATTERN SPREADING AND LAYOUT

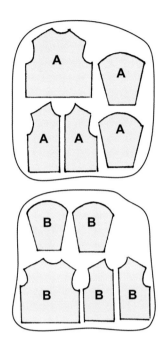

Spreading 166
Spreading techniques 167
Spreading symbols 168
Spreading machines 169
Cutting 170
Parcel formation 171

Spreading

Introduction

The layout or spreading of the pattern on the fabric is an operation carried out when making a series of garments. The rolls of fabric are un-rolled and placed on a table made just for cutting the layers, placed one over the other, and aligned along the sides and the top. This group of layers or plies, called a lay, makes it possible to cut multiple pattern pieces at the same time, reducing production time and guaranteeing that all pieces are consistent.

Spreading methods

You may layout or spread the fabric by hand, with a table and a manual or automated spreading machine. The latter provides continuous fabric spreading for fabric in rolls, layers, tubes or fabric that has been opened.

Hand spreading

When hand spreading, the plies are pulled manually along the cutting table, stacked, lined up and then cut as required. This system may be supported by mechanised equipment to easily unroll and cut the pieces of fabric. Hand spreading is common in small companies and is suitable for creating short plies of fabric, or when frequent changes in the colour or type of fabric are required.

Spreading with a manual spreading machine

With this method, the rolls are placed in a specifically designed holder on the spreading machine and unrolled manually by moving the machine back and forth. This type of spreader, also often used by small clothing producers, smooths each layer and aligns the fabric's edges. It is particularly useful when working with long, wide plies and when the rolls of fabric are changed less frequently.

Spreading with an automated spreading machine

These spreading machines are fully automated and computerised, and are used by large garment production companies. They provide highly precise, rapid spreading and cutting. In their basic configuration, they can be equipped with a traditional bar to hold the roll, but also with a cradle-feeding load mechanism, thus eliminating the need for a bar. They may also have a threading device that allows the fabric to be positioned automatically through the feed rollers until the cutter; a system for layering the fabric face to face and back to back; a cutting program; a cutting program with a meter-counter; meter-counter; rotating turret; a lay counter, etc. For knitwear taken from plies of fabric with a separating thread and for small pieces of knitwear, the stacking operation isn't done by machine. Such small size pieces of fabric are usually spread by hand.

In order to carry out the spreading in a logical way, guaranteeing high quality garments, the fabric should have already undergone the size stabilisation process beforehand, as well as have been checked for defects.

It is necessary to stabilise the size of the fabric so that the fabric doesn't arrive to the spreader with abnormal tension which may produce defects (which can be quite significant). All fabric has a certain amount of "springback", and it is necessary to ensure that the fabric will not shrink during the steps that come after spreading and cutting.

One mustn't think that a pre-existing tension in the fabric can be eliminated during spreading.

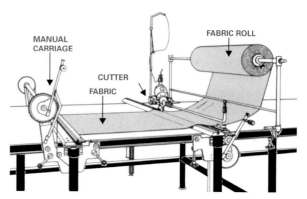

Manual spreader

Travelling spreader carriage

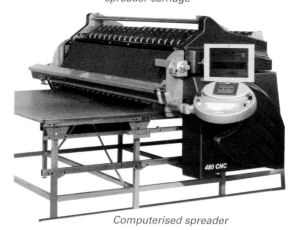

Computerised spreader

It's a good idea to remember that a proper spreader, that is, a machine equipped with an efficient fabric feeding mechanism, spreads the fabric with the same tension that it had before being put in the machine. For tubular fabrics, the stabilisation phase serves to guarantee that the height of the fabric is consistent along the entire piece. Checking for defects is meant to streamline the spreading operation and to avoid the possibility that a defect goes unnoticed before or during the spreading or that it passes unobserved until the final inspection of the finished garment. Checking for defects has yet another essential function: it ensures that the fabric is stored in the warehouse in the best condition possible, either rolled up or folded in layers.

When fabric is folded into layers as it is checked for defects, it isn't exposed to tension as when rolled, but there is the chance that the colour will be altered along the folds.

Spreading techniques

Methods for layering the fabric
The fabric may be placed in the following types of layers:
- A single ply, when only one piece of fabric is necessary (for example, to cut one pattern at a time);
- A lay: when the various plies of fabric are piled one on top of the other;
- A stepped lay: when the lay is made up of plies of fabric in various lengths, for example when there are multiple cuts in different quantities.

Spreading or layering systems
In clothing production, fabric may be spread by use of various systems, according to the characteristics of the fabric and the garment to be made:
- Zig-zag spreading; - Spreading with front side against back; - Spreading with front to front or back to back.

Zig-zag spreading
In zig-zag spreading, one layer of fabric is placed over another, without cutting to separate one layer from the next at each end of the lay. With this spreading system, the spread layers are placed 'face to face'. This means that the right side of the fabric faces the right side of the layer before it, and the knits point in opposite directions.

This spreading system is commonly used to make underwear and cut outer garments which do not require the knit or the nap of the fabric to be aligned. Characteristics of zig-zag spreading are:

1) It does not respect knit or nap orientation.

2) The right and left parts of the garment are made by superimposing the fabric in a single pack.

3) The right and left parts are perfectly equal as they are cut in a single operation.

4) Because the left and right pieces of the same garment are cut far away from each other on the strip of fabric, according to the length of the ply, it is possible that the pieces will have slight colour variations.

5) This is the quickest spreading method.

Spreading fabric 'face up'
Fabric spread with the face up (the right side against the back) requires that the plies of fabric are cut between one layer and the next.

With this spreading system, after the separating cut is completed at the edge of the ply, the fabric is brought back to the head of the ply (where the spreading began on the previous layer) without stretching it.

In this case, the knit or the top of the fabric are all facing the same direction.

This spreading system is used when it's necessary to see the top of the fabric, the nap or the knit, and to also separate the right and left parts into two distinct packs. Characteristics of spreading with the right side against the back:

1) The head or top of the fabric, knit or nap are always facing the same direction.

2) The right and left parts are separated into two different packs.

3) The right and left parts may differ, in that they are cut in two different operations.

4) The tonality and colour is generally the same, as the parts of the same garment are generally located next to each other.

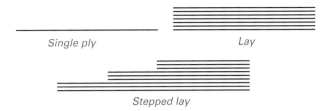

Single ply   *Lay*

Stepped lay

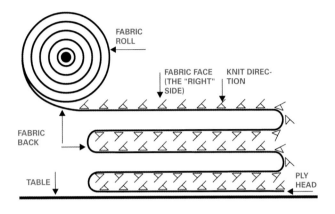

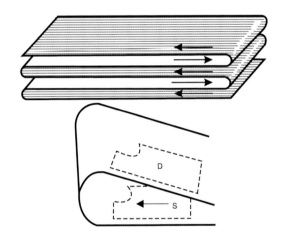

Zig-zag spreading

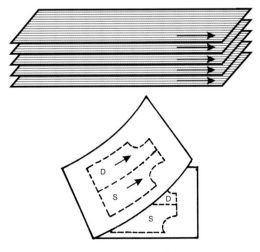

Face up spreading

5) It requires almost double the time of zig-zag spreading.

167

SPREADING SYMBOLS

Spreading fabric 'face to face'

To spread fabric with the two right sides facing each other (face to face), the same process is followed as for fabric which is 'face up' (i.e., with fabric stacked with all faces pointed in the same direction), with one difference: the roll of fabric is rotated 180 degrees before each ply is spread.

The coupling of the layers of fabric is analogous to the coupling of zig-zag spreading, but differs in that the direction of the nap or knit surface always has the same orientation.

This spreading method is mainly chosen based on the following factors: 1) the fabric's characteristics, in terms of the orientation of the direction or the knit; 2) Manufacturing needs which require the right and left parts of the garment to be overlapped in a single parcel or separated into two different parcels.

Characteristics of spreading fabric 'face to face':

1) The head of the fabric or the knit is always facing the same direction.

2) The right and left parts are obtained from overlapping a single parcel.

3) The right and left parts are perfectly equal as they are cut in a single operation.

4) The tonality of the colours may be different as the right and left parts making up a single garment may be distant from each other depending on the length of the lay.

5) This spreading system is slower than the others.

Spreading symbols

In order to avoid errors and defects during fabric spreading and pattern layout, it is helpful to use symbols to indicate the type of layout or spreading method to adopt each time, as needed.

Below you'll find the symbols used by a few companies, but this may vary by the form and type of indication.

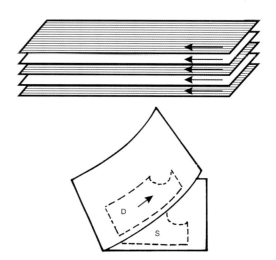

Face to face spreading

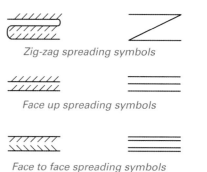

Zig-zag spreading symbols

Face up spreading symbols

Face to face spreading symbols

BASIC SPREADING SYMBOLS

SYMBOL CHART

FABRIC				CUTS	
	A	Fabric without a face (front or 'right' side), back or direction.			Cuts arranged in the same direction.
	B	Fabric with a face (front) and back but without a direction.			Cuts arranged in opposite directions.
	C	Fabric with a semi-constraining face (slight nap or pile, small print).			Cuts arranged freely.
	D	Fabric with an obvious, constraining face (velvet, prints, etc.)		SPREADING	**1.** Zig-zag spreading 'face to face', in opposite directions.
	E	Fabric with particular characteristics (checks, tartans, etc.)			**2.** Cut spreading 'face to face', in opposite directions.
PATTERN		Parts of the pattern which align.			**3.** Cut spreading 'face to face', in the same direction.
		Parts of the pattern which do not align.			**4.** Cut spreading 'face up', in the same direction.
		Parts of the pattern laid in the same direction.			**5.** Cut spreading 'face up', in opposite directions.
		Parts of the pattern laid in opposite directions.			**6.** Custom spreading with specific instructions.

SPREADING MACHINES

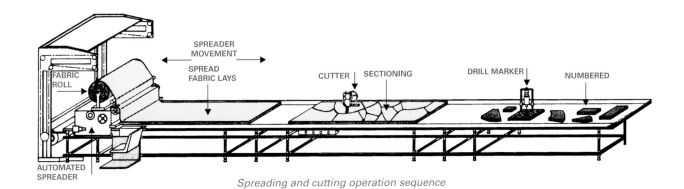

SPREADER MOVEMENT • SPREAD FABRIC LAYS • FABRIC ROLL • AUTOMATED SPREADER • CUTTER • SECTIONING • DRILL MARKER • NUMBERED

Spreading and cutting operation sequence

Spreading machines

The use of spreading machines is important because it allows you to reduce the time and costs related to spreading.

Spreading machines are, at their base, made of a spreader carriage that runs along the table, equipped with a cradle to carry the roll of fabric that is to be spread.

After affixing the fabric on one end of the table by using the automatic gripper, the carriage is moved to the opposite end of the table, causing the fabric to be unrolled and placed on the plane of the table. Once extended for the desired length of the lay, the spreader stops and, for zig-zag spreading, the fabric is blocked by a gripping device. The machine, returning to the departure point, continues to lay the fabric across the table surface as it travels. However, in the case of 'face up' spreading, a separating cut will be made before the machine returns to its departure point (of course without spreading any fabric on the return). For 'face to face' spreading, it is necessary to use a rotating roll cradle that so that the roll can be turned 180° after the creation of the separation cut. Again in this case, fabric is not spread on the carriage's return to the starting point.

Spreading machines are equipped with devices that facilitate and quicken spreading and which ensure that the plies are aligned, that the spreading takes place without tension on the fabric and that the separation cut is executed correctly, etc.

The various devices found on spreading machines may be engaged by hand or engaged automatically through electronically-controlled electromagnetic commands or through computer software. The former are semi-automated spreading machines; the latter are fully automated spreading machines.

Fabric feeding

The fabric needs to be fed so that it can move from the roll to be spread on the table without tension. Feeding may be made possible by a few counter-rotating bars covered in non-slip coating and pushed one against the other by a spring. The fabric thus passes between the two bars, which unroll the fabric by their rotation and deposit it on the table.

Device to align the fabric edges

Because of the need to pile the fabric as high as possible for the cutting phase, the edges of one layer must be perfectly aligned with the edges of the layers below it.

Automatic edge alignment device

For open fabrics or large-size tubular fabrics, for which an alignment guide may not be advised, the edges are aligned by appropriately moving the roll carried to the right or left during fabric spreading.

Movement of the carriage and the feeding bars by a pair of photo-electric or laser cells. The fabric is aligned when its edge runs between the two cells during spreading.

Cutters

For 'face up' and 'face to face' spreading, the cut is made with a circular blade cutter which runs along a transversely fixed track, placed on the front part of the spreading machine. The cutter's electric motor, in addition to propelling the blade, provides the energy to move the cutter device parts from one side to the other of the spreading machine.

Spreading a ply of fabric

Rotating cradle for 'face to face' spreading

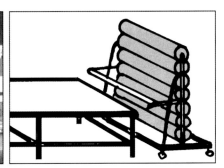

Roll stand

Cutting

After studying the layout, the spreading of the fabric and the marker making, the lay is ready to be cut. "Cut" is understood to mean the trimming of the pieces of the pattern as they are marked on the layout graphic, on the various layers of overlapping fabric. Usually the layout graphic, created according to various techniques (drawn, traced, sprayed, glued or sewn) is placed on the first layer of the stack.

Cutting is broken down into two operations: sectioning, that is sub-dividing the lay into smaller, more manageable parts so that the following operation of cutting the curves into the fabric is easier; and the cutting into the precise, exact shapes of the individual pieces. Precision mainly depends on the type of equipment used for cutting. The lay is cut with electric table cutters and belt-run saw cutters if done manually, or with a cutter incorporated into the spreading machine if done automatically.

Electric table cutters are divided into two categories: circular blades and vertical blades.

- Circular blade cutters: this type of cutter is used for the division of small or medium thickness lays. It cannot be used to cut the curved portions of a pattern as it is too difficult to trace sharply arched lines and corners in particular, due to the shape and thus the footprint of the blade itself.

- Vertical blade cutters: this type of cutter is useful for the division of small, medium and thick lays as well as for cutting the curves of a piece. This is possible thanks to the reduced footprint of the blade and its alternating vertical movement which allows it to closely and precisely follow the edges of a pattern.

Belt-run saw cutters are used for ultra-precise cutting, especially for the smaller pieces of a pattern. With these cutters or saws, the pieces are easier to move and manipulate as the operator can use both hands to control the lay as s/he cuts.

This last machine may be equipped with two blade rotation speeds: the slower speed is used for cutting fabrics with a high percentage of synthetic fibres in order to avoid melting.

The cutting or the dividing of the lay may be done directly on the spreading table with technologically advanced equipment which carries out the complete operation with maximum precision and notable speed.

In this case, the next lay is spread after the first stack of fabric is moved by conveyor belt to the adjacent cutting table.

Numbering the pieces

"Numbering" is understood to mean the placing of a small label or tag on every cut piece of fabric which makes up a garment. Numbering is useful to avoid sewing pattern pieces cut from different plies of fabric, thus avoiding possible colour defects in the same garment.

The label or the tag contains certain data or numbers which, as a code, may help identify the fabric. For example: the client's name, the order number, the cut, how many garments are included in the order, the colour, the operator that created the numbering, other instructions from the company, and the layer number, etc.

The machine used for this operation is the Saobar, the maker of which is based in America.

Spring clamps for fabric

Pressurie grip clamps for fabric

Vertical blade cutter

Circular blade cutter

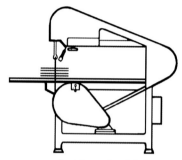

Band saw for fabric

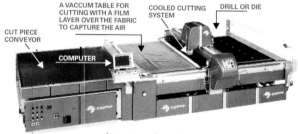

A VACCUM TABLE FOR CUTTING WITH A FILM LAYER OVER THE FABRIC TO CAPTURE THE AIR

COOLED CUTTING SYSTEM

DRILL OR DIE

CUT PIECE CONVEYOR

COMPUTER

Automated cutting machine

Cutter with sharpening and flexion controls

Die-cutting or punching device

PARCEL FORMATION

The creation of parcels is intended to bring greater security when cutting, so that the pieces are not confused during the production process.

You can create the parcel before or after numbering, according to the type of layout.

If there is just one garment in one size on the layout, you can send it on to be numbered immediately. If, on the other hand, the same layout ply has two or more sizes or numerous garments of the same size, you must first subdivide the pieces and then send them for numbering.

To facilitate subdivision, each piece within the layout should have its size clearly labelled on it. If there are numerous garments to be cut, it is incredibly important that there is an additional number or letter or symbol which can identify how the pieces are to be grouped.

A possible example of the letters/numbers/symbols to be written on each piece (for example, with 3 garments all in the same size) is as follows:

1) Sz.46/A Sz.46/B Sz.46/C

After the pieces have been numbered, you must prepare for the subdivision into many other parcels (or rolls if the parcels are small), which may be grouped:

1) By colour.
2) By the number of clients they will be sent to.
3) By the factories that will produce them.
4) By the production lines to be fed.
5) By the needs of each company

Binding the parcels or rolls

To organise the pieces of the parcel, consider two systems:

1) Tying the smallest parts (flaps, loops, pockets, etc.) with elastic, twine or adhesive tape and eventually putting all the parcels in a single bag. This system is costlier, including during subsequent production phases, but it is more secure as the pieces are less likely to be lost.

2) Stacking the pieces. Place the largest piece at the bottom then, one by one, stack the smaller pieces on top. Roll everything together and tie with a strip of fabric, twine, adhesive tape, etc.

This system costs less, but the pieces within the roll may slide out, thus increasing the chance of mixing them up or losing them.

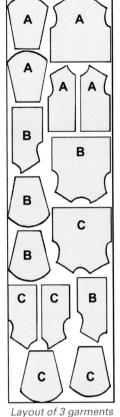
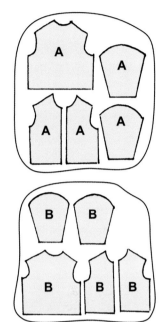

Layout of 3 garments

Subdivision of pieces with the same symbol

Cord with a hook

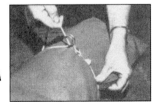

Stacking the pieces   *Tying the pices*

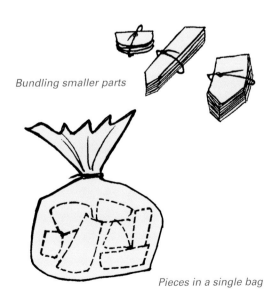

Bundling smaller parts

Pieces in a single bag

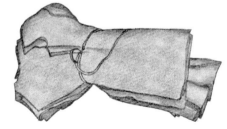

Parcel tied with elastic

CHARTS

Numbers	1/2	1/3	1/4	1/6	1/8	1/10	1.12	1/3.14	2/3.14	4/3.14	Numbers
20	10	6.6	5	3.3	2.5	2	1.6	6.4	12.7	25.5	20
22	11	7.3	5.5	3.6	2.7	2.2	1.8	7	14	28	22
24	12	8	6	4	3	2.4	2	7.6	15.3	30.6	24
26	13	8.6	6.5	4.3	3.2	2.6	2.1	8.3	16.6	33.1	26
28	14	9.3	7	4.6	3.5	2.8	2.3	8.9	17.8	35.7	28
30	15	10	7.5	5	3.7	3	2.5	9.5	19.1	38.2	30
32	16	10.6	8	5.3	4	3.2	2.6	10.1	20.4	40.8	32
34	17	11.3	8.5	5.6	4.2	3.4	2.8	10.8	21.6	43.3	34
36	18	12	9	6	4.5	3.6	3	11.5	22.9	45.9	36
38	19	12.6	9.5	6.3	4.7	3.8	3.1	12.1	24.2	48.4	38
40	20	13.3	10	6.6	5	4	3.3	12.7	25.5	51	40
42	21	14	10.5	7	5.2	4.2	3.5	13.4	26.8	53.5	42
44	22	14.6	11	7.3	5.5	4.4	3.6	14	28	56	44
46	23	15.3	11.5	7.6	5.7	4.6	3.8	14.6	29.3	58.6	46
48	24	16	12	8	6	4.8	4	15.3	30.6	61.1	48
50	25	16.6	12.5	8.3	6.2	5	4.1	15.9	31.8	63.7	50
52	26	17.3	13	8.6	6.5	5.2	4.3	16.6	33.1	66.2	52
54	27	18	13.5	9	6.7	5.4	4.5	17.2	34.3	68.8	54
56	28	18.6	14	9.3	7	5.6	4.6	17.8	35.6	71.3	56
58	29	19.3	14.5	9.6	7.2	5.8	4.8	18.5	36.9	73.9	58
60	30	20	15	10	7.5	6	5	19.1	38.2	76.4	60
62	31	20.6	15.5	10.3	7.7	6.2	5.1	19.7	39.5	79	62
64	32	21.3	16	10.6	8	6.4	5.3	20.4	40.7	81.5	64
66	33	22	16.5	11	8.2	6.6	5.5	21	42	84.1	66
68	34	22.6	17	11.3	8.5	6.8	5.6	21.6	43.3	86.6	68
70	35	23.3	17.5	11.6	8.7	7	5.8	22.3	44.6	89.2	70
72	36	24	18	12	9	7.2	6	22.9	45.8	91.7	72
74	37	24.6	18.5	12.3	9.2	7.4	6.1	23.6	47.1	94.2	74
76	38	25.3	19	12.6	9.5	7.6	6.3	24.2	48.4	96.8	76
78	39	26	19.5	13	9.7	7.8	6.5	24.8	49.7	99.3	78
80	40	26.6	20	13.3	10	8	6.6	25.5	50.9	101.9	80
82	41	27.3	20.5	13.6	10.2	8.2	6.8	26.1	52.2	104.4	82
84	42	28	21	14	10.5	8.4	7	26.8	53.5	107	84
86	43	28.6	21.5	14.3	10.7	8.6	7.1	27.4	54.8	109.5	86
88	44	29.3	22	14.6	11	8.8	7.3	28	56	112.1	88
90	45	30	22.5	15	11.2	9	7.5	28.7	57.3	114.6	90
92	46	30.6	23	15.3	11.5	9.2	7.6	29.3	58.6	117.2	92
94	47	31.3	23.5	15.6	11.7	9.4	7.8	29.9	59.9	119.7	94
96	48	32	24	16	12	9.6	8	30.6	61.1	122.3	96
98	49	32.6	24.5	16.3	12.2	9.8	8.1	31.2	62.4	124.8	98
100	50	33.3	25	16.6	12.5	10	8.3	31.8	63.7	127.4	100

Total or partial reproduction is prohibited, even if the source is cited.

ENGLISH MEASUREMENTS CONVERSION TABLE

From yards to metres	From metres to yards	From inches to centimetres	From centimetres to inches
¼ yd = 0.229 m	0.25 m = 9 7/8"	1" = 2.54 cm	1 cm = 3/8"
½ yd = 0.457 m	0.50 m = 19 5/8"	2" = 5.08 cm	2 cm = 3/4"
¾ yd = 0.686 m	0.75 m = 29 1/2"	3" = 7.62 cm	3 cm = 1 1/8"
1 yd = 0.914 m	1 m = 1 yd 3 3/8"	4" = 10.16 cm	4 cm = 1 1/2"
1 ¼ yds = 1.143 m	1.25 m = 1 yd 13 3/4"	5" = 10.70 cm	5 cm = 1 7/8"
1 ½ yds = 1.372 m	1.50 m = 1 yd 23"	6" = 15.24 cm	6 cm = 2 3/8"
1 ¾ yds = 1.60 m	1.75 m = 1 yd 32"	7" = 17.78 cm	7 cm = 2 3/4"
2 yds = 1.82 m	2 m = 2 yds 6 3/4"	8" = 20.32 cm	8 cm = 3 1/8"
2 ¼ yds = 2.058 m	2.25 m = 2 yds 16 5/8"	9" = 22.86 cm	9 cm = 3 1/2"
2 ½ yds = 2.286 m	2.50 m = 2 yds 26 3/8"	10" = 25.4 cm	10 cm = 3 7/8"
2 ¾ yds = 2.515 m	2.75 m = 3 yds 1/4"	11" = 27.94 cm	11 cm = 4 1/4"
3 yds = 2.743 m	3 m = 3 yds 10 1/8"	12" = 30.48 cm	12 cm = 4 5/8"
3 ¼ yds = 2.972 m	3.25 m = 3 yds 20"	13" = 33.02 cm	13 cm = 5"
3 ½ yds = 3.20 m	3.50 m = 3 yds 29 3/4"	14" = 35.56 cm	14 cm = 5 3/8"
3 ¾ yds = 3.429 m	3.75 m = 4 yds 3 5/8"	15" = 38.1 cm	15 cm = 5 3/4"
4 yds = 3.558 m	4 m = 4 yds 13 1/2"	16" = 40.64 cm	16 cm = 6 1/4"
4 ¼ yds = 3.887 m	4.25 m = 4 yds 23 3/8"	17" = 43.18 cm	17 cm = 6 5/8"
4 ½ yds = 4.115 m	4.50 m = 4 yds 33 1/8"	18" = 45.72 cm	18 cm = 7"
4 ¾ yds = 4.344 m	4.75 m = 5 yds 7"	19" = 48.26 cm	19 cm = 7 3/8"
5 yds = 4.572 m	5 m = 5 yds 13 7/8"	20" = 50.8 cm	20 cm = 7 3/4"
		21" = 53.34 cm	25 cm = 9 5/8"
		22" = 55.88 cm	30 cm = 11"
		23" = 58.42 cm	35 cm = 15 3/4"
		24" = 60.96 cm	40 cm = 15 3/4"
		25" = 63.3 cm	45 cm = 17 3/4"

PROMOPRESS FASHION COLLECTION

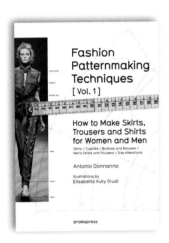

FASHION PATTERNMAKING TECHNIQUES [VOL. 1]
How to Make Skirts, Trousers and Shirts. Women / Men
Antonio Donnanno. Illustrations by Elisabetta Kuky Drudi

978-84-15967-09-5
210 x 297 mm. 256 pages

FASHION PATTERNMAKING TECHNIQUES [VOL. 2]
How to Make Shirts, Undergarments, Dresses & Suits, Waistcoats and Jackets for Women & Men
Antonio Donnanno. Illustrations by Elisabetta Kuky Drudi

978-84-15967-68-2
210 x 297 mm. 256 pages

FASHION PATTERNMAKING TECHNIQUES FOR CHILDREN'S CLOTHING
Dresses, Shirts, Bodysuits, Trousers, Shorts, Jackets and Coats
Antonio Donnanno. Illustrations by Claudia Ausonia Palazio

978-84-16851-14-0
210 x 297 mm. 232 pages

FASHION PATTERNMAKING TECHNIQUES FOR ACCESSORIES
Shoes, Bags, Hats, Gloves, Ties & Buttons. It Includes Clothing for Dogs.
Antonio Donnanno

978-84-16851-61-4
210 x 297 cmm. 240 pages

FASHION MOULAGE TECHNIQUE
A Step by Step Draping Course
Danilo Attardi

978-84-17412-12-8
195 x 285 mm. 192 pages

FASHION PATTERNMAKING TECHNIQUES HAUTE COUTURE [VOL. 1]
Haute Couture Models, Draping Techniques, Decorations
Antonio Donnanno

978-84-16504-66-4
210 x 297 mm. 256 pages

PROMOPRESS FASHION COLLECTION

FASHION DETAILS
4,000 Drawings
Elisabetta Kuky Drudi

978-84-17412-68-5
195 x 285 mm. 386 pages
Second edition in 2020

FASHION SKETCHING
Templates, Poses and Ideas for Fashion Design
Claudia Ausonia Palazio

978-84-16504-10-7
195 x 285 mm. 272 pages

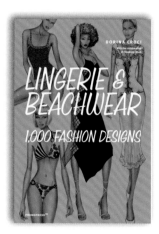

LINGERIE & BEACHWEAR
1,000 Fashion Designs
Dorina Croci

978-84-17412-52-4
195 x 285 mm. 256 pages

FASHION ILLUSTRATION & DESIGN: ACCESSORIES
Shoes, Bags, Hats, Gloves, and Glasses
Manuela Brambatti, Fabio Mencioni

978-84-17412-64-4
210 x 297 mm. 240 pages

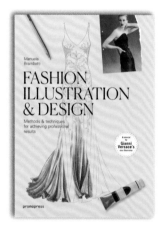

FASHION ILLUSTRATION & DESIGN
Methods & Techniques for Achieving Professional Results
Manuela Brambatti

978-84-16851-06-5
215 x 300 mm. 240 pages

COLOUR IN FASHION ILLUSTRATION
Drawing and Painting Techniques
Tiziana Paci

978-84-16851-59-1
215 x 287 mm. 320 pages

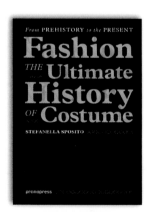

FASHION HISTORY
The Ultimate History of Costume from Prehistory to the Present Day
Stefanella Sposito

978-84-15967-82-8
190 x 270 mm. 256 pages

PALETTE PERFECT
Color Combinations Inspired by Fashion, Art & Style
Lauren Wager

978-84-15967-90-3
148 x 210 mm. 304 pages

FABRICS IN FASHION DESIGN
The Way Successful Fashion Designers Use Fabrics
Stefanella Sposito. Photos by Gianni Pucci.

978-84-16851-28-7
227 x 235 mm. 336 pages

scale 1.16

0 5 10 15 20 25 30 35 40 45 50 55 60 65 70 75 80 85 90 95 100 105 110 115 120 125 130 135 140 145 150 155 160 165

25 24 23 22 21 20 19 18 17 16 15 14 13 12 11 10 9 8 7 6 5 4 3 2 1 0

scale 1:10

scale 1:25

scale 1:10